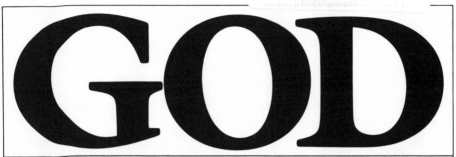

GOD

THE CONTEMPORARY DISCUSSION SERIES

ULTIMATE REALITY AND SPIRITUAL DISCIPLINE

GOD

THE CONTEMPORARY DISCUSSION SERIES

ULTIMATE REALITY AND SPIRITUAL DISCIPLINE

Edited by James Duerlinger

NEW ERA BOOKS
Paragon House Publishers
New York

Paragon House Publishers, Inc.
866 Second Avenue
New York, New York 10017
First edition © 1984. All rights reserved
Printed in the United States of America

ISBN 0-913757-08-X Pbk.
ISBN 0-913757-09-8

CONTENTS

IV/SPIRITUAL DISCIPLINES IN PURSUIT OF ULTIMATE REALITY

Editor's Introduction

James Duerlinger

E arlier drafts of most of the papers in this volume were prepared for an international conference entitled, "God: the
Contemporary Discussion II," held on December 30, 1982-
January 3, 1983 at Fort Lauderdale, Florida, and sponsored by the
New Ecumenical Research Association, an ecumenical project of
the International Religious Foundation, Inc. Scholars and students of religion, theologians, and philosophers from around the
world were invited to submit essays on one of seven preselected
topics deemed relevant to the contemporary discussion of God. The
papers on each topic were reproduced and distributed in advance
to all who had written on the same topic so that at the conference
they could devote their time to discussion. Seven discussion groups
were formed, each of which dealt with one of the preselected topics.
Each essayist also wrote a critique of another's essay in the same
group. All but two of the twelve papers included here are slightly
revised versions of essays submitted on the topic, "Ultimate Reality
and Spiritual Discipline." Of the remaining two, one is a revised
and expanded version of the critique of the first essay, and the other,
though not discussed at the conference, is composed by a partici-
pant in the original discussion.

The papers in this volume were selected for publication
because they deal with issues informative, important, and timely

enough to warrant a more general discussion, not only among university teachers and students of religion, but also among spiritual leaders and followers of the world's religions. Not all of the issues which might be raised about ultimate reality and spiritual discipline are discussed here, but many are discussed and most of these are introduced in the context of presentations of modern theological perspectives, specific religious traditions, or particular spiritual disciplines. A study of these richly textured essays, I believe, will help us to understand better how we might come to terms with our differences concerning the nature of ultimate reality and the practice of spiritual discipline, without sacrificing our own religious beliefs and practices in the process.

We live in an age in which the validity of man's spiritual search for ultimate reality is called into question by scientific and political humanistic ideologies, which advocate alternative ways of life and conceptions of ultimate reality, and by disagreements between the religions themselves about matters of religious practice and theory, disagreements which tend to undermine confidence in the efficacy of their spiritual practices and in the soundness of their conceptions of ultimate reality. It is assumed by the authors of the essays in this volume or by the viewpoints they present that there is an ultimate reality that can be experienced with the help of the practice of spiritual discipline. Their essays, from different points of view, may be seen as attempts to cope with one or another of these and other such forces which challenge this assumption. These attempts involve a great number of interrelated issues and perspectives not all of which can be illuminated by any one thematic arrangement of the essays. The themes I have chosen for their arrangement, therefore, are best construed as a convenient means by which further connections between the essays are to be discovered and explored by the reader. In what follows I shall simply summarize the contents of each of the essays in accord with their place within my thematic arrangement. Thus, with the help of these summaries the reader may decide, if he is so inclined, to read the essays in an order that reflects his own thematic preference.

In Part I, entitled "Ultimate Reality and the Nature of Spiritual Discipline," the authors try to explain how religion and spiritual discipline are related to ultimate reality. Robert Kress offers a definition of religion which he believes shows, without prejudice, how it is related to ultimate reality, and argues, against elitist views of spiritual discipline, that everyday life can be one of the disciplines of religion just because ultimate reality is immanent in such a life; James Duerlinger offers an alternative account of religion and its disciplines which he believes not only avoids the bias and elitism Kress opposes, but also serves better the purposes of ecumenism; and Arabinda Basu distinguishes the natures of both morality and religion from that of spiritual discipline, gives an account of the relationship between spiritual discipline and ultimate reality, and presents a way to resolve disagreements among religions concerning the nature of ultimate reality.

By drawing on recent developments within Roman Catholic thought Kress attempts to help us avoid bias in the definition of religion and elitism in the criteria used to identify spiritual activity or discipline. Religion, he argues, is human life as a whole organized on the basis of a reality perceived as ultimate, regardless of whether the reality so perceived is God, the ultimate reality, and by implication, spiritual discipline is activity pursued for the sake of this perception, regardless of whether it involves the explicit recognition of God. If we accept this definition and its implication, he believes, we shall see that there is no reason for members of one religion to deny the spiritual or religious character of the disciplines practiced in another, or for some special set of practices in any given religion, to be classified as spiritual to the exclusion of others. Kress analyzes the changes that have taken place in the criteria used in Christianity to determine what spiritual activity is, and sees in these changes a tension between elitist and anti-elitist views of spiritual practice which he believes can be resolved by an appeal to a doctrine espoused in the Second Vatican Council and its theological elaboration by Karl Rahner. The Council recognized the possibility that an atheist can be holy and be saved, a doctrine that Rahner explains in terms of the theory that one can achieve the goal of Christianity insofar as he makes his ultimate concern in his everyday life the good of his fellow man, living thus in a Christ-like way. In such a life, he claims, there is already graced transcendence in communication and communion with God, since it accepts those whom God created in his own image. In this way, Kress argues, we can see how everyday life, even if not explicitly lived for the sake of union with God, can be recognized by the

Catholic Church as a spiritual discipline leading to salvation. In like ways, he suggests, the followers of each religion might reinterpret the disciplines of others as disciplines of their own, capable of achieving their goals.

Duerlinger objects that Kress's account of religion, its disciplines and their relation to ultimate reality, inadvertently plays into the hands of secular opponents of religion. In its place he offers views which he believes retain more traditional assumptions and yet effectively handle the problems of biased definition and elitist conceptions of spiritual discipline. He defines religion as human life organized in pursuit of the divine life, which he equates with an eternal blissful state of consciousness of ultimate reality, and defines spiritual discipline as activity which is believed to be an effective way, when performed properly and regularly, to attain the divine life. Duerlinger stresses that his definitions allow for the fact that although religions offer their own interpretations of the exact nature of ultimate reality, yet they agree, in opposition to secular conceptions, that ultimate reality is what is experienced in the divine life and is permanent rather than impermanent, unlike the reality man experiences in his everyday life. Kress's attempt to show that everyday life lived in accord with love for one's fellow man is already a communion with God Duerlinger interprets as a sign of Kress's need to compensate for the lack of reference in his definition to a transcendent ultimate reality, and maintains that the basis of ecumenical discussion and cooperation among the great religious traditions should be a common commitment to the restoration in the modern world of the pursuit of the divine life and of belief in the special reality and values this pursuit assumes.

Basu draws on the Hindu religious tradition to offer yet a third view, one in which spiritual discipline is distinguished from both morality and religion, while ultimate reality is identified with a supreme Self whose impersonal and personal aspects can be integrally experienced. He defines morality as the discipline by which man seeks to purify himself of vice and to internalize virtue for the sake of right action, religion as man turning toward superior forces and beings in prayer and worship for the sake of assistance, and spiritual discipline as the means by which man experiences his true spiritual nature, which is uncreated, immortal consciousness free from the defects of man's body, life, and mind. Morality, he

4

argues, is necessary for spiritual discipline, while religion can be helpful if genuinely spiritual in intent and practice. Basu also contends that there is an ultimate reality, a supreme Self with which the liberated individual spiritual self can be associated by fuller realization of selfhood. When this ultimate reality is experienced in its impersonal aspect, the individual self experiences identity with it, and when it is experienced in its personal aspect, as a God possessed of transcendent Knowledge, Action, and Enjoyment, the individual self attains close union with it and may become a living instrument of its Will. According to Basu, when ultimate reality is realized merely through the spiritually illuminated mind, its impersonal and personal aspects cannot be integrated, but a superior capacity can be evolved by man, with the grace of God, which will allow him to possess an integral realization of ultimate reality. Religions offer different conceptions of ultimate reality, he contends, insofar as they rely solely on the mind to inform their conceptions.

In Part II, entitled "Ultimate Reality and the Efficacy of Spiritual Discipline," the authors discuss whether and how the practice of spiritual discipline can bring about its intended results, especially with regard to its goal of achieving consciousness of ultimate reality. Huston Smith defends the practice of spiritual discipline against the charge that it is not an effective means for uncovering ultimate reality; Philip Novak attempts to explain why it can be effective for this purpose; and James Gaffney calls attention to impediments to its effective practice arising from the need for its institutionalization.

Smith defends the practice of spiritual discipline as an effective way to achieve insight into ultimate reality by answering a number of objections to its claims of efficacy, and argues, in addition, that its practice, in spite of important differences of emphasis to be found in different religious traditions, is the means by which the same basic virtues are developed and the experience of the same transcendent ultimate reality is achieved. To the objection that only God through His grace can grant salvation he replies that the need for grace, both on a theistic and a nontheistic interpretation, need not preclude the use of spiritual discipline. To the charge that the practice of spiritual discipline is prompted by a subtle form of willfulness or ego-involvement, which is the very thing to be destroyed in the practice, Smith replies that although the practice must begin in this way, as it progresses this prompting is left behind. A third charge, that it fosters spiritual pride, he reduces to a warning which must be heeded by applying the proper countermeasures.

Once such charges are put aside, there remains the question of whether the practice of spiritual discipline enables its practitioner to experience ultimate reality. Novak attempts to explain why it can do so. He argues that although morality, love, intellectual insight, etc., are important aspects of spiritual discipline, the use of active, nonreactive sustained attention to ego-centered mental activity is the key to its efficacy. He first examines a number of important disciplines in the world's religions, finding in them a central use of sustained attention of two types, concentrative and receptive, to achieve spiritual self-transformation, and then asks how it enables the self to undergo such change. Since man's ego-centeredness, he argues, is what keeps him from the experience of divine ultimate reality, ego-transcendence is the means by which this experience is to be achieved. The problem, however, is that man needs to perform the difficult task of destroying his most deeply habituated egoistic predispositions in order to achieve this goal. Novak argues that by the systematic practice of active, nonreactive attention to our ego-centered mental patterns of activity we can slowly starve them of the psychic energy they need to survive, and hence become free to experience ultimate reality.

Finally, Gaffney talks about how the institutionalization of the practice of spiritual discipline affects its efficacy. He first suggests that Plato, one of the first Westerners to discuss the standardization of spiritual discipline, failed to provide for the spiritual needs of all members of the institution he established for this purpose, primarily because of his elitest assumption that very few are capable of practicing all of the disciplines. The most basic problem of institutionalizing spiritual discipline, Gaffney argues, is that in spite of its considerable advantages for the spiritually unresourceful, it often leads to the despiritualization of its practice to the point where the practitioner's mind becomes dulled and bored and the institution itself may in effect be treated by him, as he comes to rely on it, as ultimate reality. Gaffney also finds in Plato's works the recognition that it is not by any institution, but ultimately by his own efforts, that the individual will achieve the divine life, and he concludes that because of the truth of Plato's insight, a way will eventually always be found past the hazards of institutionalization.

In Part III, entitled "Ultimate Reality and Spiritual Discipline in a Secular World," the authors respond in very different ways to what they take to be modern secular man's need to accept and practice a spiritual discipline that leads him to the experience of ultimate reality. Ursula King offers a possible foundation for spiritual disciplines practicable in modern secular society; Dagfinn Aslid introduces, to those who have rejected as other-worldly the ideas of ultimate reality and the practice of spiritual discipline, a new religion in which spiritual discipline itself is the attempt to actualize ultimate reality in this world; and Seyyed Hossein Nasr, in response to the secularization of the very concept of ultimate reality, argues for both the reinstatement of the idea that God is ultimate reality and the acceptance of the traditional means by which He is known.

King believes that present-day confusions about the choice of appropriate spiritual disciplines can be overcome not by a revival of traditional practices, but rather by the adoption of new spiritual disciplines which are integrated into man's attempt to build a more peaceful secular society. The adoption of spiritual disciplines of this sort, she believes, can be justified by appeal to Teilhard de Chardin's theory of the phenomenon of spirituality as the emergence and development of spirit within the natural process of evolution, culminating in the union of human consciousness with the spirit of God. King argues that if we regard spirituality in this way, rather than as an unchanging timeless state, we can more easily see that the contemporary call for relevant spiritual guidelines is best answered by new forms of spiritual discipline which take into account the knowledge, experience, and sensibility of our age. She claims that such spirituality can be seen as a worldwide developing energy resource which can be used to weld humankind into a closer-knit community. The most powerful agent of unification within this resource, according to King, is love, and by the exploration of this energy source it may be possible for a concrete, creative mysticism to emerge in which the spiritual disciplines and mystical insights of the great religious traditions are joined with social action to meet the complex requirements of modern life.

Aslid also believes that our modern world requires more relevant, this-worldly forms of spiritual discipline. He first calls attention to the widespread rejections of the traditional idea of ultimate reality as a transcendent God and of the practices used to transport us to His reality, and then draws on the philosophy of Alfred North Whitehead and Unification theology to offer an alternative ideal of ultimate reality and spiritual practice which he believes will be more acceptable to contemporary man. Aslid argues that the Unification idea that ultimate reality is the Heart of God, conceived as the divine experiential relationality of all things that requires for its full actualization intimacy with all things, lends itself, in a way that the traditional idea of a transcendent substantial divine intellect does not, both to the modern holistic and ecological perspectives and generally to the new age movement, while it avoids the traditional unhealthy bifurcation of man's intellectual and emotional life that cuts him off from the aesthetic and mythopoeic dimensions of religion whose inspiration he needs. That God's Heart will be actualized, he believes, is certain, but how it is to be actualized is not, and depends on the practice of appropriate disciplines performed by man, who has the responsibility to make the earth fit for divine cohabitation. Spiritual discipline is man creating a harmonious, loving world, participating as a human being on intrapersonal, interpersonal, and universal levels, thus experientially becoming sensitive to and receptive of the Divine Heart.

Nasr adopts a more traditional response to the contemporary secularity. He draws on the resources of Islamic theology to attempt a rescue of the concept of ultimate reality from its modern empiricist prison. Spiritual discipline, he says, is the means dispensed by a qualified master to enable those capable of practicing it to gain a realized knowledge of ultimate reality. He identifies ultimate reality with God himself, who is at once absolute, infinite, and good or perfect, and explains the world which is God's creation as a veil that at once manifests him as relativity and hides his absolute nature. After appealing to God's infinity as the source of all possibilities to resolve the perennial doubt about whether God's perfection can be reconciled with the existence of evil in his creation, Nasr explicates both God's absolute, infinite, and good or merciful creative nature and the relative and illusory nature of his creation. To recapture this knowledge of absolute and relative

8

reality, he concludes, the modern empiricist and rationalist perspectives, which have occasioned religious skepticism and relativism, must be abandoned and the traditional sources of divine knowledge, revelation and intellection, must once again be accepted. These ideas concerning God and his creation, Nasr claims, lie at the heart of all true religions.

In Part IV, entitled "Spiritual Disciplines in Pursuit of Ultimate Reality," the authors explain how a variety of spiritual disciplines have been or can be employed to enable their practitioners to experience ultimate reality. William Cenkner shows how the Indian poets Rabindranath Tagore and Sri Aurobindo Ghose used their art as a spiritual discipline to experience ultimate reality as each conceived of it; Ruth Tiffany Barnhouse gives an account of how the Spiritual Exercises of St. Ignatius may be given a modern interpretation which, since they provide a transcendental reference for our value systems, can be used to help us achieve spiritual maturity; and Robert Thurman shows how in Tsong-Khapa's account of Buddhist spiritual discipline both the transcendent and the immanent dimensions of ultimate reality are to be realized.

Cenkner first employs Mircea Eliade's views on the nature and function of ritual to explicate the spiritual dimensions of the creative activities of Tagore and Aurobindo, and then explains how the ritualization of the aesthetic imagination of Tagore and Aurobindo, as each conceived of it, transformed their art into a spiritual discipline. He argues that Tagore's ritualized practice of writing poetry was the means by which he strove to experience the immensity of the interrelatedness of all things, while Aurobindo's ritualized practice was the vehicle by which he surrendered to and aspired for the divine life in which there is unity with divine consciousness and experience of its descent into man. This fusion of art and religion are possible, Cenkner claims, because when ritualized, both can enable their practitioners to transcend the limitations of the empirical self and achieve self-transformation. He shows that Tagore and Aurobindo both sought the realization of their spiritual selves through the use of the aesthetic imagination, but had different conceptions of the nature and role of this imagination and of the metaphysical status of this self. Nevertheless they agree, he concludes, that the creation of poetry can be a practice which brings one to experience the mystery of ultimate reality.

Barnhouse argues that the Spiritual Exercises of St. Ignatius

9

are Christian spiritual disciplines which can be adapted for use by non-Christians to satisfy their spiritual need to be anchored in the divine ultimate reality. The purpose of the Exercises, she says, is to attain spiritual freedom from the tyranny of the false self and establish the true spiritual self. Throughout her exposition she calls attention to Ignatius' use of profound psychological techniques which facilitate spiritual freedom. She is especially concerned to show that the contemplations of sin or "unfreedom," when properly understood and adapted to the modern temperament, are a purgative essential for spiritual growth, preparing us both to appreciate the nature and possibility of a Christ-like life in which all obstacles to freedom are overcome and to submit ourselves willingly and without reservation to God's care and love in order to attain this life. Also important in the Exercises, she shows, are the development of compassion for the suffering of others and the cultivation of love of God, which motivate us to engage in loving and redeeming action in the world. These Exercises, or some adaptation of them, Barnhouse claims, can accomplish what no secular psychotherapy can: a spiritually free, caring human being in communion with ultimate reality.

Thurman calls attention to the need for every religion to acknowledge both the transcendent and the immanent aspects of ultimate reality and shows how the Tibetan saint, Tsong Khapa, integrates them into Buddhist spiritual discipline. The discipline, he shows, is divided into the development of transcendental renunciation, the supreme spirit of love and compassion, and the wisdom of selflessness. He emphasizes, as Barnhouse does, the psychological profundity of the discipline explicated, the transcendental grounding it gives to loving action in this world, and its adaptability to practice by the members of other religions. However, the discipline he explains also deals more extensively with the practitioner's attempt to experience ultimate reality in its purely transcendental character. To this end he describes in detail the steps by which the Buddhist meditator achieves insight into selflessness, which is a person's transcendental reality, and argues that this denial of self is not inconsistent with professions of the existence of a spiritual self so long as it is understood that this profession is solely an expression of the immanence of ultimate reality rather than a disguised attempt to reinstate the egocentric self-habit.

I

ULTIMATE
REALITY
AND THE
NATURE OF
SPIRITUAL
DISCIPLINE

Everyday Life
and Spiritual Discipline

Robert Kress

*I*n an attempt to have an ecumenical discussion about religion
and God, or spiritual discipline and ultimate reality, etc., we
are immediately faced with the problem of definitions. What
do these words really mean? It is not a problem restricted solely
to discussion of these matters, for our most important words, such
as "love," "peace," "justice," "marriage," "leader," and "hero,"
all tend to be difficult. Nevertheless, religious words and definitions might be more difficult precisely because religion is *so*
important, both to those who are for it and to those who are against
it. To facilitate discussion, I want, first of all, to offer a definition of
religion which shows, without prejudice, how it is related to
ultimate reality. Then I shall consider the problem of how to
determine membership in a religion, and so, how to tell what
counts as spiritual practice or discipline; and finally, within the
context of a discussion of the Christian religious tradition, I shall
propose an account of the relationship between religion and the
everyday life and practice of Christians which I hope will shed
light on the relationship between Christianity and the spiritual
disciplines practiced by members of other religions.

The Definition of Religion
Not infrequently both opponents and proponents of religion

are pleased to define religion as narrowly as possible, thus restricting it to very limited and often exotic populations. For opponents this is advantageous, for it definitely marginalizes religion as a human reality. If, for example, one can identify religion with the historical Jim Jones or the fictional Elmer Gantry, one can readily dismiss it. On the other hand, for proponents of religion the temptation is to identify religion with the particular religion (or church) to which they belong. Thus, their own religion is easily equated with religion as such, and deemed to be the one true religion. All others are error and corruption in various degrees. Their narrow definitions of religion they contrast to others, which they accuse of being so vague and sweeping that the term ends up being completely without identifiable content. But however narrowly or widely religion is defined, it will be necessary for the definition at least to indicate what kind of actions its practitioners are to perform. That is, the definition also implies the criteria by which the practice of and membership in a religion can be judged. The definition of religion is, then, my first task, but it immediately entails my second, which is to establish and describe the criteria of religious practice and membership.

How is religion to be defined? First of all, we should note that the word "religion" is basically a Western word, coming from the Latin word *religio*. However, to know that the word comes from the Latin does not help us very much. All attempts to explain what religion is on the basis of the word's etymology have failed. Indeed, the etymology itself is unclear. Does the word come from *religari* (to bind back together) or *relegere* (to pay special attention to something) or *reeligere* (to choose again or often or repeatedly)? Such famous thinkers as Cicero, Augustine, and Lactantius used this etymological approach.[1] Later on, Thomas Aquinas found a common thread running through all three Latin words and concluded that "properly speaking, religion means having the right order to God, to whom we must be chiefly bound (*religari*) as to our never ceasing beginning; to whom our choosing must also be diligently directed (*relegere*) as our ultimate end and goal; whom, should we have 'lost' him by sinning, we must regain, rechoose (*reeligere*) by faith and witnessing the faith."[2] Although Aquinas composed this "definition" within the context of a particular religion, we shall see that, with a few modifications, it is not inapt to describe what all religions really want to be and accomplish.

But, first, we should recall how complicated the study of religion is. There is comparative religion, the history of religion(s), and the psychology, sociology, anthropology, and philosophy of religion.[3] Furthermore, in any of the humanities one can focus on the religious aspects of literature, music, art, economics, history, etc. I mention all this, not for the sake of encouragement or discouragement, but to emphasize how all-pervasive religion seems to be. One may like religion, one may dislike it, but one cannot avoid it. Religion has been and is an important dimension of human life.

Against this background we can legitimately have recourse to what is known as the phenomenological or anthropological definition of religion.[4] This approach abstracts from the crucial and critical questions of truth and error, good and bad, and simply treats religion as observable human behavior. But what precisely is *religious* human behavior in contrast to all other kinds of human behavior? What distinguishes religion from everything else is its concern with the total, the whole, the all of human life and existence. For years Dionne Warwick has sung the song from the movie *Alfie*, "What's it *All* About?" And in *Jesus Christ Superstar*, Mary Magdalene is also inspired to ask the same question. The answer, both theoretical and practical, to this question is precisely what religion is. When we study religion, we study how the *whole* of human existence is lived and explained. Some definitions emphasize the human reaction to the experience of limitation; others emphasize the experience of suffering; still others the experience of the need for redemption or salvation; and finally, others emphasize that religion is the human effort to discern the dictates of conscience and to live accordingly.[5] None of these is wrong, and each is correct in its own way. Furthermore, we should not expect to find one, perfect definition of religion.

I prefer to define religion as the organization of one's whole life, individual and social, on the basis of values and insights perceived to be ultimate. In this definition "organization" is not to be understood as signifying some sort of elaborate filing system. It signifies, rather, how one organizes one's life—that is, how one spends one's energies, how one uses one's talents and abilities, how one treats oneself, other people and the world. (It even signifies how one treats God, as we shall see.) I use "values" to refer to what is thought to be good, what we hold dear, treasure, want to be with, want more of. "Insight" is another word for "truths," and signifies what makes sense, what makes life intelligible and meaningful. The word "perceived" is used to emphasize that religion is really a human enterprise, something human beings do. Religion is to some extent a human product; it depends on human perceptions.[6] Since human beings experience and perceive the world differently, there can be different religions *legitimately*. That is, differing religions do not have to result from the bad will and dim wit of others (their sin and ignorance). They can and do result primarily from the different experiences people have of the world and their different interpretations of their experiences. This positive explanation of religious diversity makes ecumenical dialogue easier and mutual understanding and cooperation among different religions more likely, without requiring them to give up their particular identities.

Finally, we come to the key word in the definition—"ultimate." Whenever I have proposed the above definition, two questions, which very often are really objections, have been raised. The first is that the definition makes no reference to God, and the second is that it makes everyone and every society religious. My explanation of "ultimate" will deal with both of these questions or objections.

Is reference to God really absent from my definition? Yes and No. I have deliberately chosen to omit the word "God" in favor of "ultimate" as an adjective modifying "insights" and "values" because God is indeed the ultimate truth or insight and good or value for those who accept or believe that God is the ultimate reality, but this does not mean that those who refuse to use or accept the word "God" do not have ultimate values and insights (that is, an ultimate reality upon which they rely). Everybody has an ultimate reality, a final value and insight which is no longer negotiable.[7] This is the case even for those who deny that they have an ultimate, since their very denial implies and reveals that they do have one.[8] One of Karl Rahner's great services to this discussion has been to point out repeatedly that some atheists are convinced that they have to be atheists for the sake of the same values and truths that convince other people that they have to be theists.[9] This does not mean that either is right or wrong, but that everybody accepts an ultimate reality of some sort. It also means that the detailed explanations people give of their ultimates can differ, even conflict, although the truths and values they think are ultimate can have great similarity. In any case, these ultimate values and insights, however different they may be and however differently they may be explained, play the same role in the lives of the people who espouse them. That is, whatever the values and truths might be, they provide the reality which structures the daily lives, decisions, and actions of people. People arrange their lives in view of and on the basis of what they perceive to be ultimate reality.

Support for my not making explicit reference to God in the definition of religion has been provided by the civil courts of the United States of America.[10] According to the Supreme Court, secular humanism, which by definition excludes belief in the personal God of traditional theistic religions, is a religion. In a 1965 conscientious objector case, the Court accepted that belief in a lower case supreme being (god) plays the same role in people's lives—and in the public value system of the nation—as does belief in a higher case Supreme Being (God). The Court was not ruling on whether or not God exists. It was simply asserting that *even* those who deny the traditional supreme value and insight called God, nevertheless have an ultimate value and insight (a god) which functions in their lives the way God functions in the lives of traditional theistic believers. In the same spirit, the Ninth Circuit Court of Appeals recognized as religious belief "man thinking his highest, feeling his deepest and living his best." In the following year the same Court described as religious those human beings who believe in "goodness" or "livingness" at the heart of the world and all beings in the world. According to the *Seeger* decision the test of a "religious belief" is "whether a given belief that is sincere and meaningful occupies a place in the life of the possessor parallel to that filled by orthodox belief in God."

Support for the omission of explicit reference to God in my definition of religion is also provided by the actual history of religions and the comparative study of religion. There are, in fact, religions, recognized by all as religion, which do not have a personal God like the God of theistic religions.[11] To the ultimate true and good "being" of these religions one cannot say "God, our heavenly Father" or "God, our heavenly Mother." But the members of these so-called "God-less religions" have patterns of behavior which are quite similar and parallel to those of the traditional "God" religions.

Finally, it should also be noted that even people who use the word "God" to describe their ultimate reality differ widely in their understandings of God. Even religions like Judaism, Christianity, and Islam, all of which claim Abraham as their historical father, have differing explanations of who and what the God of Abraham is. All this is not intended to provoke discouragement and despair, cynicism and skepticism. It is, rather, to emphasize the point that when one observes the behavior of human beings, one discovers that human life is extraordinarily rich and varied, and complicated too. Nowhere is this more so than in regard to the human response to the question, "What's It All About?" This response we call religion.

But the second question or objection can still be urged. Is it fair to classify all people (and societies) as religious, even if and when they do not want to be religious? Is this not an imperialism which fails to respect the freedom and identity of others and imposes my will, my understanding on them—again, against their will? I do not think so. First of all, this approach does not require anybody to belong to any particular religion. Secondly, it does not assert that one religion is better than another or all others. In fact, it does not even say that religion as such is always or necessarily good. By its own principles, this approach would have to allow for the existence of what some people would call corrupt or perverted religion. As religion is a formation of human life and being, so can it also be a deformation. The phenomenological and anthropological approach speaks about the positive nature and essence of religion as well as its negative possibilities, its un-nature.[12] It simply asserts that, if one compares populations (cultures, societies, sub-societies) which seem to be very diverse, one still finds certain common patterns of behavior among them. One is that people organize their lives on the basis of values and insights perceived to be ultimate. Traditionally, in theistic religions this ultimate value and insight has been called God. How-

ever, empirical observation shows that people can and do so organize their lives even when they do not believe in the traditional
theistic personal God. This life-organization is called religion.

Some theologians have called these new, nontraditional religions pseudo-religions. However, since "pseudo" has such negative
overtones (false, cheap, phony, bogus, fradulent, counterfeit, insin-
cere), it is better omitted. Paul Tillich suggested that "quasi-
religions" would be a good term to describe modern secular
movements, whose members are in a "state of being grasped by an
ultimate concern, a concern which qualifies all other concerns as
preliminary and which itself contains the answer to the question of
the meaning of life."[13] Again, this statement does not judge the
truth, goodness, and beauty of such "states of being." It merely
observes that such states of *ultimate* concern with the *meaning of
life* do really exist—even when they do not take the form and shape
of the traditional religions more familiar to most of us.

Common to both the old, traditional, theistic religions and
the new, secularist, nontheistic religions is their desire to save
human beings, individually and corporately. As Raimundo Panikkar has emphasized, "The aim of any religion is to save or free Man.
No matter how we interpret this salvation and liberation, religion
is always the means whereby Man arrives at his destination..."[14]
This desire for salvation is so human that it is present not only in
the traditional theistic religions like Judaism, Christianity, Islam,
Hinduism, and others, but is also clearly present, both theoretically and practically, in modern secular versions like Marxism,[15]
Pragmatism and Ethical Culture and in "eastern countries which
feature a number of religious and pseudo-religious movements."[16]
Even the classical critique which Ludwig Feuerbach, Karl Marx,
Friedrich Nietzsche, and Sigmund Freud made of traditional religion is religious, for it wished to save people from a false, imaginary and unreal salvation.

These critics said that the traditional, theistic religions were
basically elaborate psychological mechanisms used to console
oppressed people without changing their oppression and its causes.
This so-called consolation was deceptive, for it was achieved only
by postulating another, higher life or world after death where
everything would be fine and dandy. The classical critique of
religion wishes to save humanity from this delusion, this illu-

sionary salvation, and replace it with true salvation. If, in the process, it replaces the Savior-God of traditional theistic religions with the Savior-Man of modern secularist religions, it remains committed to the salvation of humanity.[17] A traditional theist may not find the various salvations offered by secular humanist interpretations of the world and humanity appealing, but this does not mean that they are not presented as salvations.[18]

Even in materialist societies, one can discern among human beings a "fundamental need for meaningful fulfillment beyond the mere satisfaction of material needs...They look to ends which transcend individual existence."[19] Another way of saying this is Alfred North Whitehead's description of religion as humanity's search for "what is permanent in the nature of things."[20] Some find this transcendence and permanence inside the cosmos and its history; others find them beyond; still others find them inside and beyond. What is clear in all three cases is that human beings share a common quest. This quest is properly called religion—a quest in which all human beings engage. Hence, as Luigi Korinek has pointed out, the question is never whether human beings are religious or not—only whether they belong to and practice this or that religion.[21]

The Criteria of Religious Practice and Membership

As we have seen, human beings as such are religious. This general religious nature of human beings takes on many different concrete forms and shapes. Indeed, the variety is so great that sometimes one religion can have difficulty recognizing others as religions. This diversity exists in both religious theory and practice. Diversity in the practical dimension is more obvious, and here the question of the criteria of religious practice and membership easily and quickly arises.[22]

Some religions are highly organized, even complicated, in their ritual and worship, ministry and office, doctrine and devotion, while others are not. The same is true of the criteria whereby the degrees of participation and membership in any given religion can be discerned and measured. These criteria vary from religion to religion. The more complicated a religion, the more complicated will be its criteria of participation and membership. It is also important to note that within a religion the criteria can change from time to time, place to place. These criteria help both the members inside and nonmembers outside to understand the religion. Hence, they serve both theoretical and practical purposes. It is not fanciful to propose that the history of a religion can be read as the history of the discernment, establishment, revision and application-practice-enforcement of such criteria. I do not mean to imply that the majority of religionists have done this with explicit reflection. Since religion is primarily a way of life, a living practice, many practitioners may very well not reflect upon it in special ways. But they do participate in the reflection and practice of the entire membership, the corporate body.[23]

This lack of explicit reflection on the part of some, perhaps many, members in a given church can give rise to a serious problem. Does the distinction between explicitly reflecting members and nonreflecting members divide them into two different classes or grades? Is one of these classes better than the other? In any large society the population is differentiated. Not everybody is like everybody else, not everybody acts like everybody else. Diversity in unity and unity in diversity is a noble sentiment. But its actual practice has been difficult. It is not easy to be different and basically equal. We very easily slip into an attitude in which "different" automatically means "inferior," "subordinate," or "second rate." The other is not only other than us, but worse. Difference easily produces not a communion of the many, but a division into separate castes. We are familiar with this in regard to sex and race.

Unfortunately for its proponents, religion has not always escaped this kind of cleavage. This is partly the reason I have suggested that the history of a religion can be read as a debate about criteria of membership and practice. Who belongs? And who lives the religion the best? The King? The Prophet? The Priest? The Guru? The Ascetic? The Monk? The Pastor? The Preacher? The Scholar? The Specialist? The daily Communicant? The person who spends much time in church? The person who works in the slums? The sick person who endures without complaint? The charismatic reformer? The martyr? The ordinary, everyday "common man," doing his/her work and vocation conscientiously?

The problem of criteria is complicated because religion has a double dimension—interior and invisible, exterior and visible. The inner attitude and the outer action are supposed to correspond.

As Jesus admonished, true religion demands that external sacrifice and ritual worship be the true reflection and expression of inner righteousness—reconciliation with God and neighbor (Matt. 5:20-24). But who would want to claim to have achieved full correspondence between the two? Likewise, who would claim that the good intention in our hearts is always adequately put into practice in our everyday lives? An additional problem arises. Are people who look "more religious" really more religious? For example, are priests and ministers whose full-time jobs require them to be occupied with "obviously" religious matters like preaching and worship really more religious than the mother whose life is taken up with the care of her children and who may have little time for the "obviously" religious activities? Are people who reflect explicitly on religious life and practice, and who may therefore know more about the religion, in a privileged status compared to the simple believers?[24] The question becomes all the more critical because, and insofar as, these explicitly reflecting religionists tend to provide the theoretical explanations, the practical directives, the criteria for the religion as a whole. It would not be surprising were they to establish criteria which directly reflect and embody the understandings and practices most familiar and most dear to them. And, one must also concede, easiest for them to perform. We need not suspect them of hypocrisy as such. That is another matter, and we need not expend our time and energy on the deliberate hypocrites, who simply feign interest in religion. They are not a serious problem for our consideration.

I want to apply these general considerations to the Judeo-Christian religious tradition with which many of us are more familiar. Several New Testament texts illustrate a theme that is present from the very beginning of the Bible. What are the criteria of the true worshipper of God (John 4:23), the true son of Abraham (Matt. 3:9), the true Jew (Rom. 9:31-33)? What Christians call the Old Testament is simply filled with similar texts, all dealing with the same question: How do I live properly? What is God's will for me? What must I do to be saved? What must I do to be holy?[25]

Here the problem of differentiated membership arises. Are all called to holiness, or only some? Does membership in a certain class require, enable, assure holiness? This problem exists within each religion, but it also exists between religions. Can one religion understand the criteria of holiness in other religions? Can it accept them as valid for the other religions, without surrendering its own principles and identity? Can a given religion find a way to discern the gifts of God, which it believes itself to have received, to be also available to other religions, present in a different way, of course, but nevertheless truly present? A way was in fact found by the Roman Catholic Church at the Second Vatican Council (1962-64). This Council accepted as official Church doctrine the idea that someone can be an atheist and still satisfy the criteria for holiness and salvation.[26] This expansive view of holiness and salvation required revision of the traditional or customary criteria, a revision whose implications I wish now to explain with the help of a brief survey of the history of these criteria, especially in Western Christianity.[27]

At the beginning of Judeo-Christianity stands the exhortation of God to Israel, "Be holy, for I am holy" (Lev. 19:2). Jesus takes up this idea when he tells his disciples, "You must be perfect just as your heavenly Father is perfect" (Matt. 5:48). The early Church continues the same theme: "Be holy in all you do, since it is the Holy One who has called you" (1 Peter 1:16). "What God wants is for you all to be holy...We have been called by God to be holy" (1 Thess. 4:3, 7). It is indeed clear that we must be holy. But, the question immediately arises, how do I become holy? What must I be, what must I do? Jesus was often asked this. For example, "One of the scribes...put a question to him, 'Which is the first [greatest] of all the commandments?' Jesus replied, 'This is the first...you must love the Lord your God with all your heart, with all your soul, with all your mind and with all your strength. The second is this: You must love your neighbor as yourself. There is no commandment greater than these'" (Mark 12:28-31). Similar and parallel narratives can be found in Matthew 22:34-40 and Luke 10:25-28. This answer is correct, of course, but it is not very definite and concrete. In Luke, Jesus explains it with the parable of the Good Samaritan. That is, one loves one's neighbor by helping those in need whom one meets during one's life journey. In another scene a rich person asks Jesus, "Good Master, what have I to do to inherit eternal life?" Jesus replies that he knows the [ten] commandments and should keep them. The man replies that he has kept them since he was very young. Jesus then tells him to sell all that he owns, give it to the poor and follow Jesus (Luke 18:18-22).[28]

These two incidents from the Gospel illustrate both the purpose and the problem of criteria. Parallels can be found in all the religions. To understand that one must be holy does not automatically tell one how. Even to have some knowledge of how does not mean that one has enough. In every religion there is the need for even greater specification in regard to the criteria of holiness, for these criteria are at the same time the means whereby one lives a holy life. The Ten Commandments, with which many of us are familiar, are specifications of the more general command to be holy. But even these ten are still quite general and vague. We want and need more information, more specifics. Just *how* do I know my Father and Mother? Even the negative commandments (Thou shalt not) are in need of clarification, although they tend to be more concrete than the affirmative ones. It would be something of an oversimplification, but it would not be wrong, to say that much of the Bible is a commentary on the general command to holiness and the Ten Commandments. Or, from another angle, that the command to holiness and the Ten Commandments are symbolic summaries of the whole Bible. A note of caution may be fitting here. It is possible to overemphasize actions and good works to the neglect of the inner disposition and "belief." Nevertheless, we need always to recall that it is difficult to know what we really think until we put our thoughts into words and actions. That is where we find out how clearly we think and how strongly we treasure our thoughts. This is why the Epistle of James is right on target when it proclaims "that faith without good deeds is useless, dead" (2:1-26). Our internal faith and holiness achieve their full being and identity in our external actions.

And here the question immediately resurfaces: Which actions are reliable criteria indicating the existence of inner faith and making it really present in the world about us? Since the disciples of Jesus and the early Christians were a distinct minority, it may have been a bit easier for them to discern these criteria. If you accepted Jesus as the true prophet, then you had to stay close to him, follow him, and imitate him. It may not have been easy to do this, but at least you know what you were supposed to be doing.

Indeed, that it would not be easy to be and do like Jesus became clear fairly quickly, for you could end up being a martyr like Jesus.

In fact, the martyr was regarded as the true Christian, the true model for Christians. How better fulfill the first and greatest commandment of loving God above all else? This martyr love for God also frequently entailed the second commandment, love for one's brothers and sisters. And we know that many of the first Christians were indeed martyrs. Even those who were not actually martyred had nevertheless to be ready always. It is immediately clear, however, that even this readiness is not as clear-cut a criterion of holiness and the love of God as the act of martyrdom itself.

But what happens when the age of martyrs is past? Who then is the model Christian? How am I to know what to do, how to be, so that my inner faith is truly being lived in the world? This was a true and crucial crisis for the Church. What was to be the new criterion for religious interest and commitment? Of course, there was still the original command to be holy and the Ten Commandments and the example of the martyrs and many exhortations and admonitions both in and out of the Bible. But how was one to put all this into practice? How was one's inner faith to take shape, acquire a form (*Gestalt*) in the real world?[29]

A solution was found in the acceptance of the role of monk. Symbolically the monk replaced, indeed, became the martyr. Like the martyr, the monk "died" to the world, for God. The monk did not marry and have children; the monk did not own anything, having surrendered ownership to the monastic community and the abbot; the monk even surrendered his own will to the abbot—all this constituted a symbolic death to sin and the world, for God. It was truly a witness to the monk's faith and commitment. The import of the traditional three monastic vows of obedience, poverty, and chastity is precisely death to the world, symbolic martyrdom. The monastic life has a foundation in the New Testament and a legitimate role in the Christian religion.

But like many good things in the history of religions, monastic life soon exceeded its original purpose and its proper nature. Rather than being a symbolic expression of Christian living and a challenge to others, it came to be regarded as *the* Christian way of life, and others were regarded as lesser and inferior. This process was further complicated when and insofar as priests, the official ordained ministers, adopted a lifestyle which was more and more monastic—celibacy, distinctive "religious" clothing, separate housing, full-time church employment. The external actions performed by priests and monks were no longer inspiration and exhortation, but models and patterns to be followed and imitated as closely and literally as possible. The criteria for being a Christian became, then, the vows of poverty, chastity and obedience as these were practiced by the monks and, in their own proper way, by the priests, and the frequent devotional and liturgical practice which these states in life made possible. This way of being a Christian, legitimate in itself, was not balanced by another classic triad in Christianity, namely, prayer, fasting, and almsgiving. The monastic mode of performing even these three actions ceased to be one mode among many and became the way, the only way.

An unfortunate, but inevitable consequence of this is that religion became unworldly and the world became increasingly unreligious. Only a few people, a select few, were really religious. Everybody else was at best marginally and peripherally religious. Holiness came to be the specialized enterprise of some rather than the vocation of all. One of the aims of the Protestant Reformation was to de-monasticize the Church. Its success, though, was moderate. And in some cases it succeeded only by dividing the Church and the world into two separate kingdoms.[30] One consequence of this separation was to reinstate highly specialized, "obviously religious" criteria, resulting again in the establishment of a caste of explicit, professional religionists. And these became once again the true believers, the really holy people.

I know that this may seem overly critical. I do not intend it to be so, and I do not claim that I could have done it better. I mean it as a case lesson in the need to be aware, and wary, lest we take what is positively a legitimate criterion and make it into the only and absolute criterion of religious living. This absolutization of a particular criterion, to the effective exclusion of all others, necessarily produces a division within the membership of a religion. And with this division comes a separation or schism of the religion, the elevation of some (few) members into an elite, the reduction of most to an amorphous and nameless mass. "Elitism" connotes not people who have developed great skills and abilities, but a group or caste who claim superiority over all on the basis of one or more specialized, if not superior, skills. These elite people generally claim to be a privileged group, not merely other, but better than others. It is possible for this claim to be better than others to develop to the extent that others are not only inferior but even excluded from the possibility of becoming holy, achieving salvation, however holiness and salvation might be understood in the various religions.

The danger inherent in elitism is that it will *a priori*, by definition, exclude or marginalize certain sub-populations from holiness and salvation. The difficulty with this is that it contradicts the inner universalist dynamism of the salvation religions as such. As Etienne Cornelis has noted, "It is clear, then, that we can speak of a salvation-religion as soon as this religion, through its sacred doctrines, rites and other elements, undertakes to enable the human being—all human beings—to understand how to escape effectively from a common and universal situation of misery which afflicts the existence of humanity whole and entire."[31] The history of any given religion, and all religions, can be read as the temptation to elitist exclusivism and the struggle against it.

Of course, anti-elitism has its own inherent danger, namely, that of a universal levelling, a monolithic and monochromatic uniformity, in which everybody is forced into the same patterns and mold. The difficulty with this is twofold. First of all, people simply are not all the same, merely many different members of the same one model. Secondly, excessive anti-elitism deprives people of the variety of models and inspirations which would correspond to their own real diversity and which would inspire and challenge all these diverse people to develop their own gifts as best they can, and thus come to the holiness and salvation proper to them. The Christian practice of saints is a good illustration of this anti-elitist diversity.[32] The saints vary so much in their personalities and personal histories that no one can complain that he or she is not called, not able to be, a saint. Likewise, in Roman Catholicism the many different *religious* orders, as they are called, the Benedictines, Franciscans, Dominicans, Jesuits, Maryknollers, to name but a few of the more known ones, all illustrate the diversity of ways to the same saving holiness.[33] Unfortunately, as we noted earlier, in Catholicism the religious orders came to be the exclusive ways of holiness. Nevertheless, the history of the Catholic Church can also be read as a history of the struggle to avoid the perils of both exclusivist elitism and uniformist anti-elitism. While defending the legitimacy of the religious state of life, Thomas Aquinas also emphatically insisted that

> The precept (or command) of the love of God, which is the ultimate purpose and end of the Christian Life, is not narrowed or restricted by any boundaries whatsoever, as if one could say that so much love of God falls under the precept, but greater love, surpassing the limits of the precept, would come under the counsels. Rather, each one is commanded to love God as much as he can. This is evident in the very form of the command, "You shall love the Lord your God with your whole heart."[34]

Most recently the Second Vatican Council also recalled that "Thus it is evident to everyone that all the faithful of Christ of whatever rank or status are called to the fullness of the Christian life and to the perfection of charity."[35] If this is so, then criteria must be provided which enable "all the faithful" to put this call into practice. The monastic and clerical criteria of the past will not be suitable for this universalization of holiness. New universal criterion will have to be developed. Does the Catholic Church have the means to develop such criteria?

As we have seen, to discover that human being as such is religious is not enough. Further explanation is necessary, and this explanation can result in elitist and caste divisions within the religion. This can happen although the religion may very well have resources within itself which counter such elitist divisiveness. I think that Catholicism does have these resources.

We can illustrate this and prepare for our third section at the same time. The Christian religion grew out of the Jewish religion, which was about two thousand years old when Christianity began. Over the years Judaism had developed many laws, rites, doctrines —many criteria, we would say—of religious membership and belonging. It is legitimate and very enlightening to read the Gospels as arguments between Jesus and his contemporary Jews about the true criteria of the Jewish religion.[36] Which are most important, precisely how does one fulfill them, etc.? As complicated as Judaism had become two texts stand out for their universalist dynamism and simplicity. The Epistle of James emphasizes that "Pure, unspoilt religion, in the eyes of God our Father is this: coming to the help of orphans and widows when they need it, and keeping oneself uncontaminated by the world" (1:27). However, James spends several pages in detailed explanation of how such a pure religionist behaves, for he certainly knew that not many people's lives are likely to be taken up with the care of needy orphans and widows. "Keeping oneself uncontaminated" by evil is so general and vague that it is hardly helpful as a criterion of religious practice. Nevertheless, there is something utterly correct and sufficient about James's simple statement. Since everybody is religious, the criteria of religious practice must be available to everybody. Therefore, all articulations and elaborations in religion, all complications of the religion, we could say, are secondary, must serve and be subordinate to the first and greatest commandment, to love God, and its immediate corollary, to love one's neighbor.

I find this to be confirmed by the last parable Jesus tells, often called the parable of the last judgment, about the separation of people into sheep and goats and their reward. It is clearly a parable about the criteria of being religious, becoming holy, attaining salvation. And the criteria are certainly universalist and simple. The virtuous sheep who enter heaven are those who fed the hungry and thirsty, welcomed strangers, clothed the naked, visited the sick and prisoners. Certainly these are criteria which human beings can generally accomplish: one need not be extraordinarily talented or the privileged member of an elite to perform these actions. Parents, for example, would perform them perforce. What is perhaps most surprising is that the people who did this were not even explicitly aware of what they were doing. For when they did this to the "least," they did it to Christ. For our purpose, this is enormously important. It means that those who explicitly and especially reflect on the religious tradition and elaborate doctrine and policy are not an elite, not privileged in regard to religion, holiness and salvation. Were they not to so reflect and elaborate, they would have failed their proper role in the religion, their proper vocation. But their fulfillment of this task does not make them better or higher than the other members, only different, and, of course, holy, but not necessarily holier. For the Gospel makes it clear that holiness is not a matter of one's state in life, but of one's dedication to God and one's neighbors.

Everyday Life as Spiritual Discipline and Mysticism

In this third section I want to make these more general insights about religion and religious criteria more concrete. To do so I shall have recourse to the Catholic interpretation of the Judeo-Christian religious tradition, with special reference to the theology of Karl Rahner. One of Rahner's great concerns has been to explain theology so that the "man in the street" would be able to understand it: "At the beginning of Rahner's thought stands not a theological, doctrinal proposition, but contemporary man, with his own proper and typically modern self-understanding and *Weltanschauung*."[37] Although Rahner's thought can be difficult, his basic desire has not been to be an erudite academician, but a priest and pastor, dedicated to the "care of souls."[38] In an interview Rahner once emphatically insisted that "the primary end of theology is the salvation of man...not the contemplation of truth."[39]

Rahner has articulated his theology so that all believers, indeed, all human beings can understand that their lives—their ordinary, everyday lives—are the means whereby God communes with them and whereby they do God's will, become holy, attain salvation. Those who are called to more striking, unusual, extra-ordinary ways of becoming holy are the full-time religious professionals such as monks, ascetics, gurus, priests, ministers. But most people are called to be and become holy in and through their ordinary, everyday lives. In the fulfillment of their states in life as husbands and wives, parents and children, drivers and doctors, farmers and physicists, teachers and students, most people can and must become holy. In these "mundane" activities they can and must find God.[40] Rahner's theology has been the quest to find, in the Christian tradition, genuine criteria of religious participation and membership which would enable all Christians and all human beings to be able to experience God in their daily lives, and to know that they do so.

Let us now clarify our terminology and then briefly show why and how Rahner's understanding of Christianity enables him to advocate this position.[41] For Rahner the term "spiritual discipline" would be the equivalent of "spirituality," "piety," or "devotion." All of these words are liable to misinterpretation, especially because of certain overtones they have picked up in the course of history: spirituality is not immateriality or incorporeality, nor is a spiritual person one who always and perfectly follows the Holy Spirit; the pious person is not necessarily removed from the world, passive or otherwise retiring, although the word "piety" frequently conjures up images of bloodless statues swooning in garlands and grottoes; and devotion is not a purely interior attitude, certainly not precisely an intensely and enthusiastically emotional approach to religion. With varying emphases, these terms are used by Rahner to represent the relationship of a human being to God, the ultimate reality. They all imply an inner dimension (attitude) and an outer dimension (actions, whether ethico-moral or ritual-liturgical).

What distinguishes spirituality from religion in general is its focus on the concrete conditions of the particular human being. Religion can be thought of as the genus of spirituality, whose specific difference is those historical, psychological, sociological, economic, cultural, temperamental, educational, vocational, religious elements which conspire to constitute the precise identity of an individual or homogenous group of individuals. Spirituality is religion as it is realized, actualized, practiced, embodied here and now in particular people. In Rahner's own words, "Spirituality embraces the whole, entire Christian person's existence (*Dasein*) as a particular, individual human being, with special emphasis on the person's precise relationship to God."[42]

In more traditional Christian terms, Rahner describes "spirituality [as] the deliberately, consciously chosen and, to some extent or other, systematic, methodical development of Faith, Hope, and Charity."[43] Faith, Hope, and Charity are themselves key concepts in the history of Christian theology.[44] They describe and constitute what it really means to live the Christian life. To perform these three attitudes and acts is to live one's Christian existence really and truly.[45] We must keep in mind, however, that Faith, Hope, and Charity are also culturally conditioned, and so can be understood in different ways over the years.

Faith has customarily been understood as belief in God and acceptance of God's revelation as true because God can neither deceive nor be deceived. Correct in itself, this is certainly a bare bones definition, much in need of enrichment.[46] For Rahner, Christian faith is the "later" historical form (articulation) of an "earlier," original way or dimension of being human or "existential." This means that because human beings are finite, they are not in charge of their own beginning, and hence must rely on someone else. In the Christian view, this someone else is God the Creator, who is utterly reliable. Since the world has been created by God, it too is reliable or trust-worthy. Human beings can, therefore, live in it confidently. Precisely because the world has been created by a gracious God, there is possible for human beings "a fundamental, original, originary trust [*Urvertrauen*] in the comprehensive meaning and meaningfulness of [even finite, contingent] human existence."[47] "When and insofar as this *Urvertrauen* is intensified and takes on the form of a movement into immediacy (intimacy) with God, it is called Faith, Hope and Charity."[48] Since this fundamental trust (an original human existential) in the meaningfulness of finite, even fallen human existence, takes place in a graced cosmos, Rahner can further describe faith as "the acceptance and embracing of the flow (the to and fro) of everyday life."[49] Elsewhere he also explains faith as the courage to face the difficulties and challenges, as well as the joys and pleasures, of everyday life, for these daily events mediate God's saving initiative and will to us.[50] Hence, once again, holiness and salvation are not events on the margin of our real lives. Grace, God's special communication and communion with us, is not a series of infrequent and isolated intrusions from above into an otherwise secular, pagan world. Rather, in the divinely graced world, ordinary human life is already a school of holiness, as monasteries were once called.

Rahner bases this position on the doctrine of the universal saving will of God who "wants everyone to be saved and reach full knowledge of the truth. For there is only one God, and there is only one mediator between God and mankind, himself a man, Jesus Christ" (1 Tim. 2:4-6). On the basis of this and similar biblical assertions, Rahner understands that the world must always have been graced. That is, the human race, whole and entire, has never been without the means to be holy and saved. Because of God's gracious initiative, God's creation has never been merely natural. It has always been supernatural. This means that the grace of holiness and salvation has always been offered to human beings,

32

whether they accept or reject it. Rahner calls this universal offer of grace the "supernatural existential," for this gracedness truly belongs to and constitutes human nature as it actually exists in history. This is also the source of Rahner's theory of "anonymous Christianity," which is not a sneaky attempt to get more Christians at a time when official Church membership is declining, nor an imperialist imposition on others who do not want to be Christians in the first place, but, rather, the theological attempt to see whether and how the divine gifts of grace, holiness, and salvation which Christians believe themselves to have received are also available to others, indeed to all humanity. The alternative, of course, is to believe that only explicit Christians can be holy and saved. That *is* imperialistic![51]

The theology at the base of the theory of "anonymous Christianity" is important not only for the relationship of Christianity to non-Christians. It is equally important for those who are already explicitly Christians. Anonymous Christianity requires a positive understanding of creation as the means and symbol of God's communication and communication with that which is not purely and simply God. By virtue of creation, the world is already the image and likeness of God, where God shares being and life with what would (could) otherwise not exist on its own (Gen. 1, 2). Even sin has not totally destroyed or corrupted this state of affairs. Indeed, sin has been the occasion for God's continued and even greater communication and communion with humanity (Gen. 3-12). This communication and communion of the divine with the human reaches its peak in Jesus, who is the sacrament (sign and cause) of God's saving will in the world (Rom. 5:12-21; 1 Cor. 15:20-58). According to St. Paul, Jesus is God's Yes to all His divine promises to the world (2 Cor. 1:20). Because of this divine affirmation of the human, everyone who also affirms the human is already being God-like and consequently also Christ-like. This is the case, as Jesus reminded us in Matthew's Gospel (25:31-46) even when the human affirmers are not explicitly aware of their God- and Christ-likeness. In this context it is clear that although Love of God and Love of Neighbor are not simply identical, they are equally inseparable.[52] In this context it is also clear that to follow one's conscience sincerely and diligently is already to have faith, to be a believer.[53] Why? To follow one's conscience and to love one's neighbor in the ordinary activities of everyday life is already to accept this God-given world. This acceptance requires and implies that trust and commitment that we traditionally demand of and describe as faith. Since this accepting and trustful commitment happens in a world graced by the universal saving will of God, it is also sanctifying and saving. It is Faith—and Hope and Charity, too.[54]

For this reason, Rahner returns repeatedly to the "Mysticism of Everyday Life."[55] He is convinced that "the religious person of tomorrow will be a 'mystic' who has 'experienced' something, or he won't be at all."[56] Basically Rahner seems to agree with the Greek Church Father, Origen, that "every knowledge of God is in some way or other mystical."[57] Rahner is intent on enabling us to understand that we encounter and experience God in many ways. These ways are not restricted to extraordinary, ecstatic experiences or to special moments of formal, ritual, liturgical worship.

Rather, in the *seemingly* secular experiences of everyday life, we encounter and experience God, who has made the world precisely in such a way that we can meet God *in* it:

> Basically, I really want to say only this one thing to my readers. Human beings are always, in every place and at every moment, directed to the ineffable mystery of their life, which we call God. This is the case whether human beings know it or not, whether they reflect on it or not. Furthermore, because of the crucified and resurrected Jesus, human beings are able to hope that they will attain (be with) this God as their own proper and unique fulfillment, already now and even more so after death.[58]

If this is so, then what role do such important religious realities as sacraments, sacred scriptures, rituals, monasteries and such play? Are they superfluous at best, hindrances at worst? Rahner has been concerned with this problem throughout his career. It takes different forms. One is fairly simple, like the relationship between the "sacramental" and "personal" dimensions of piety. Both are important. Each individual must find the proper proportion.

Rahner has often insisted that "the Christian life does not simply coincide with the sacramental life."[59] That is, the sacramental does not exhaust the entire Christian reality. The sacramental is the more intense, sensibly perceptible celebration, in time and space, of the divine saving grace which is always present and active. In this usage "sacramental" is restricted more or less to the special seven sacraments (Baptism, Confirmation, Holy Eucharist, Penance, Anointing of the Sick, Marriage, Holy Orders). However, there is another and more expansive way to use the word "sacrament." In this wider sense, it means that God's grace in the world always has some sort of "worldly" shape. How could it not, if it is to be truly present and effective in the real world? The ultimate basis for this more general usage of the term "sacramental" is the doctrines of creation and incarnation. They tell us that when God communicates with the world, God also gives a sign or symbol of this communication.[60] Hence, the created world is already the image and likeness of God (Gen. 1:27). As the image and likeness of the invisible God, his divine Father (John 1:14-18, 14:8-21; Col. 1:15-20), Jesus is the special sacrament of the divine presence in the world from the very beginning. Jesus does not appease an angry God and transform Him from a vengeful punisher to a gracious forgiver. Rather, Jesus reveals that God has always been gracious to the world, even in its fallen state. Jesus reveals that priesthood and sacrifice are both personal and ritual. The heart of the priestly and sacrificial is not to offer holocausts and similar oblations, but to do the will of God (Heb. 10:4-10).

The temple, where the true worship of God takes place, is no longer a special, separate place, cut off from or out of the rest of the world as the Greek word for temple (*temenos*) implies.[61] Rather, as Jesus had told the Samaritan woman, true worship is restricted to neither a sacred city nor a sacred mountain. No, it takes place in spirit and truth (John 4:15-24). This, of course, does not forbid or downplay public, liturgical worship. It simply emphasizes that such ritual worship must always be the genuine expression of the personal doing of God's will. In principle, there is no rivalry, no conflict between the personal and the sacramental. Likewise, in principle the historical and categorical is not opposed to or separate from the transcendental. Indeed, it is precisely in the historical and categorical realities of creation that the transcendent creator is mediated to us. The divine transcendence is not for the sake of God's separation from us, but for the sake of our communion with God. As St. Paul preached in the Areopagus, "Yet in fact He is not far from any of us, since it is in him that we live and move and exist" (Acts 17:27-28).

This truth, the nearness of the transcendent God to us, so that God is truly not only transcendent to the world but also immanent in it and intimately present to human beings—this truth enables us to speak of creation and incarnation, grace and holiness, supernatural existential and anonymous Christianity, everyday life as spiritual discipline and "the Mysticism of Everyday Life"— in a word, salvation.

This is truly religion—truly for everyman and everywoman.

NOTES

1 See Michael Nicolau and Joachim Salaverri, *Sacrae Theologiae Summa I* (Madrid: B.A.C., 1955), 64-75.

2 Thomas Aquinas, *Summa Theologiae*, II-II, q. 81, a. 1.

3 The various articles on religion in *The New Catholic Encyclopedia* (New York: McGraw-Hill, 1967), 240-72, are a very helpful introduction.

4 See Wolfgang Riess, *Glaube als Konsens* (Munich: Kösel, 1979), 173-78.

5 Bernhard Stoeckle points out that the need (*Bedürftigkeit*) for redemption is universally present among human beings, even if they do not explicitly feel this need (*Bedürfnis*), "*Erlösungsbedürftigkeit des Menschen und Vorauswirken der Erlöslung,*" *Mysterium Salutis*, II, ed. Johannes Feiner and Magnus Löhrer (Einsideln: Benziger, 1967), 1024-39.

6 But this does not make it as such sinful pride and a work or trick of the devil, whereby human beings close themselves off to the true revelation given by God. This approach, which can be traced back to Soren Kierkegaard and which peaked in the early Karl Barth, has also been very influential in theologians such as Emil Brunner, Helmut Thielicke and Dietrich Bonhoeffer who proposed that a "religion-less world" would provide a sterling opportunity for the Christian faith, the true path to God, alone the true path in their view. This negative approach to religion and the religions of the world has been deemed too narrow and inadequate by even the *Taschenlexikon Religion und Theologie*, 3, ed. Erwin Falhbusch (Göttingen: Vandenhoeck und Ruprecht, 1971), 261. If one does not subscribe to this negative view of religion, then one also need not subscribe to Paul Ricoeur's contention that there must be a "death of religion" (similar, one assumes, to the death of God, which was so popular at the same time), so that true, genuine, and mature faith might flower. Paul Ricoeur, *The Conflict of Interpretations* (Evanston, Ill.: Northwestern University Press, 1974), 441 (*Le Conflit des interpretations* [Paris, 1969]).

7 See Robert Johann, *Building the Human* (New York: Herder and Herder, 1968), 15-17.

8 This is similar to the problem of absolute skepticism, when one absolutely denies that there are absolutes, when one knows that no one can know anything. Already Aristotle knew that such assertions contradict themselves. In a famous conundrum: "You say one must philosophize. Then you must philosophize. You say one should not philosophize. Then (to prove your contention) you must philosophize. In any case, you must philosophize." From Jacques Maritain, *Introduction to Philosophy* (New York: Sheed and Ward, 1947), 104, with references to the original Greek text.

9 Karl Rahner, "Kirche und Atheismus," *Stimmen der Zeit* 106 (1981), 3-13.

10 The decisions referred to are the following: Torcaso v. Watkins, 397 U.S. 488 (1961) at 495, n.11; United States v. Seeger, 380 U.S. 193 (1965); Peter v. United States, 324 F. 2d 173 (9th Cir. 1963); Macmurray v. United States, 330 F. 2d 928 (9th Cir. 1964).

11 For example, Theravada Buddhism. See Huston Smith, *The Religions of Man* (New York: Harper & Row, 1965), 132-39.

12 Bernhard Welte, "Wesen und Unwesen der Religion," *Auf der Spur des Ewigen* (Freiburg: Herder, 1965), 279-96. Welte speaks of the *Wesen* (the nature or essence of religion; this is good) and the *Unwesen* (the un- or anti-nature/essence; this is bad).

13 Paul Tillich, *Christianity and the Encounter of the World Religions* (New York: Columbia University Press, 1961), 4.

14 Raimundo Panikkar, *Myth, Faith and Hermeneutics* (New York: Paulist, 1979), 408.

15 Louis Dupre, *The Other Dimension* (New York: Seabury, 1979).

16 Iring Fetscher, "State Socialist Ideology as Religion," *Christianity and Socialism*, ed. J. B. Metz and J. P. Jossua, *Concilium* (105), 85. See also *Häresien der Zeit*, ed. A. Böhm (Freiburg: Herder, 1961), 215-374; Lilly Weissbrod, "Religion as National Identity in a Secular Society," *Review of Religious Research* 24 (1983), 188-205.

17 Bernhard Casper, *Wesen und Grenzen der Religionskritik* (Würzburg: Echter, 1974), 40.

18 That these nontraditional or quasi-religions really are religious and really want to be such can also be discerned in the fervor with which they try to eradicate and supplement the traditional ones. A classic case, with systematic persecution toward the elimination of the traditional religions, is Albania, strangely if deliberately overlooked in the Western media. See Heiner Emde, "Scheinfriede und brutale Gewalt," *Weltbild* 3 (4 February 1983), 38-41. See also Thomas Molnar, "Desacralization in Modern Society," *Catholicism in Crisis* 1, no. 4 (February 1983), 3-4. The same issue of this journal has a short report on a Sandinista (Nicaragua) memo either to eliminate Christmas or to transform it into a political symbol (pp. 5-6). See also Serge Schmemann, "New Soviet Rituals Seek to Replace Church's," *New York Times* (15 March 1983), A9. In the course of his *The Spirit of Democratic Capitalism* (New York: Simon and Schuster, 1982), Michael Novak often has occasion to note the religious claims and thrust of socialism (pp. 50, 59, 65, 91, 104, 187-214 and *passim*). See also Robert Nisbet, *History of the Idea of Progress* (New York: Basic Books, 1980), 357, where he goes so far as to speak of "the sheer lure of the political-ideological 'church'...The Church of Politics." Here (p. 331) and elsewhere (*Twilight of Authority* [New York: University Press, 1975], 205), he speaks freely, and correctly, of the "lay clergy of the West—the intelligentsia that began in the eighteenth century to succeed the clergy as the dominant class so far as citizen's beliefs are concerned."

19 Fetscher, "State Socialist," 85.

20 Alfred North Whitehead, *Religion in the Making* (New York: World, 1960), 16.

21 Luigi Korinek, "Psicologia della negazione di Dio," *Psicologia dell' atheismo* (Rome: PUG, 1967), 42, 74.

22 For a detailed examination of this question, see Hervé Carrier, *The Sociology of Religious Belonging* (New York: Herder and Herder, 1965).

23 Ninian Smart, *The Phenomenon of Religion* (New York: Herder and Herder, 1973), 36.

24 Nowadays, however, the case is slightly different. As Karl Rahner, certainly an excellent and erudite theologian, has often pointed out, today's knowledge explosion has made it impossible for one person to have command over even one specialty in theology, much less all theology, even much less over all human knowledge. Karl Rahner, *Grundkurs des Glaubens* (Freiburg: Herder, 1976), 20; *Foundations of Christian Faith* (New York: Crossroad, 1978), 8.

25 On this, see Robert Kress, *Christian Roots* (Westminster, Md.: Christian Classics, 1978).

26 *Lumen Gentium,* 16; *Gaudium et Spes,* 19-22; *Ad Gentes,* 7. See Karl Rahner, "Atheismus und Implizites Christentum," *Schriften zur Theologie* 8 (Einsiedeln: Benziger, 1967), 187-212. The documents of this council are referred to by both Latin and English titles, of which the above three documents, with the English short reference form in parentheses, are *Dogmatic Constitution on the Church* (*The Church,* 16), *Pastoral Consititution on the Church in the Modern World* (*The Church Today,* 19-22); *Decree on the Church's Missionary Activity* (*Missions,* 7). The paragraphs of the texts are numbered. Hence, page references are not necessary. There are two editions and slightly differing translations available in English. *The Documents of Vatican II,* ed. Walter Abbot (New York: America Press, 1966). *Vatican Council II,* ed. Austin Flannery (Northport, N.Y.: Costello, 1975). Both contain some commentary and supporting documents.

27 For extensive elaboration and documentation of this, see Robert Kress, *The Church: Communion, Sacrament and Communication* (Washington, D.C.: University of America Press, 1983), chap. 4.

28 On the tensions in earliest Christianity between the wandering charismatics (like Jesus, Peter, Paul) and more sedentary local communities, see Gerd Theissen, *Sociology of Early Palestinian Christianity* (Philadelphia: Fortress, 1978).

29 As St. Paul said, "My children! I must go through the pain of giving birth to you all over again, until Christ is formed in you" (Gal. 4:19). Here "formed" means taking shape in the world; in Greek, *morphē,* in German, *Gestalt.* See Franz Schupp, *Glaube—Kultur—Symbol* (Düsseldorf: Patmos, 1974), 31-39.

30 In the Lutheran tradition one speaks of the Two Kingdom Doctrine.

31 Etienne Cornelis, "Soteriologie und nichtchristliche Erlösungsreligionen," *Mysterium Salutis* III/2 (1969), 607.

32 For all its lack of balance among men and women, nations and cultures, etc., see Lawrence Cunningham, *The Saints* (San Francisco: Harper & Row, 1980). According to Karl Rahner, *Schriften* 3 (1956), 120: "What Christian holiness is is revealed in the life of Jesus and his saints...They are the initiators and

creative exemplars of precisely that holiness which is required by and proper to any given age."

33 An analogous diversity can be discerned in Protestant denominationalism and sectarian formation. Of course, within Protestantism the unity of diversity in unity is not as clear.

34 St. Thomas Aquinas, "Contra Pestiferam Doctrinam Retrahentium Homines a Religionis Ingressu," in *Opuscula Theologica* II, ed. R. Spiazzi (Turin: Marietti, 1954), 165 (#759).

35 *The Church*, 40.

36 See Kress, *Christian Roots*, 41-63.

37 Karl Heinz Weger, *Karl Rahner* (Freiburg: Herder, 1978), 4.

38 Paul Imhoff and Hubert Biallowons, "Vorwort," *Karl Rahner im Gespräch* I (Munich: Kösel, 1982), 16. Unfortunately, spiritual theology and systematic theology have tended to lead separate lives, to the distress and disadvantage of both. As Dietrich Rössler has pointed out, "In any case, in theology piety [spirituality] has not been a focal point, central concern. Piety is not one of the distinguishing themes of the great Church reformations, renewals or the various theological schools, with the exception of Pietism...but Pietism is not primarily a theological school, but a church-religious movement, which influenced theology...In Catholic theology the situation is somewhat different, but nevertheless comparable...However, piety is not a major concern of either Catholic dogmatic theology or official church doctrine." Dietrich Rössler, "Frommigkeit als Thema der Ethik," *Handbuch der christlichen Ethick,* II, ed. Anselm Hertz, Wilhelm Korff, Trutz Rendtorff, and Hermann Ringeling (Freiburg: Herder, 1978), 506-7. Rahner stands in stark contrast to the situation described by Rössler.

39 In an interview with Patrick Granfield, *Theologians at Work* (New York: Macmillan, 1967), 43.

40 A favorite theme of Ignatius of Loyola and his spirituality is "to find God in all things" ("hallar Dios en todas las cosas"). *Spiritual Exercises of St. Ignatius,* trans. Thomas Corbishley (New York: Kennedy, 1963), 79-80 (#233-37). Unfortunately, the few pages on these paragraphs in Rahner's *Spiritual Exercises* (New York: Herder and Herder, 1965), 270-77, are not very helpful. Much more helpful is his "Die Ignatianische Mystik der Weltfreudigkeit," *Schriften* 3 (1956), 329-428.

41 For elaboration of all that follows, I refer the reader to Robert Kress, *A Rahner Handbook* (Atlanta: John Knox, 1982).

42 Karl Rahner, "Formale Grundstrukturen der Heilsvermittlung," *Handbuch der Pastoraltheologie*, II/1, ed. F. X. Arnold, et al. (Freiburg: Herder, 1966), 63.

43 Karl Rahner, *Schriften* 12 (1975), 335.

44 Karl Rahner, *Schriften* 13 (1978), 310 (Schlusselbegriffe).

45 *Schriften* 13, 255: "den einen ganzen Vollzug christlicher Existenz."

46 John Macquarrie, *Principles of Christian Theology* (New York: Scribner's, 1977), 373-84.

47 Karl Rahner, *Wagnis des Christen* (Freiburg: Herder, 1974), 28; *Herausforderung des Christen* (Freiburg: Herder, 1975), 85; *Schriften* 10 (1972), 286, 293-97, 417.

48 Karl Rahner, *Wagnis*, 30.

49 Karl Rahner, *Schriften* 10, 417.

50 Karl Rahner, "Faith as Courage," *Meditations on Freedom and the Spirit* (New York: Seabury, 1978), 7-29; *Schriften* 13, 252-68. See also *Schriften* 13, 239-43 where Rahner describes, with examples from ordinary human experience, "the Mysticism of everyday living, the finding of God in all things" (p. 243) in terms of human, philosophical transcendence which has been supernaturally graced by and in the Holy Spirit of God. Also *Schriften* 9 (1970), 161-76; 10, 133-44; 3, 105-10.

51 See Kress, *A Rahner Handbook*, 56-61. I note here immediately that, when asked how he would react to being termed an anonymous Zen Buddhist, Rahner replied: "Of course, from your standpoint you may and you must do so. I could only feel honored by such an interpretation, even if I would nevertheless have to regard it as mistaken, or presuppose that, correctly interpreted, genuine Zen-Buddhist-Being and correctly understood Christian-Being are identical at that (ontological) level which is actually and immediately intended by such statement." It should also be noted that Rahner speaks of an anonymous relationship to God (*Schriften* 6, 27), anonymous Lutherans (9, 78), anonymous theism (9, 185), anonymous Lutherans and anonymous Catholics (10, 500), anonymous Buddhists, (12, 276), anonymous and unthematic knowledge of God (*Grundkurs*, 32; *Foundations*, 21).

52 On this entirely fundamental theme see explicitly Karl Rahner, "Über die Einheit von Nächsten- und Gottesliebe," *Schriften* 6 (1965), 277-98, and *Herausforderung des Christen*, 137), where he explicitly defends himself against accusations of having simply equated the two.

53 Karl Rahner, "Kirche und Atheismus," *Stimmen der Zeit* 106 (1981), 12.

54 Karl Rahner, "Herz Jesu Verehrung heute," *Korrespondenzblatt des Canisianums*, 116/1 (1982/83), 7.

55 Karl Rahner, *Schriften zur Theologie* 13, 243-45; *Schriften* 14 (1980), 236. The words mystic and mysticism are among the most difficult of all religious terms. Their meaning in Rahner has been examined by Harvey Egan, "Rahner's Mystical Theology," *Theology and Discovery*, ed. William Kelly (Milwaukee, Wisc.: Marquette University Press, 1980), 139-58. A classic treatment is offered by Evelyn Underhill, *Mysticism* (New York: New American Library, Meridian Books, 1955). An easier introduction is David Knowles, *The Nature of Mysticism* (New York: Hawthorn, 1966). *Mystery and Mysticism* (New York: Philosophical Library, 1956) is an interesting collection of articles on Christian mysticism. Of special interest are the two articles by Louis Bouyer on the

history of the word "mysticism" (pp. 119-37) and its relationship to the fundamental Christian term *mysterion*, whence come both mystery and sacrament in the Christian vocabulary (pp. 33-46). This book is older, but not dated. We should also mention a brief comparison of Christian mysticism with mysticism in general or other mysticisms by Henri de Lubac, "Preface," *La Mystique et les mystiques*, ed. A. Ravier (Paris: Aubier, 1965). The preface and entire book contain rich bibliographies.

56 Karl Rahner, *Schriften* 7 (1966), 22.

57 Karl Rahner, *Schriften* 11 (1975), 128. See also Klaus Fischer, *Der Mensch als Geheimnis* (Freiburg: Herder, 1974), 21-30.

58 *Karl Rahner im Gespräch*, 301.

59 Rahner, *Handbuch der Pastoraltheologie*, II/1, 71; also *Schriften* 6 (1965), 31.

60 Robert Kress, "Worship" and "The Church," *Options in American Catholicism*, ed. Nathan Kollar (Washington, D.C.: University Press of America, 1982).

61 Heribert Mühlen, "Sakralität und Amt zu Beginn einer neuen Epoche," *Catholica*, 26/1 (1972), 71.

Religion, Its Disciplines, and Their Relation to Ultimate Reality

James Duerlinger

P rofessor Kress rightly calls attention to the need to avoid religious bias and elitism in an ecumenical discussion of ultimate reality and spiritual discipline. He is especially concerned that we avoid definitions of religion which favor a theistic conception of ultimate reality over others, and avoid paradigms of religious practice or discipline which exclude the activities of everyday life. To this end he defines religion as human life as a whole organized on the basis of insights and values perceived as the ultimate reality, and, by implication, spiritual discipline as any activity in which one conscientiously engages for the sake of his ultimate reality. After explaining the changes that have occurred in the criteria by which spiritual disciplines have been identified in Christianity, he then draws on the views of the Catholic Church and Karl Rahner to support the idea that a spiritual discipline in which one lives everyday life in accord with his own perception of ultimate reality is already a mystical communication and communion with God, the divine ultimate reality, since such a life is an acceptance of a world infused with His grace. Thus, Professor Kress argues that everyday activities are spiritual disciplines insofar as they are conscientiously performed by persons for the sake of their most fundamental goals, even if they do not themselves acknowledge the existence of God or consciously engage in traditional religious disciplines designed to bring them closer to God. He further argues that these activities are also *Christian* disciplines insofar as they are mediated communications with the divine ultimate reality with which Christians also seek to communicate directly. In this way, Kress argues, Christians can believe not only that non-Christians practice a religion, but also that, as anonymous Christians, they may attain Christian salvation to the extent that they follow their conscience and act out of love for their fellow man. This view, he insists, is not an imperialist conversion of the world to Christianity, but an attempt to rid Christianity of the prejudice that only recognized Christians may be saved. He thinks that this view shows the way in which other religions may try to free themselves of exclusivist dogmas and elitist conceptions of spiritual discipline.

Most of us, of course, wish to avoid the religious bias and elitism Professor Kress explains in his richly documented essay, and for his penetrating analysis of these failings in the Christian tradition we can all be grateful. I must take exception, however, to his own attempt to overcome them, and for the purpose of laying a firm foundation for ecumenical discussion and cooperation among religious leaders I shall here explain my reservations and propose an alternative view which I believe will not involve the problems I find with Professor Kress's proposals.

What is primarily lost by the acceptance of his proposed definitions of religion and its disciplines is the very thing I believe it is most important for the traditional religions to preserve. For what distinguishes religion and its disciplines from other forms of organized life and discipline is precisely the spiritual nature of the ultimate concern they involve, and his definitions fail to specify this nature. It is difficult, however, to specify without prejudice what this distinctive ultimate concern is. A specification is impossible, Professor Kress rightly stresses, if one insists upon including, as theists may wish to do, reference to an all-good, all-knowing, and all-powerful God who creates and sustains the world, since not all religions accept his existence. But in his attempt to avoid this difficulty Professor Kress goes to the extreme of omitting from his definitions any reference to a spiritual value or insight which distinguishes religious ultimate concern from secular. He resorts to making the fact that one *has* an ultimate concern of some sort over the course of his life the mark of his possessing a religion, when he needs only to give a non-prejudicial specification of the spiritual ultimate concern that separates religious people from nonreligious. As a result, he must accept the idea that all people are religious and defend this idea against objections.

According to Professor Kress's definitions, it is clear, political ideologies and materialistic philosophies are religions and the activities performed to achieve their goals are spiritual disciplines, in spite of the fact that religions in the past have regarded them as nonreligious in character. In seeming acknowledgement of this historical circumstance Professor Kress himself is willing to speak of them as secular religions or as quasi-religions, but he still insists that they are religions because of what strikes him as their important similarities to the traditional religions, e.g., their concern for the whole of life and its meaning, reliance on values being held as ultimate, etc. The point, however, needs to be made that the similarities on which he fixes his attention do not of themselves warrant the reclassification of these ideologies and philosophies as religions; it must be decided, as well, what the advantages and disadvantages are to using these similarities as the basis for a reclassification, to whom it will be advantageous or disadvantageous, and why. With regard to ecumenism, however, I do not see that the decision to classify secular ideologies and philosophies as religions will be very useful. To be sure, Professor Kress's definitions avoid bias against nontheistic religions and elitist conceptions of spiritual discipline, but the losses for religions incurred by their acceptance, as I shall argue later, far outweigh their gains. For the moment I want only to emphasize that the work the words "religion" and "spiritual discipline" should do in an ecumenical discussion among religious leaders is to mark off themselves and their practices from what they themselves have always regarded as nonreligion and nonreligious practices, and I see no good reason for them to sacrifice these distinctions in order to avoid making reference to God in the definitions of religion and spiritual discipline.

Professor Kress's failure to isolate the spiritual nature of religion and its disciplines in his definitions is camouflaged somewhat by his reinterpretation of religion and its disciplines from his own Christian-theistic perspective. His motivation, presumably, is to show Christian theists how they may free themselves from the notion that they alone will be saved, but his reinterpretation also has the effect of making his definitions more acceptable to such theists who will have difficulty accepting the idea that there can be a religion or spiritual discipline without some intimate connection to God. It would seem that he resolves the conceptions of religion and its disciplines into the genera to which they belong, namely, the conceptions of organized life and activity each pursued for the sake of an ultimate concern, and then, for the sake of enlightening Christian theists, with whose view Professor Kress himself agrees, he interprets all such life and pursuit in terms of the Christian theistic perspective. Does not this maneuver, however consciously well-motivated, show us that Professor Kress himself may be sensing that the distinctively spiritual nature of religion and its disciplines has not been captured by his definitions? Christian theists, I suspect, do not really think that religion is the way man organizes his life in relation to whatever he happens to *think* is ultimate reality, but the way man organizes his life in relation to God himself, and if they accept Professor Kress's definition of religion, I believe, it will be because they think that he has somehow reduced whatever man happens to think is ultimate reality to ultimate reality itself. I do not myself see how this can be a valid reduction, since the acceptance of God's creation is not the acceptance of it *as* God's creation, and only if it is accepted *as* his creation can a so-called secular religion be reduced to that of the theist. For this reason I have said that Professor Kress's reinterpretation camouflages the nonspiritual character of his definitions.

Presumably, members of nontheistic religions could also reinterpret Professor Kress's definitions so they imply that all religious people are anonymous members of their own religions, e.g., Buddhists could reinterpret them so that all religious people are anonymous Buddhists, etc. But what is the point of these definitions if we must resort to this means of recapturing the spirituality religious people sense is lost in them? In particular, is it really helpful to the cause of cooperative understanding among the religions of the world to secularize the conceptions of religion and its disciplines so that any religion can then give them a spiritual meaning according to its own metaphysical religious perspective?

Religion and its disciplines, I contend, do in fact have a

specifiable spiritual nature, and so in what follows I shall make suggestions of my own about the definitions of religion and its disciplines and their relation to ultimate reality. It is my belief that these suggestions, or some version of them, will be acceptable to representatives of the world's religions as a basis upon which they can recognize other religions as religions, without at the same time being forced to admit various secular movements as religions or to reinterpret one another according to their own metaphysical perspectives in order to assert their spiritual nature.

The world religions are organized attempts, inspired by the lives and teachings of their founders, to realize a life for man in which he experiences forever things as they really are, not as they ordinarily appear, and achieves eternal blissful freedom from the suffering which attended his separation from consciousness of ultimate reality. Such a life they have regarded divine in the sense that it is life lived in permanent blissful consciousness of ultimate reality, free from the suffering incurred by a life in which something else is taken to be ultimate. Different interpretations of the nature of this ultimate reality are made by these religions, and there are often considerable disagreements about its nature even within the same religion. For instance, some identify ultimate reality with God, who is the all-powerful, all-good, and all-knowing uncreated creator and sustainer of the world and who himself possesses divine life; others identify it exclusively with an ineffable nature of all things which man must experience if he is to live the divine life, and either construe God as the highest manifestation or distinguishable aspect of the ineffable nature or deny his existence altogether.

To what extent religions can reconcile these and other opposing views concerning the nature of ultimate reality is debatable, but it is clear in any case that they seem to have important doctrinal differences. In this situation, if cooperation between the major religions is to take its start from an agreement about what is and what is not a religion, no special conception of ultimate reality, as Professor Kress points out, can be specified in the definition of religion. This means that each religion must free itself of the idea that religion must involve an attempt to commune with ultimate reality exactly as it conceives of that reality. It does not mean, however, that in a definition of religion we must resort to the idea

that the ultimate reality with which religious man seeks to commune is merely what he *perceives* to be ultimate. There is no need
to surrender to the forces of modern skepticism a reference in the
definition to an ultimate reality which not all persons perceive or
accept. In spite of their differences concerning the nature of ultimate reality, religions do seem to agree that this reality is permanent and is not the very same thing as the impermanent things which
ordinarily appear to us, even if they hold that such things are
sustained by the ultimate reality, that they are appearances of the
ultimate reality itself, or that the experience of ultimate reality
transforms how such things appear, etc. The point is that spiritual
realization involves a liberating perception of a permanent ultimate reality not reducible simply to the finite world just as it
appeared before the realization.

My own suggestion, therefore, is that religion is to be found, if
anywhere, in man's organized pursuit of the divine life, one in
which he perpetually enjoys an eternal blissful state of consciousness of ultimate reality, a reality whose nature has been
differently conceived by different religious traditions and even
within the same traditions, but which transcends things as they
ordinarily appear and which frees him when he perceives it from
all sufferings. What is ultimate about this reality, these religions
seem to agree, is that it is what is experienced by man at the acme of
his spiritual quest and is more permanent than what he once took to
be real. Spiritual discipline, accordingly, may be defined as activity which is believed to be an effective way, when performed properly and regularly, to attain the divine life. It is essential, moreover, that such activity be performed for the sake of entering the
divine life if it is to have a spiritual nature. Thus even prayer,
fasting, almsgiving, Eastern forms of meditation, etc., are not
spiritual disciplines if performed for secular reasons.

Consequently, in my view, not everyone is religious and those
who are religious not only believe that there is a divine life which
can be attained, but also use spiritual disciplines for the sake of
attaining it. By defining religion, its disciplines, and their relation
to ultimate reality in this way, we do not exclude any genuine
religion, nor do we marginalize religion as a human phenomenon.
However, we do exclude as religious those who believe that consciousness perishes at the end of this earthly life, those who deny

that in any sense there is a permanent reality or that if there were we could never experience it, those who believe that suffering for man can never be eliminated, etc. In short, we exclude those whose basic beliefs and values are purely secular.

But what of those who spend their lives in loving and helpful communion with their fellow man, never aiming at anything beyond the good effects of their actions in earthly life? Such people are not religious or spiritual, and if we say they are we have simply abandoned the distinction between being moral and being spiritual or religious. We must recognize that morality, even profound love of mankind, is possible without religion. For some, a moral code is itself their only ultimate concern, and to this extent, they are moral rather than religious. Others, of course, follow a moral code because to do so facilitates the attainment of the divine life or is commanded by God, and to this extent are moral because they are religious. Again, some make the understanding of the world their ultimate concern, others make it the establishment of a utopian state; but in all such cases, because of the absence of reference to the life divine in their explicit goals, religion has no part. If particular religions accept the dogma that such people cannot achieve the divine life, either they must abandon the dogma or be subject to the disapproval of those who find it objectionable.

I would now like to set my disagreement with Professor Kress about the nature of religion, its disciplines, and their relation to ultimate reality into the larger context of the central problem that I believe all of the religions of the modern world must unite together to solve. I think this problem shows what is at stake in our dispute. The most basic and common problem of religions today, I believe, does not concern how they can avoid bias and elitism between and among themselves, but how they can best help man achieve the divine life in a secularizing world that denies or doubts the very existence of a divine life and promises a more meaningful life to those who devote themselves to the achievement of various secular goals. Denials of the existence of a divine life have arisen from many quarters, not the least of which are anti-spiritualistic political ideologists and modern scientific humanists, and doubts concerning its existence are fed by strong disagreements between and within religions concerning the exact nature of the divine life and the means by which it is achieved. Utopian dreams of what can be accomplished in this world by social, political, and moral action are gradually supplanting spiritual ultimate concerns, and fear of nuclear holocaust, compassion for the world's many hungry, poor, and needy, and outrage at the pervasiveness of man's inhumanity to man have diverted many of man's higher energies into the attempt to solve the problems of this world, away from the attempt to solve the problem of his spiritual deprivation. This potent mixture of open hostility to religion, doubt about its doctrines, utopian fantasies, and diverted spiritual energy can be ignored by religions only at the price of a further serious depletion of the world's spiritual resources. The challenge these religions face is to find a way in common to respond to the denial of and doubt about the very possibility of a divine life and to the adoption and pursuit of secular ideals to the exclusion of spiritual ones.

The advantages and disadvantages of Professor Kress's account of religion, its disciplines, and their relation to ultimate reality must be evaluated in the light of this challenge. He himself is concerned primarily to counteract Christian bias against other religions and elitism within Christianity itself, and derivatively to suggest to other religions the use of similar ways to reduce bias and elitism. His proposals, if accepted, might have the advantage of reducing friction among and within religions, and perhaps with less such friction religions could better deal with a secularizing world. But he would have them achieve less friction by defining away religious dogma about the divine life and how it is best achieved, and accepting as religion man's life-long organized attempts to implement the values he happens to regard, whether explicitly or implicitly, as giving life its meaning. Through the pursuit of insights and values deemed ultimate, man will, Professor Kress assures the world religions, communicate with the divine and so will be religious (in something more like the old sense) in spite of himself. But how, we may ask, does this approach deal with the problem of the modern man abandoning religious ideals and pursuits for the sake of secular ones? Indeed, not only does it ignore these problems, but it appears to play into the hands of the hostile forces of despiritualization by granting full religious status to their secular goals and activities, while consoling religions with the view these goals and activities can, after all, be given a religious interpretation.

Professor Kress, it seems, has himself come under the spell of a secularism which promises an "objectivity" with regard to values. The secularizing force to which he has succumbed appears under the guise of a phenomenological or anthropological approach to religion, an approach which limits itself to observable human behavior, and hence becomes blind to the difference between spiritual and secular values. But how likely is it that we shall eliminate bias and elitism in religion by calling on the services of a spiritually blind third-party arbitrator? The solution to this problem, surely, must come from the members of each religion attempting to purge their own religions of bias and elitism by the resources within their own religions. In the second and third parts of his paper Professor Kress performs this task with regard to his own religion, but in the first part, which is really logically independent of the remaining two, he does not. I fully agree that Christians can and should find within their own dogma the means by which to accept the spiritual nature of other religions and practices, and, if possible, even the possibility of spiritual accomplishment in other religions. But let us by all means resist the impulse to solve these problems by recourse to "scientific" or "objective" approaches which pretend to eschew all value judgments, including those shared by all religions. For that matter, the decision to restrict the description of religion to what can be observed about human behavior is itself based on a set of secular values.

What marks off the religious from the nonreligious life is the practice of spiritual discipline, and without the acceptance of the dogma of a divine life, the dogma which supplies the basic theoretical support to this practice, there is no reason to adopt the religious life. Therefore, if we value the practice of spiritual disciplines as effective means to spiritual fulfillment, the contemporary challenge to religious belief cannot be met by setting aside all religious dogmas. It will be necessary, however, to reject religious dogmatism, especially the dogmatic rejection of the spiritual nature of other religions, if religions are to cooperate in an effort to meet the challenge of secularism. We must not go to the extreme of defusing the power of this dogma to motivate effective religious practice by claiming that it is just one among many possible beliefs we can use to help us lead a "religious" life.

Belief in the existence of divine life is the basic motivating force in religious life, and to lose that belief is to fall away from religion and its disciplines.

The definitions I propose can play a central part in the response of religions to a world which is increasingly more attracted to secular ideals than to the possibility of a divine life. What religions need to do, I believe, is to make a strong *spiritual* response in which they rally in common around the idea that they all teach of a divine life and ways in which it may be achieved. Although in fact they may differently conceive the details of the nature of that life and advocate somewhat different practices for its attainment, these differences are not nearly as important as their common denial of the belief that the physical world is the only reality and that man is simply a temporary transformation or evolute of this physical reality, capable of achieving temporary happiness and no more. Central to the success of this sort of spiritual response would be the revitalization of the practice of spiritual disciplines within the traditions themselves, for it is through the proper and regular practice of these disciplines that their followers in fact are believed to achieve the divine life, and to the extent that these followers develop the virtues such practices produce, intelligent human beings will find themselves once again drawn to religious values on the basis of their irrepressible admiration for their extraordinary effects on the lives and personalities of religious people.

One of the major reasons so many moderns have turned toward secular rather than spiritual values is that there is nowadays so little spiritual accomplishment evidenced within the religions themselves. If man is to believe in the possibilities of his spiritual fulfillment by the use of spiritual disciplines he must be inspired to belief by the accomplishments of their seasoned practitioners. It was, after all, the belief in the spiritual achievements of the representatives of Eastern religions that has recently drawn so many in the West to these Eastern religions. This shows us, I believe, that the best way for religions to encourage the pursuit of the divine life in the modern world is to rejuvenate their spiritual resources and create strong spiritual communities which can inspire the rest of the world to follow them.

There is a place within the religious life, of course, for the pursuit of social, political, and moral goals, but it is essential for such a life that one's spiritual goals explicitly provide the underlying motivation for the pursuit of the others. Religions, I believe, should be adding to contemporary social, political, and moral movements a spiritual dimension rather than granting them a spiritual or religious status. Similarly, they should spiritualize everyday life rather than reinterpret everyday life as spiritual discipline. Whether or not it is the very same ultimate reality the different religions seek to help us experience we may never know, but whatever these religions may or may not decide about this matter should not stand in their way of working together to promulgate belief in the divine life and man's attainment of it among those who seek only secular ends in life. In this way each religion can retain its uniqueness while working in concert with the others to develop man's spiritual potential. Let them proclaim loudly together that religion is the path to the highest good for man, the life divine.

Moral Life, Spiritual Disciplines, and Union With God

Arabinda Basu

Morality and religion are human phenomena. They belong to the human situation. Religion, of course, is directed to something more than human. Nevertheless, God does need religion; it is man who has to take resort to it to realize the nature of the ultimate reality. The mutual relationship between morality, religion, and spirituality is of crucial importance. Before discussing that point, it is necessary to say something about morality because the other two, religion and spirituality, presuppose it. However, since morality is human activity, it is essential that there must be a clear idea of the nature of man.

An external view of man reveals that he is a composite creature of matter, life, and mind. He has a physical body; there is a force in it which carries on the physical, nervous, and vital functions, and he has a capacity to think, feel, and will. It is possible to distinguish a higher aspect of the mind, which will be designated intelligence or intelligent will. Mind is primarily concerned with coordinating the functions of the senses. The intelligence interprets the images that mind forms from the reports of the senses in contact with the objects of the external world. It ascertains what they are and decides on the course of action to be undertaken. There is also another principle in man which will be called the ego. It is not an essential reality, but a temporary and constructed sense of self-identity which distinguishes one human being from another.

All of this constitutes man's personality, which is the same as his nature. But the real man is something qualitatively other than his personality or external nature. That is the *ātman,* the spiritual self. The self is by definition uncreated, immortal, and free from the defects and limitations of all the elements that constitute his personality, his nature. It is of the nature of consciousness, which is other than the intelligence mentioned above. Nothing in nature has a light of its own, but everything is revealed, manifested, known in the light of consciousness which is self-luminous, undeniable, even indubitable. It is by reflecting the self that the intelligence appears as conscious.

It is obvious that man does not know his true being, though he can do so. The reason for this lack of direct knowledge of the spiritual self need not be discussed here. But it is to be noted that through the ego, the *ātman* falsely identifies itself with the elements of his external personality. Due to this ignorance of his true self, man feels a basic dissatisfaction and lack of fulfillment. Even when he has almost everything that worldly life can offer him, he is not really happy. This sense of want leads him to desire things of the world—physical possessions, fame, power, position, adulation, love—and craving for these things eggs him on in life. This craving shapes his conduct to a great extent. His conduct and relations with his fellows are determined by what he considers to be his good. But man is not known to have lived in complete isolation, even in primitive times, which means that he always has had some consideration for others. This may be taken as an indication of the fact that man is not inherently selfish. But from a subtler point of view, he is still egoistic, understanding the term "ego" in the sense explained above. In other words, the cave-man took care of his mate because she was *his* mate. The ego stresses the sense of "I" as distinguished from others. But it can enlarge itself to include the family, the clan, society, nation, even humanity.

As man grows in his consciousness, his sense of the right and the good becomes more and more refined and purified. He comes to see that the right must be done because it is right, not because it is to his interest to do so, neither in fear of punishment nor in expectation of reward. The principle of the act becomes more important. Thus man evolves as a moral being.

It is a matter of common experience that human intelligence varies in quality in all three aspects of its operation—cognitive, conative, and affective. From the intellectual point of view it is either refined, open, and bright and is capable of acquiring knowledge, or it is restless or distorted and if it knows, it does so not objectively and dispassionately but with an eye to practical results because it is motivated by self-interest. Or it is dull and gross and unable or unwilling to know. From an emotional point of view man is either content, happy, balanced, relatively at peace with himself and with others, or restless, unhappy, unbalanced, and habitually dissatisfied and disgruntled. There are still others who are insensitive and incapable of emotions. Similarly some men have a great deal of push and drive and are dynamic, though their energy is not always directed and controlled by reason, while there are others who are discriminating and know what and when and how much they should do which they get done without being perturbed. Still there are others who are lazy, lack in enthusiasm for work and procrastinate. It can be easily seen which type of man is morally superior among the three classes briefly described above.

In Indian classical psychology the collective name for mind, intelligence and ego is *citta,* which may be described as the basic conscious stuff in the external empirical personality of man. It is said that the *citta,* the basic conscious stuff in man, flows in two directions—towards *pāpa,* vice, sin, moral ill-being, and *kalyāna,* virtue, righteousness, and moral well-being. If man applies himself sufficiently to the task of resisting his evil impulses, he can turn his consciousness towards moral well-being. The process is inherent in the intelligence and moral discipline progressively enabling man to attain that purification. Consequently his intelli-

Usually with most men morality is confined to action and character. We might say, to use a colloquial phrase, it is skin deep. But what has been said above about the purification of intelligence in all its three aspects, i.e., intellectual, volitional, and emotional, should make it clear that there is also such a thing as interior morality. It is not enough to control conduct and shape behavior in accordance with certain principles. It is also necessary to deal with the inner springs of action and that is why the purification of intelligence is of paramount importance. A moral man is truly a cultured man not so much in the sense that he is an intellectual in the ordinary sense of the term or a creator or appreciator of beauty but in this, that he is primarily a man of refined sensibility and therefore in control of his external behavior.

None of this is spirituality. The life of spirituality would be devoted to the realization of the spirit. Needless to say, an immoral person cannot be spiritual. The reason simply is that his intelligence, being full of immoral tendencies and unethical impulses, is not capable of that purity, steadiness, and equilibrium which is essential for spiritual realization. Thus spirituality presupposes morality but goes much further beyond. In the context of spiritual life ethics has a different significance than it has in the ordinary human life. The true being of man has to be elevated from the moral to the spiritual plane. Mere virtue and righteousness and the purity of conscience are not sufficient means for attaining spiritual realization. Even the belief in God is not enough. The question may be asked whether man can be truly moral by his own effort. Is not the Grace of God indispensable for attaining the true moral life? Surely the Grace of God may and does help man to turn from immorality to morality. But that in itself is not spirituality. Disciplines which are specifically designed to turn man's moral and refined consciousness towards a direct realization of the spirit as the true being in man must be practiced. For mere morality does not make man's consciousness capable of such realization.

Religion may be placed between morality and spirituality. Man turns to forces and beings he considers superior to himself in knowledge and power and the capacity to grant his prayers, which may be for transitory or eternal values. At its best, religion may open the way for man to union with a supreme Being. But man does not always seek God for the sake of union with him but for what he can get from him to fulfill his desires for ordinary things. In other words, religion as such may not be spiritual. More often than not it loses its way in a plethora of rites and ceremonies and is encrusted by creed and cult. A truly spiritual aspiration may take its start from religion, but just as it leaves morality behind, so also it goes beyond religion. Morality, religion, and spirituality are the three great sign-posts in man's long way towards the realization of the supreme good of his life—self-realization and God-union.

It is not necessary here to describe in detail the various kinds of spiritual disciplines that are practiced by seekers of spiritual realization. Intense and sincere aspiration is of course the first step one must take. Faith in the possibility of direct experience of the spirit strengthens such aspiration. Not to have desire for transitory values, and to reject such desires when they do occur and try to deflect man's consciousness from the spiritual end, is a necessary discipline. This should not be misconstrued to mean that the desire to realize ephemeral values has no place in life. Before one has heard the spiritual call, one must seek to improve the quality of one's life. And this seeking is not inconsistent with morality, provided excesses are avoided. There is nothing wrong with the wish to be rich. There is everything wrong with wanting to make money by unfair and corrupt means. To seek fame as a writer or musician is legitimate. But bribing a journalist to buy a spot on television is certainly immoral. Contemplation, meditation, concentration, and chanting the name of God are other well-tried methods. Rejection of anti-spiritual tendencies has to be constantly carried out. For even after a seeker is launched on the spiritual path, his nature is still subject to tendencies and impulses which run counter to his main purpose. Even if he does not have any immoral propensities, there is still a gravitational pull towards the ordinary human life, which, however decent and cultured and ethical, is not spiritual. There are spiritual methods described in many books which belong to different religious traditions. Despite differences of outlook and emphasis, they display an astonishing agreement with regard to the actual methodology and technique.

The end of spiritual life is being, while that of moral life is doing. It is true that we speak of the moral being, but the moral being is part of becoming, of our internal personality and nature. The spiritual self, *ātman*, on the other hand *is*, is true being.

The *ātman*, spiritual self, can be experienced and realized differently, the common element among which is that it is true being and pure consciousness. It may, however, be known as personal or impersonal. Though essentially free from association with intelligence and other constituents of the external personality, it has its own kind of knowledge, action, and enjoyment, though it can be experienced as devoid of them. The more important question is whether the liberated individual spirit, *ātman, relates itself to a supreme Ātman*. There are realizations in which this relationship can be discovered. This is a further enrichment of the realization of the spirit. The supreme *Ātman* itself may be realized as impersonal or personal or having a status beyond both and yet inclusive of these two aspects. If stress is put on the impersonal aspect, then the individual spirit will realize its identity with the supreme Spirit. If, however, the personal aspect is emphasized, then the individual self will be in a state of and enjoy a close union with the ultimate Spirit which in this aspect may be called God. In this state of union the individual spirit may become a channel of his Power—for the supreme Spirit can be realized as static or dynamic or simultaneously both—and an instrument for his work in the world. The work may take the form of philanthropy and service to man. But of the spirit in union with God the motive is service and pleasure of the Divine Being. The individual spirit gets joy from doing the will of God and the service is rendered to the universal Spirit in man and in the world. The holding together of the people is a high motive and the liberated spirit, surrendered and willing instrument of God, contributes to the progress of humanity. He is engaged in doing good to all creatures. The most complete and perfect realization would be that in which both the identity and the union in distinction are simultaneously experienced as real. This is possible because the ultimate Reality is pure Identity, which by its inherent dynamic Force manifests itself as the individual Divine or individual self. Thus the liberated individual spirit can know itself as both identical and distinct from the Divine, and in the latter case, there may be more stress either on the unity with God or on distinction from him. But in any case there is no separation between the individual self and the supreme Spirit.

Once God has been realized as dynamic and the world is seen as his manifestation, it is possible to realize his presence in everything in the world. But it is also realized that though the world is a manifestation of the Divine, God is not manifest in it. He is secret and hidden behind the mask of matter, life, and mind. Man is primarily a mental being. Even in his spiritual search, mind is his chief and best developed means. But the mental consciousness is incapable of being entirely free of the sense of duality and division.

Consequently when man experiences God through the spiritually illumined mental consciousness, he fails to realize all the aspects of the Divine. He cannot unify in one realization the transcendent, universal, and individual aspects of God, far less see him as a presence and sustaining power of all things in the world, even less as that which is emerging out of a sleep in matter to a fully manifest aspect of his universal being. This is why there are so many different experiences and realizations of the ultimate Reality, different religions and philosophies.

But if God has created or manifested the world, it is not difficult to see that he did so by a knowledge and a will superior to mental knowledge and will. This superior knowledge and will must be involved even in the lowest term of universal existence, that is, matter. On the other hand, life and mind are patent realities in the world which have evolved from matter. They must have been present in a subtle and unmanifest way in matter. For otherwise they could not have evolved out of it. Mind, which is now the highest emergent in the world, can neither understand it nor control life in it, because it did not create or manifest them.

Mind itself is an intermediate level of consciousness holding in itself a higher level of it, a superior knowledge and will without the limitations from which the mind suffers. In relation to God the superior Knowledge-Will is his own self-awareness and world-awareness and his own energy of action.

If man can evolve and release in himself this divine supramental Knowledge-Will, he will be able to realize God more completely than mental-spiritual man can. He will also be able to see how this Knowledge-Will is waiting to manifest itself on the lower planes of mental man's being, namely, body, vitality, and mind. The manifestation of the supermind will really mean the evolution of God in Matter. For one consequence of the emergence of the supramental Knowledge-Will will be that Matter itself will become capable of releasing the secret and involved Conscious-Force in it and thus know its reality in relation to the Divine, the ultimate Reality. This can be described as union with God even in enlightened conscious Matter. Not only uniting with the Divine beyond all manifestation, not only realizing him as the Self of the universe, not merely knowing him as the self of the individual beyond the evolutionary word and also as the evolving soul in it, but God's knowing, realizing, and manifesting himself as a dynamic Presence and Power in transfigured matter, life, and mind, is the ultimate and integral union with God that man can and should aspire to in this life.

In spiritual life and discipline, vis-à-vis morality, the emphasis need not be on *Brahman* or *Ātman,* the supreme Self conceived either as impersonal or personal or both. The stress is on *ātman,* the individual self. This self, which is not the soul as conceived in Western thought or in the Semitic religions, is not the mind, however much purified, turned to morality and religion and God. The goal of the spiritual life is the realization of the *ātman*—and in some systems of philosophy and yoga, also union with God, the supreme *Ātman*—which entity, to repeat, is in essence uncreated and immortal and free from the defects and imperfections of the external man's nature, constituted by body, life, and mind. If God or a supreme *Ātman* is accepted, it must be said that the individual *ātman* is of the same nature as the Divine Being, and thus, is essentially free from moral struggle. Man can, by practicing proper spiritual disciplines, realize this true being as his reality.

Experience of the ultimate Reality can be extremely varied because of its many aspects. It can be realized as completely transcending the universe, as immanent in it, or simultaneously as both, as static or dynamic or both at the same time, as the Self of the world and that of the individual and also of the collective being, as a living Presence in everything and the dynamic Power behind all movements of cosmic Nature, as apparently unconscious and then as sub-conscious, partly conscious and fully conscious Force, or as the substance of matter, life, and mind, which are seen to be the media of its progressive self-manifestation in the world. This does not mean that everything is divine, but that everything is from the Divine and *essentially,* but not actually, Divine now. The full self-manifestation of God in these lower but now imperfect means of his manifestation will be divinized when he evolves his own supramental Knowledge-Will in and out of Matter, and embodied man consequently becomes capable of realizing God integrally and of manifesting him in all parts of his being and nature. It is possible, and that is what normally happens in the world of religious search, to have partial experiences and realizations of the ultimate Reality. That is because man is a mental being and his religion and spirituality are mind-dominated. And mind, being basically a divisive consciousness, cannot realize the Divine integrally. But mind need not be for all times the instrument of religious and spiritual experience and knowledge and actions and enjoyment. A superior capacity can be evolved by man, with the Grace of God, which will enable him to realize his own supreme Reality, the integral Divine, integrally.

II

ULTIMATE REALITY AND THE EFFICACY OF SPIRITUAL DISCIPLINE

In Defense of Spiritual Discipline

Huston Smith

"A lot of people are looking at maps. Few seem to be
going anywhere." This wry remark by John Updike shows
us at once one of the reasons why it is so important for
us to discuss spiritual discipline and ultimate reality. An oasis is
of no avail while it is distant, and the same holds for reality; for it
to empower us we must be joined to it. But we are normally not so
well joined, as the myths of exile and fall, sleepwalking and
estrangement, persistently remind us. Something must be done to
effect the needed union, and for the purposes of our present discussion, discipline is the name for that doing. It is the journeying
that carries us from exile to our spiritual home.

Discipline as Requisite
To say that this journeying is always in order is an understate-
ment; it is needed, for never for long are we exactly where we
should be. There are intervals when we seem to be where we
should be; these are the "times of inherent excellence" Wallace
Stevens speaks of,

> As when the cock crows on the left and all
> Is well, incalculable balances,
> At which a kind of Swiss perfection comes...[1]

Such times do indeed come, and when they do we do not know whether the happiness they bring is the rarest or the commonest thing on earth, for in all earthly things we find it, give it, and receive it. But we cannot hold onto that happiness. This hardly needs arguing, but two giants can be quoted to drive the point home. "Whoever thinks that in this mortal life a man may so disperse the mists of bodily and carnal imaginings as to possess the unclouded light of changeless truth, and to cleave to it with the *unswerving* constancy of a spirit wholly estranged from the common ways of life," St. Augustine wrote, "he understands neither what he seeks, nor who he is who seeks it" (italics added). St. Teresa's formulation of the same point is as follows: "If anyone told me that after reaching this state [of union] he had enjoyed *continual* rest and joy, I should say that he had not reached it at all" (again, italics added). There seems to be no permanent abode this side of Eden. Even Jesus prayed, and the Buddha continued to sit after his enlightenment.

This initial point is important enough to repeat, exchanging the metaphors of travel, oases, and home for the actual object of the spiritual quest, which is knowledge. No desire is more deeply embedded in us than the desire to know; to see things as clearly and completely as is possible. Buddhism recognizes this by asking us "to see things in their suchness," while a *hadith* of Muhammad runs, "O Lord, show me all things as they truly are."[2] In our present state, though, as St. Paul admits, "we see in a mirror dimly" (1 Cor. 13:13). As a boy growing up in China, that was a vivid image for me, for quicksilver mirrors had only recently arrived and the reflections afforded by the traditional mirrors of burnished bronze were murky at best. To "see face to face" is not our present lot, but we can polish our mirrors, or (in Blake's alternative wording) cleanse the doors of our perceptions. If we take seriously our human opportunity (which the Indian tradition never tires of reminding us is "hard to come by") we may wonder whether anything unrelated to this cleansing is worthwhile.

Light cannot penetrate a stone, and is barely reflected from a black surface. For truth's light to enter us, our petrified selves must be turned into crystal: correlatively but in altered imagery, if our lives are to reflect truth's light, black bogs must be changed into fields of snow. Such alchemical changes require doing. They require discipline.

Objections to Discipline

Those who have urged the importance of spiritual disciplines
—be they the Buddha with his Eight-fold Path, Patanjali with his
Raj Yoga, Buddhaghosa with his *Visuddhimagga (Path of Purification)*, St. Ignatius with his *Spiritual Exercises*, John Wesley with his
Method-ism, to name a representative sample—have had to face a
number of objections, three of which are recurrent.

The first of these is the charge that such regimens preempt for
man the credit for change that belongs to God. Approaching salvation as if it were a condition to be achieved rather than a gift to be
received, they shift the accent from grace, where it belongs, to
self-effort.

A number of rejoinders are in order here, and I will proceed
from the most obvious to ones that are less so.

To begin with, not all disciplines have subjective change as
their aim. When the Qur'an enjoins the Muslim to "hymn the
praise of thy Lord when thou uprisest, and in the night-time also
hymn His praise, and at the setting of the stars" (LII:48-49), it
foreshadows what is probably the most widely-practiced spiritual
discipline on our planet today, the canonical prayers of Islam.
These prayers unquestionably have an effect on those who offer
them, but that effect is not their direct intent which is, rather, to
honor Allah with the adoration that is his due. A cynic could of
course claim that though that is the right reason for prayer, the real
(in the sense of operative) reason is the celebrant's wish to get to
heaven. To this the answer is: that although this is so for some,
motives for praying cover a wide spectrum, reaching to the prayer of
the sufi saint Rabi'a, which has become classic:

> O God! if I worship Thee in fear of Hell,
>   burn me in Hell;
> And if I worship Thee in hope of Paradise,
>   exclude me from Paradise;
> But if I worship Thee for Thine own sake,
>   withhold not Thine everlasting beauty!

Proceeding to the more subtle point, even when discipline
does include self-transformation in its object, it does not follow
that the program excludes grace or even tips the scales away from
it.

The model in this second instance is the athlete. No one supposes that an Olympic contender can stay in the running unless he works out regularly. Are we to suppose that spiritual attainment is less demanding; that it does not require its "spiritual exercises," to invoke Ignatius's phrase which fits perfectly here? Both cases call for effort, but athletes are not normally concerned with the relation of that effort to empowerment from other sources,[3] whereas "spiritual athletes" have to give thought to that question because "relation to reality" is their central concern. Where do they come down on the question? What *is* the relation between grace and self-effort?

It is easiest to state the conclusion negatively. The relation is not a disjunctive one, such that the more you have of one the less you have of the other. It's closer to the opposite: not either/or, but both/and.

Given a space that is finite, say an empty hat box, the more black marbles it contains the less room there will be for white ones and vice versa. But for the way human activity is related to God's, this model won't work: a new logic is required. To begin with, there is no human action which is not empowered, which makes every human act in some way God's act as well. This initial point is simple, but it opens quickly onto paradoxes and then mysteries. There is no hope of fathoming these here, if indeed the rational mind can ever dissolve the mysteries that are involved. What it can do, to repeat, is see clearly that either/or logic in this domain is "pre-Riemannian." With Ramakrishna's "the winds of God's grace are always blowing, but you must raise your sail" and St. Paul's "in His service is perfect freedom" we approach paradox, but if we keep going we are confronted with what, to the rational mind, must look like absolute contradictions. Spinoza's equation of freedom with determinism is one of these; Pauline theology another. I once heard a New Testament scholar compress the latter into a sentence that was vivid though earthy: "You have to work like hell because it's all been done for you."

In an important essay that originally appeared in 1968 but has recently been republished, Marco Pallis details the reciprocal relationship between grace and self-effort as they interact in Buddhism.[4] Early, Theravadic Buddhism provides a good test case on this issue, for a perspective that does not include the idea of a personal God seems at first glance to leave little room for the idea of grace as well. Can merciful action from above, defined as an unsolicited gift that is extended to human beings independent of their own effort, be reconciled with the workings of karma as the inexorable law of moral cause and effect? Pallis shows that it can be. For as the Buddha said: "There is, O monks, an unborn, an unbecome, an unmade, an uncompounded," without which there would be "no escape from the born, the become, the made." This "uncompounded" on which the Buddhist quest is founded and to which it leads, stands prior to all human doings as something that is simply given to us. Our discernment of the uncompounded initiates our spiritual quest, but again we must ask into the anatomy of this discernment. When we gaze on the Grand Canyon, how much of what we see is of our own doing? We make the journey to see it, we can say; but would we have done so had we not heard reports of it and been endowed with sensibilities to respond to those reports? Above all, would we have journeyed and responded had it not been *there*? In the case of enlightenment, were it totally beyond our reach we could no more respond to its summons than an ox can feel drawn to astronomy, which shows that the capacity for enlightenment has been given us as a gift. Meister Eckhart put this matter in perspective when he wrote that "in the course of nature it is really the higher which is ever more ready to pour out its power into the lower than the lower is ready to receive it"; for as he goes on to say, "there is no dearth of God with us"; what dearth there is, "is wholly ours who make not ready to receive his grace." Eventually this point finds Buddhist statement in the assertion that the Buddha-nature is with us from the start.

All of the Buddha's emphasis on self-effort and exertion—"be ye lamps unto yourselves"; "work out your salvation with diligence"—should be seen in the context of a gracious matrix that inspires the religious quest and assures its fulfillment. There is not space here to go into Pallis's discussion of the ancillary "means of grace" in Buddhism; the skillful means (*upayas*) that range from the compelling example of the Buddha's own life, through the sutras and other scriptures, to art (notably the sublime iconography of the Buddha himself) which can put us ahead of ourselves by relaying to our dispositions the beauty that impacts our senses. Even if we do not include the Boddhisattvas who are grace personified, these gifts are strewn about almost carelessly in Buddhist civilizations—free for the taking. But though I must pass over these proximate supports, I do want to note before completing this Buddhist excursion that Marco Pallis's analysis was in important ways foreshadowed by Daisetz Suzuki's study of Shin Buddhism. As a development that stresses other-power (*tariki*), Shin had from the first to argue that it is truly Buddhist, for original Buddhism (as we have seen) *seemed* to lean heavily towards self-power (*jiriki*). Suzuki argues Shin's case historically by saying that in our preoccupation with the Buddha's teaching we should not overlook his example which leaned heavily towards helping others. From the moment of his enlightenment, he was occupied with his mission: what he could do for others and the benefits that could accrue to them from that. But beyond this historical point, Suzuki argues the logical point we have seen Pallis making: self-power and other-power, self-effort and grace, prove under inspection to be reciprocal; each entails the other in principle. Other-power *must* be received, while self-power rides on a supporting context that *is* received inasmuch as the self did not create it. Moreover, it is possible to advance to the point where each component is recognized as its opposite. The Shin believer pronounces the formula that saves him (*nembutsu*), yet he doesn't; Amida, the saving Buddha, pronounces it using the believer's lips while being simultaneously the faith/compassion that rises in the believer's breast.[5] Meanwhile, the Zen Buddhist, whose strenuous zazen places him at the opposite end of the grace/self-effort spectrum, is brought to the same point the Shinnist reaches. He urges self-effort, but what happens to self when it discovers that it is nothing less than the Buddha-nature in phenomenal guise?[6]

I have spent what may seem like disproportionate space on the interplay of discipline and grace because, respecting the topic at hand, this is the point at which theological confusion is most likely to arise. In four steps, let me summarize the argument I have used Suzuki and Pallis to get before us: In the first, we notice that segments of experience are suffused with feelings of effort or ease that can stand in sharp contrast. There are times when it seems that if anything is to come our way it will have to be through our own initiative, and there are times when we simply sit back and ride the Glory Train—Shinran's image is taking a boat ride; it is so easy and pleasant. The second step is to recognize that these episodes do not last. Effort eases, but then that ease too crumbles like something in a fairy tale when the clock strikes twelve. Nothing in life can be understood without introducing the element of time, and time brings rhythms and oscillations. We wake to work; later we lie down to sleep. We stretch our legs and then relax them. Thirdly, we see, if we look closely, that apart from these pendulum swings which show both reception and exertion to be parts of life's story, self- and other-power entail each other in principle. Other-power must be received, and self-power presupposes a supportive context which the self did not create. Finally, we conclude that each of the two components is actually experienced as being also its opposite. Whereas the preceding point was that Amida's saving power requires the *nembutsu,* now the point is that in pronouncing that formula the Shinnist realizes that Amida is pronouncing it through him. Comparably with the Zennist. It is not just that his zazen presupposes a supporting context. The line between his sitting and what cushions that sitting, we might say, disappears.

Disciplines have been subject to a second criticism; namely, that they are prompted in the end by a subtle form of willfulness.

A natural tendency of the ego is its wish to have things differ from the way they are. The West is inclined to see this as a problem because we want things to differ in *our* way, not God's way, but there is a view that holds that the problem lies deeper. According to this second view, the ultimate cause of the human problem is our wish to have things differ in any way from the way they are. Buddhism argues this most explicitly with its claim that the source of suffering (*dukkha*) is desire or craving (*tanha*), but we can find the point in every tradition if we look carefully enough. Eckhart's teaching that we should not even wish that we had not sinned is readily misunderstood, but in the context of his complete theology its function is to take the final step in closing the ought/is divide. Beginning by acknowledging God's omnipotence—recognizing that in the last analysis he is the author of everything—it goes on to affirm that that omnipotence is perfect. Islam, for its part, compresses the logic in question into its very name. Unique among the world's faiths in being named by a common noun, that noun designates a spiritual attitude: submission. Uncapitalized, *islam* simply means submission; capitalized it designates the company of those who have dedicated their lives *to* submission.[7] Run-of-the-mill under-standings of submission ride on master/servant imagery, but meta-physically submission calls for aligning the human heart with the way things are. The test of this alignment is total affirmation; not passive acceptance, but the active affirmation of everything, exactly as it is and will be.

The bearing of all this on discipline is not far to seek. To the extent that spiritual exercises aim at self-change, this second criti-cism argues, they exacerbate the is/ought divide rather than amelio-rating it. That the posited "ought" is in this instance a noble one—self-improvement and eventually liberation—only camou-flages the trap it overlays: the ego has a deep-rooted tendency to co-opt and appropriate even the process of liberation; it thrives on such appropriations and we are presented here with a clear instance. In Buddhist terms, the desire to be desireless is itself a desire and therefore contradictory. The Sufi, Hasan Esh-Shadhili makes the same point in theistic idiom when he writes: "The desire for union with God is one of the things which most surely separates from him."[8]

As in the first charge against disciplines, there is much in this second charge that is true—everything, in fact, save its presumed conclusion: that spiritual disciplines are misguided. "To desire to be desireless" may sound contradictory, but until we *have* tran-scended desires—while we continue to dangle from their puppet-strings—it is crucial to discriminate among them.[9] Some desires— the Bodhisattva's vow to save all sentient beings, and yes, the desire to reach enlightenment oneself—are better than others. To over-look this simple fact is to betray one's ignorance, the deadliest form of which is to think that one has completed the spiritual journey when one is still a traveler on its way.

As for the Sufi version of the warning-against-desire that was quoted above, is it true that desire for union with God actually separates us from him? The answer depends on the nature of the union anticipated. If it focuses on a finite ego which is destined to be flooded with rapture and who knows what other good things when the beatific vision dawns, desire for a union that places this grandi-ose ego stage center does indeed separate. As disguised egoism, it is simply another variant of Chogyam Trungpa's "spiritual material-ism." But if eyes are kept steadfastly on God, allowing his presence to expand until, filling the horizon, it leaves no room for the self that inherits the view, it is difficult to see how this second mode of desire, radical to the point of seeking the ego's extinction (*fana*), could backfire.

A third charge against disciplines is that they foster spiritual pride. This is indeed a danger; spiritual pride is pride's subtlest form. But the religious have known this, while adding that this final adversary is best countered with a light touch. When William Law proposed some measures for deepening the contemplative life, a clergyman responded with an angry sermon "On the Wickedness and Presumption of Attempting to be Righteous Overmuch." Law replied, "Perhaps, Sir, if you try to be a saint, you may succeed in being a gentleman."

To summarize this central section of my paper: If the reproaches that have been directed against disciplines are read as warnings they can be useful. It would be a mistake, though, to see them as proscriptions. The alternative to discipline and the effort it requires is "quietism," a technical term in the vocabulary of mysticism for a state that comes perilously close to doing nothing. Even Taoism, whose concept of nonvolitional activity (*wu wei*) skirts the brink of that state, recognizes that the state itself is disastrous.

The Common Thrust of Spiritual Techniques

Having devoted most of my space to answering objections to spiritual disciplines, I can only touch on four other points, beginning with the sense in which such disciplines point in the same general direction.

To broach the prospect of unity in the world's religions is to raise the spectre of syncretism, but fortunately Professor Hossein Nasr has in his Gifford Lectures staked out the guidelines for avoiding its pitfall.[10] Syncretism plays upon universal yearnings for brotherhood and understanding to reduce the "strong meat" of divine revelation to innocuous pablum; it levels the great traditions to their lowest common denominator, as if there were nothing more to God's (in ways terrible) word than the Golden Rule and vague belief in "a something or other" that is greater than ourselves. In important ways the revealed traditions are *not* alike, and to insist prematurely on their resemblances is to play down these "importances" in favor of resemblances that are secondary and derivative.

As Professor Nasr points out, the most vocal champions of ecumenism often turn out to be persons who, having lost faith in the revealed character of traditions *per se,* their own included, have retreated to common sense values—brotherhood and understanding—which are secure in that no one could possibly take exception to them. Thanks to its advocates of this stripe, ecumenism (for all its lofty ideals) often spreads relativism and strengthens secularism's already heavy hand.

Still, it seems most unlikely that there is not some important sense in which the great religions are one; for one thing, would God have permitted them to endure for millennia, nourishing the spirits of untold millions, if they were not in some sense vehicles of his all-including will? As Nasr, following Schuon, rightly notes, the way to acknowledge this authentic unity while avoiding the pitfall of syncretism is to locate the unity in a transcendent realm, beyond the kataphatic, positive (as in the *via positiva*), articulated theologies whose differences should be honored and kept sharply edged.[11] In his keynote address to last year's God Conference, Heinrich Ott made a parallel move by suggesting that interfaith dialogue be anchored in the notion of mystery.[12] If, as Noam Chomsky and his fellow transformational grammarians are arguing, human languages with their surface variations derive through the application of unconscious rules or "transformations" from a deep linguistic structure that is common to the human species—programmed into its members, one might say—might there be a comparable universal religious "grammar" which the great religions illustrate as different languages?[13]

This is not the place to explore that question, and in any case I have already argued my (affirmative) answer in a book-length study.[14] I shall note only that a common direction in which spiritual disciplines point seems clearly discernable; it comes to view when we attend to the virtue they all seek to cultivate. Asia, characteristically, describes these negatively by way of the vices that stand in their way; in Buddhist terms these are the Three Poisons: greed, hatred, and ignorance. The West is less reticent about invoking the virtues directly; they are humility, charity, and veracity, and it is easy to see that they are simply direct expressions of the virtues Buddhism approaches indirectly. Selfishness or greed is the opposite of humility, which has nothing to do with low self-esteem, but is rather the capacity to distance oneself from one's private, separate ego to the point where one can see it objectively, and therefore, accurately, as counting for one, but not more than one. Obviously love is the opposite of hatred, and veracity or truth the opposite of ignorance.

Variations on the Universal Theme

Several times I have acknowledged that not all disciplines aim at self-change. The belief that pious observances, regularly performed, are "the food of the gods" is widespread, and in disciplines thus outwardly directed the accent is on the objective, cosmic consequences of our acts, not their subjective deliveries.[15] But discipline tends to suggest self-discipline, and admittedly it is this side of praxis that this paper has primarily in mind. When the Surah of the Rock tells us to "worship God till certainty comes to thee," an important reflective consequence of worship, balancing its objective, "food of the gods" intent, is brought squarely to view.

The preceding section called attention to the uniform direction in which spiritual disciplines point, but the invariance of that direction does not preclude significant differences in the multiple paths that honor it. These paths can be identified as the world's great religions; as they differ from one another in ways that are isomorphic with the differences in the civilizations they serve, we are not surprised to find that each has its own distinctive path (*marga*) as well.[16] Thus orthodox Judaism centers in a discipline which, in its call for observance down to the Torah's minutest details, conforms the self to a holy mold which prayers *keep* holy. Christianity, by contrast, foregoes a good part of that law to focus on an inward spirit which, through love and devoted service, it seeks to open to Christ's incursion. Buddhism takes yet another tack; the distinctiveness of its discipline emerges in its attention, not to what the mind believes, but to how it works. If we could understand this working, not just theoretically but experientially, we would see how we bring our unhappiness on ourselves and would be released from our self-imposed sentence. Islam's distinctive mode is anchored in its Five Pillars. The *shahadah*'s twofold testimony fixes the Absolute in its place and, through its Messenger, anchors the relative world in that Absolute. Prayer marks the submission of the relative to the Absolute. Fast is detachment with regard to desires and so with regard to the ego. Almsgiving is detachment with regard to things, and so with regard to the world. Finally, pilgrimage is return to the Center, to the Heart, to the Self.

A different typology emerges if we attend, not to differences between religions as integral wholes, but to different spiritual personality types that surface in varying ratios everywhere. With her theory of the Four Yogas, India has taken the lead in this way of "slicing the pie." *Jnana yoga* is for those who want most to know God, *bhakti yoga* for those who want to love him, *karma yoga* for those who want to serve him, and *raj yoga* for those who want to experience him directly through psycho-physical exercises. My colleague Agehananda Bharati insists that this tidy scheme goes back no further than Swami Vivekananda, but the fundamental division, between *bhakti* and *jnana,* can be traced at least to the Upanishads.

Returning for a moment from diversity to oneness, the universality of invocation is too conspicuous to forego mention: the *mantram* in Hinduism, Buddhism's *om mani padme hum* and *nembutsu,* the "Jesus Prayer" in Christianity, and Islam's *dhikr.* "There is a means of polishing everything, and of removing rust; what polishes the heart is invocation..." "The invocation of Allah," that *hadith* concludes, but each tradition could provide its own appropriate ending.

Stages on the Path

If an intentional or disciplined life, taken as one that places itself under a rule involving prescribed acts in some kind of time frame, is likened to a journey with a destination of some sort in view, a question suggests itself. Does the journey admit of stages? Does the scenery change in predictable ways? Are there landmarks that show how far one has come and how far one has yet to go?

Of the several facets of our topic I have discussed in this paper, this is the one I am least clear about. One reads of demarcations, beginning with the traditional Hindu claim that the castes (*varnas*) themselves show how far one has progressed on life's total odyssey. If for present purposes we pass over that reincarnational claim and content ourselves with the present life, we can begin by noting the sequences in Patanjali's *raj yoga,* the final steps of which are roughly paralleled by Buddhism's higher *jhanas,* most clearly delineated perhaps by Buddhaghosa. Beginning with unwavering attention to a single object, one proceeds in this program to eliminate, first the subjective awareness of oneself as the meditator who is experiencing the object being attended to, and then that object itself, whereupon the "intentionality" of Brentano and his phenomenological successors collapses and one is left with a state of consciousness without an object.[17] In Christian spirituality we encounter the stages of vocal prayer, mental prayer, affective prayer (prayer of the will), and the prayer of simplicity wherein words are silenced and images foregone. Covering not prayer only but the aspirant's life as a whole are the stages of purgation, proficiency, and union. The Sufi counterpart of these is more complex, but its subdivisions fall into two categories: stages (*magamat*) and states (*ahwal*). The former of these are the stages through which the wayfarer must pass in his strivings after perfection and in his efforts to dispose himself for the flooding of mystical graces. Being moral and spiritual purifications and realignments that can and must be effected by the disciple's own efforts, they are said to be "acquired" rather than "infused," and are subject to slippage. In these respects they differ from the states which are mystical graces: sheer gifts of divine grace and generosity to a soul which has stripped itself of all self-seeking and self-regard. Henceforth it is not so much the earnest striving and pressing forward of the pilgrim himself that is in the foreground; it is the victorious and irresistible attraction of the divine beloved, sweeping the traveller off his feet and carrying him along in states that are not easy to describe.

The clearest account of these stages and states that I have encountered is given by Cyprian Rice,[18] who lists the stages as seven[19] and the states as ten,[20] but there are many variations. These alternate listings within a single tradition is one thing that keeps me from getting a firm grip on this matter of progression, but there are other obstacles. Being very much a novice on the path myself, reports of its further reaches lack immediacy; they sound stylized and abstract. And when they are not "archetypal" in this way, the idiosyncratic biography and imagery of the reporter so colors his/her account that I have difficulty pegging it on a universal scale. Finally, my own odyssey has been so filled with ups and downs and the unforeseen, including sharp reversals at times, that it seems presumptuous to try to delineate the stages of pilgrimage in any but a very general way.

Ultimate Reality

It might seem that in concentrating on spiritual discipline I have neglected ultimate reality completely, but the neglect is less categorical than it appears. For in the religious life, Wisdom (about the way things finally are) and Method (as the process of adequating ourselves to that way) are inexorably linked. Birds need both wings to fly, humans both legs to walk, and religion has its two sides too. Always it is a doctrine with a view to realization, doctrine that is operative in its intent. To complete the circle by returning to Updike's metaphor, we need a map to guide our steps, and we also need to take those steps. So closely related, in fact are wisdom and method that the deeper we penetrate into the understanding of one, the more we find ourselves involved with the other until in the end wisdom begins to look like static method and method like dynamic wisdom. So if we have entered any distance at all into the understanding of discipline, the reader should have been able to read between the lines some implications concerning the way reality ultimately is, even though that way has not been explicitly discussed.

NOTES

1 *Collected Poems* (New York: Knopf, 1955), 786

2 Sayyid Haydar Amuli, *Jamehal-Asrar wa Manbuh al-Anwar*, 17, 89; *Rasa'il-e Shah Nimatullah*, 1:209; 4:23.
Shabistari's gloss on this *hadith* reads:

> Leave behind both worlds and reside
> on the highest peak of His threshold.
> God will bestow upon you whatever you want
> and show you all things as they truly are.

Quoted in Javad Nurbakhsh, *Traditions of the Prophet* (New York: Khaniqahi-Nimatullahi Publications, 1981), 32-33.

3 I say "not normally concerned," but actually such concern may be more common than we suppose. Michael Murphy has made a study of star athletes which shows that a large number of them were seriously occupied with forces beyond themselves which they felt worked in their behalf at crucial junctures.

4 "Is There Room for Grace in Buddhism," in Marco Pallis, *A Buddhist Spectrum* (New York: Seabury, 1981).

5 The Islamic version of this is contained in the *hadith*, "I have known my Lord by my Lord," which is anticipated by the Qur'anic verse, "He turned to them that they might turn"(IX:119). "For," as Abu Bakr al-Kalabdhi explains in commenting on that verse, "the cause of everything is God."

6 Suzuki's full analysis of the *jiriki/tariki* relationship is summarized on pages 142-47 of my "Four Theological Negotiables: Gleanings from Daisetz Suzuki's Posthumous Volumes on Shin Buddhism," *The Eastern Buddhist* 10, no. 2 (October 1977).

7 Arabic has no capitals. I have converted the case into English.

8 Quoted in Frithjof Schuon, *Spiritual Perspectives and Human Facts* (London: Perennial Books, 1969), 162. It will not have been lost on the reader that in introducing examples to illustrate the points of this paper I often match East with West, in keeping with the dictum: "And to God belong the East and the West. Wheresoe're ye turn, there is the Face of God" (Qur'an II:115).

9 The word "transcended" is important because it is also possible to sink to a condition that is *below* desire's reach. Both cases involve a levelling process, but in the second a dead level is reached, the psyche having lost its capacity to *respond* to anything. The difference is the absolute one between finding God everywhere and finding him nowhere.

10 Seyyed Hossein Nasr, *Knowledge and the Sacred* (New York: Crossroad, 1982), chap. 9.

11 To speak of transcendence is to suggest a hierarchical view of reality, and some will see this as relativizing the Schuon/Nasr solution (to which I also subscribe), inasmuch as it will be acceptable only to those who buy into its ontological

premise. But speaking from inside that perspective I see things differently because I do not see how it is possible to deal philosophically with spiritual matters *without* a hierarchical ontology. Those who attempt to do so, I must honestly say, look to me as if they have not thought this matter through, or are required by their ontological relativism, if they face up to it, to be ontological atheists. They may not be existential atheists, which is to say, they may make something (for which they claim no ontological ultimacy) the focus of their ultimate volitive concern, but existential can never be a match for ontological theism.

12 Heinrich Ott, "Does The Notion of "Mystery"—As Another Name for God— Provide a Basis for a Dialogical Encounter Between the Religions?," in *God: The Contemporary Discussion,* ed. Frederick Sontag and M. Darrol Bryant (Barrytown, N.Y.: Unification Theological Seminary, 1982).

13 Irene Lawrence has recently pressed this possibility in her *Linguistics and Theology* (Metuchen, N.J.: Scarecrow Press and the American Theological Association, 1980).

14 *Forgotten Truth: The Primordial Tradition* (New York: Harper & Row, 1976).

15 Some lines by Aldous Huxley, quoted in "The Uses of Ceremony: Two Views," *Parabola* 7, no. 3 (Summer 1982), will remind us, if reminder is needed, that this view is not naive: "Intense faith and devotion, coupled with perseverance by many persons in the same forms of worship or spiritual exercise, have a tendency to objectify the idea or memory which is their content and so to create, in some sort, a numinous real presence, which worshippers actually find 'out there' no less, and in quite another way, than 'in here.' Insofar as this is the case, the ritualist is perfectly correct in attributing to his hallowed acts and words a power which, in another context, would be called magical. The *mantram* works, the sacrifice really does something, the sacrament confers grace *ex opere operato:* these are, or rather may be, matters of direct experience, facts which anyone who chooses to fulfill the necessary conditions can verify empirically for himself."

16 The isomorphism is not surprising, given the fact that the religions spawned their respective civilizations.

17 This state of consciousness is analyzed by Franklin Merrell-Wolff in *The Philosophy of Consciousness Without an Object* (New York: Julian Press, 1973).

18 *The Persian Sufis* (London: George Allen & Unwin, 1964).

19 Repentance or conversion, fear of the Lord, detachment, poverty, patience, trust or self-surrender, and contentment.

20 Watching one's consciousness, realization of the nearness of God, love, fear, hope, longing or yearning, loving familiarity with God, security and serene dependence, contemplation, and certainty.

The Dynamics of Attention in Spiritual Discipline

Philip Novak

Introduction

W hen we use the phrase "ultimate reality," we implicitly confess our sense that we live in a diminished one. But authentic spiritual life is born precisely when that unsettling and unshakable feeling of distance between our actual state and that which is ultimately possible penetrates our awareness. The spiritual disciplines of the world's religious traditions are ways of life aimed at lessening that distance, of coming to realize our essential and inviolable oneness—or as the Buddhists and the Advaitins would have it, our not-twoness—with ultimate reality.

And when speaking of "spiritual disciplines" it is helpful to remember that the word "spiritual" points always to the goal of the work and not to its actual locus. For it is not the spirit that needs discipline. "Spirit" or its equivalent in other traditions points to that unconditioned dimension of ourselves which dwells in a timeless union with the Real and which is to be discovered or uncovered by means of the disciplines.

The true locus of spiritual, or as I prefer to call it, contemplative discipline, is the psyche, that interdependent network of conditioned structures which forms and informs our very states of consciousness, our identities and our varying notions of what counts as valuable and real. And contemplatives universally presuppose that the psyche is malleable. Consciousness and the structures which determine it thus comprise the pivot point between whomever we think we are and ultimate reality. Contemplative discipline aims at nothing less than the transformation of the undergirding structures of our consciousness so that their new formation allows us to awaken from the sleep of bondage and to stay awake—both for our own welfare and for that of the human community.

Studies of the contemplative dimensions of religions have in the past tended to focus too exclusively upon the extraordinary mystical experience. While denying neither the tremendous, liberating insight such an experience can bring nor its breakthrough character, I think exclusive emphasis upon it has been and continues to be a mistake. For no single experience, no matter how extraordinary, is likely to permanently reorient the deep structures of consciousness. Lacking the accompaniment of a thoroughgoing and ongoing personal transformation, the mystical experience may well fade into a happy memory, a profound insight whose power to actually change behavior will nevertheless diminish over time. The contemplative's purpose, let us recall, is not solely to reach an ultimate illumination but in his or her life to become more like the Buddha, like the Christ, like the *al-Insan al-kamil,* or Universal Man, of Islam. Conformation to such spiritual archetypes and ethical ideals requires a slow maturation of the psyche and such maturation can take place only in the gradual unfolding of the Path whether or not it is accompanied by the mystical experience. An altered *state* of consciousnesss is, after all, not the same as an altered *trait* of consciousness and, as Zen Buddhists say, the real practice begins only *after* the experience of *satori.* An altered *trait* of consciousness, then, requires nothing less than an entire way of life over a life's time.

In what follows we shall be focussing on the phenomenon of attention for I believe it to be the very heart of the contemplative way. The heart, of course, is not the entire body, and there is so much of importance that I must of necessity neglect to mention. Physical ascesis, moral purification, love, intellectual insight—all of these aspects of the contemplative way are omitted here. But by calling attention to the heart of the contemplative way I do mean to underscore its *sine qua non* character. For without mastery of the mind, in which endeavor attention is the chief tool, the deeper structural determinants of consciousness cannot be transformed. And without such transformation the journey to ultimate reality will be fundamentally impeded.

I am suggesting, then, that in the long haul of planetary evolution spiritually questing men from various cultures have commonly discovered that here in the mind's inchoate ability to remain attentive there dwelt the fundamental means of awakening to the full meaning of his existence. For attention, as I will presently and briefly suggest, is the core and common denominator of all man's higher forms of contemplative praxis. And later I will be attempting to suggest how a little thing like attention may be thought to transform even the deep and unconscious structural determinants of consciousness.

Attention in the Traditions

Our first step must be to recall briefly some of the most important contemplative practices in the world's religious traditions so as to see the centrality of attention therein. This is most easily done for the great traditions which arose in India, namely Hinduism and Buddhism. From the Upanishadic seers down to the present day there is in India an unbroken tradition of man's attempt to yoke his bodymind to Ultimate Reality. Yoga takes on many forms, but its essential psychological form is one-pointed attention or concentration (*citta-ekagatta*). Whether by fixing the attention on a mantram or on the flow of the breath or on some other object, the attempt to quiet the mind through attention is the first step and continuing theme of Hindu psychospiritual yoga.

It could hardly be otherwise for the traditions that stemmed from Gautama Buddha. The *samatha* and *vipassana* forms of meditation in the Theravada tradition require as their root and anchor an ever increasing ability to attend, to hold one's attention fast without relinquishing it to the various psychological forces which scatter it. *Samatha* is the cultivation of one-pointed attention and is the common starting point for all major types of Buddhist meditation. *Vipassana* meditation consists in the deployment of the concentrated attention developed in *samatha* from point to point within the organism, with the intent of understanding certain Buddhist doctrines at subtle experiential levels. Though the attention sought in *vipassana* meditation is not one-pointed in the sense of being fixed on a single object, it remains a highly concentrated and directed form of attention, the very antithesis of dispersed mental wandering. Likewise, the Tibetan practice of *visualization,* which is attempted only after preparatory training in *samatha,* is a way of developing the mind's ability to remain steadfastly attentive by requiring it to construct elaborate sacred images upon the screen of consciousness. The two practices central to the Zen tradition, *koan* and *skikantaza,* have as their common denominator the practice of sustained, vigilant attention. Moreover, the major contemplative schools of Buddhism stress the virtue of mindfulness, the quality of being present, aware and, in a word, attentive.

Arthur Waley tells us that by the fourth century B.C. the Taoists had already developed methods of meditation and trance induction which were probably only indirectly influenced by Indian methods.[1] They were called *tso-wang* and *tso-ch'an* and were fundamentally a training of concentration by the fixation of attention on the breath. Buddhism would likely have had a far more difficult time developing in China had it not been for such indigenous Chinese parallelisms.

When we turn to the three great Western monotheisms the phenomenon is not as starkly visible. Nevertheless it is there. Broadly speaking, spiritual disciplines in the monotheisms are not as fully developed as their cousins in the East. Often forced underground by hostile theological or theopolitical currents, many spiritual practices of the monotheisms appear to have succumbed to a process leading from esotericism, to obscurity and corruption and eventually to forgetfulness. Still, these monotheisms contain profound mystical dimensions, and it is there we must look for the practice of attention.

The actual practices and methods of Jewish mystical prayer are difficult to determine. Kabbalist scholar Aryeh Kaplan states that "some three thousand Kabbalah texts exist in print, and...the vast majority deal with theoretical Kabbalah."[2] There are also monumental problems of translation and interpretation. References to method can, however, be found intermittently in the ancient Talmudic texts, quite frequently in the works of Abraham Abulafia and some of his contemporaries, in the Safed Kabbalists of the sixteenth century, in the works of Isaac Luria and in the Hasidic texts. The key terms are *hitbodedut* (meditation), *hitboded* (to meditate) and *kavanah* (concentration, attention, and intention). The first two come from a root meaning "to be secluded." They often point beyond mere physical seclusion, however, to the seclusion beyond the discursive activity of the mind attained through concentration. *Kavanah* likewise refers to a concentrative or attentive form of prayer capable of inducing an altered, "higher" state of consciousness. For the Jewish mystical tradition as a whole, *mantram*-like repetitions of sacred liturgical words seem to be the central vehicles for the training of attention, but references to concentration upon mental images, letter designs and color and light visualizations can also be found in the texts. Concentrative exercises are also linked with bodily movements and the movement of the breath. Some of the exercises prescribed by the thirteenth-century Abulafia involve long, complex series of instructions and would seem to require massive attentive capability to perform without distraction. In this they seem akin to the Tibetan Buddhist practice of elaborate visualization.

In the Christian world we find, in Eastern Orthodoxy, the prayer of the heart, or Jesus prayer, a Christian mantram which the contemplative uses to recollect him/herself, to unify his/her attention and thereby to open the heart to the Divine Presence. The bulk of contemplative texts in the Roman Catholic tradition, like those of the Judaic tradition, are concerned with theory and doctrine rather than specifics of method. In the early Middle Ages one can find references to contemplation as a seeking for God in stillness, repose, and tranquility, but the specificity ends here. The late Middle Ages witnessed among contemplatives the growth of a prayer form called *lectio divina,* or meditative reading of the scriptures. Cistercian monk Thomas Keating describes *lectio divina* as the cultivation of a "capacity to listen at ever deepening levels of inward attention."[3] Ladders of progress in mystical prayer abound at this time, but one is hard pressed to find any advice on how actually to climb them. Practical mysticism comes more fully into bloom with the arrival of Teresa of Avila and John of the Cross in the sixteenth century. In the opinion of J. Maritain, the latter remains the prototypical practitioner of the Catholic mystical way, *the* mystical Doctor and psychologist of the contemplative life *par excellence.* And John's way was the way of inner silence, of nondiscursive prayer, of states of mind brought about by what he called "peaceful loving attention unto God." Lately an attempt has been made to popularize this kind of contemplative attention in the "centering prayer," again a *mantram*-like technique for the focusing of attention and the quieting of the mind similar to the Jesus prayer of Eastern Orthodoxy.

In the world of Islam we have the contemplative practices of both silent and vocal *dhikr*, again a *mantram*-like repetition, usually of the names of Allah, aimed at harnessing the will and its power of attention. Dr. Javad Nurbakhsh, spiritual head of the Nimatullahi Order of Sufis writes that the purpose of *dhikr* (Persian: *zekr*), i.e., the remembrance of the Divine name, "is to create a 'unity of attention'. Until this is attained the disciple will be attentive to [distracted by?] the various attachments of the self. Therefore, he should try to incline his scattered attention to the all encompassing point of Unity."[4] A more generic term for the kind of meditative attention achieved in *dhikr* is *moraqebeh*. *Moraqebeh* is described as a "concentration of one's attention upon God," as the "presence of heart with God," "the involvement of the [human] spirit *(ruh)* in God's breath" and the "concentrating of one's whole being upon God."[5] *Moraqebeh*, the Sufis say, is not only a human activity but a Divine one as well: it is because God is constantly attentive to us that we should be attentive to him.

Two men who have drawn on the traditions listed above and whose eclectic writings have had a significant impact among those interested in self-transformation are G.I. Gurdjieff and J. Krishnamurti. Crucial to the Gurdjieff work is the exercise of "self-remembering," fundamentally an attempt to develop sustained, undistracted, observational attention both outwardly toward experience and simultaneously, inwardly toward the experiencer. This particular aspect of the Gurdjieff work is very similar to the "bare attention" exercises of Buddhist *vipassana* meditation. Krishnamurti teaches that the practice fundamental to psychological transformation is "choiceless awareness." It is, again, the cultivation of sustained, observational, nonreactive attention to inner and outer experience. Looked at in isolation from the rest of Krishnamurti's teaching, this gesture of attention is not significantly different from either that of the Gurdjieff work or Buddhist "bare attention."

The preceding survey is not to be understood as implying that the training of attention is the same in every tradition nor that it occupies the same relative importance within the various traditions.

Quite to the contrary, attention is in these traditions developed in a variety of ways, to varying degrees of depth, within strikingly different contexts and to apparently different ends. Nevertheless, despite the differentiating factors surrounding the training of attention in the various traditions, there seem to be some unitive factors as well. Summarily put: the traditions mentioned above seem to be one in the understanding that the human mind in its ordinary state is somehow fragmented, unfree, and given to dispersion; they seem to be one in having evolved at least some kind of practices which lead to mental stability, unity, control, and integration; and they seem to be one in assuming that such psychological transformation can make reality and truth experientially more accessible.

Finally, it should be noted that scholars of the psychology of meditation generally agree that there are two main types, namely, concentrative and receptive. Concentrative meditation consists of the concentration of consciousness upon a single object until some sort of psychic breakthrough is achieved. The *koan* exercise of Zen and most mantra meditations would fall under this category. Receptive meditation is characterized by sustained, open and nonreactive attention to the stream of consciousness and is not limited to a single object. *Vipassana* and *shikantaza* forms of Buddhist meditation would be good examples. This distinction must not be pressed too far, however. Though I lack the space to demonstrate this point, I believe that any long-term contemplative discipline would bring both forms into play in a complementary way. Thus to label meditation forms as exclusively concentrative or exclusively receptive is probably more misleading than helpful. Furthermore, as Washburn has argued in a seminal article, the two forms of meditation are actually complementary species of a single genus, namely, says Washburn, "sustained attention, i.e., uncapitulating alertness. Sustained attention can in fact serve as the defining characteristic of meditation *per se*."[6] Given this central role of attention in contemplative praxis it will be my task in the remaining section of this paper to describe attention's basic dynamics and to suggest its peculiar psychotransformative power.

Attention and Transformation: The Awakening from Psychological Unfreedom

The question at hand is how the practice of attention, understood as regular and durative, and practiced within the context of a spiritual tradition, enables the self to undergo change, to extricate itself from the fundamental predicament which it seems contemplative traditions in general have arisen to solve, namely, compulsive ego-centeredness and the blindness to subtler and more inclusive realities which result therefrom.

The answer to this question requires that we form a general notion of the dynamics of the ego-predicament in which adult human beings are likely to find themselves. Let us remember that we are creatures of desire. There pulses in us and through all living forms a basic urge to be. It is what St. Thomas Aquinas called *desiderium naturale* and what Spinoza called *conatus:* the desire of living things to persist in and expand their being. This self-assertive or self-expansive urge, so necessary to the individuation of living forms, is in man liable to serious complication. Unlike other life forms whose self-expansive project is confined to biological scenarios, man has a psyche which requires far more than mere survival and somatic satisfaction. It hungers for identity, for worth, for esteem, for meaning, and because the domain of the psyche is virtually boundless, so is its appetite for these. Each of us longs to be special, to be a center of importance and value, to be a possessor of life's fullness, in fact, to be immortal. According to contemplative traditions, there is good reason for such longing: ultimately we share in the undying life of the Divine Nature. Unfortunately, however, the ego-*transcendence* which contemplative traditions prescribe as the only way to this fullness is usually rejected in favor of endless attempts to expand the ego through possession, projection, and gratification.

The predicament becomes acute only after infancy, after one learns to differentiate oneself from objects. Before that one lives in a magical, self-enclosed world in which all one's surroundings are extensions of one's own center. But quite soon the party is over. The individual begins to collide with very real existential limits in a world where s/he is decidedly not the center, and the agonizing struggle for secure, inviolable self-esteem is set in motion. The inner urge for importance continues unabated and the ego learns innumerable strategies for securing its sense of worth: it accumulates possessions that it can call "mine," it links itself with external loci of power and authority, with credos, causes, countries, conquests, lovers, and bank balances. The self-project also has a negative aspect, a reflex that penetrates to the deepest layers of an individual's psyche. After Ernest Becker we call it the denial of death or the denial of contingency. For in order to continue to fulfill that profound, self-expansive urge, the child learns that it must defend itself against those truths of thought and experience which emphasize its contingency while playing up those phenomena which enhance its self-project. By the time one is old enough even to begin to take an objective view of the project, one is already hopelessly enmeshed in it, with little chance to escape its incessant demands. The naked urge for importance unfolds into an egocentric system in which one's beliefs, feelings, experiences, perceptions, and behaviors are automatically viewed and assessed around one's sense of value and worth as an individual.

The assessment process, automatic and barely conscious, is basically simple. Experiences, external and internal, are divided according to whether they expand or diminish us, affirm or negate our will to be. The psyche gradually becomes a webwork of likes and dislikes, desires and aversions both gross and subtle, which manifest in the personality in the same way that black and white dots can create the illusion of a face. Time and repetition harden parts of the webwork into iron necessity. We fancy that we are walking through life freely when in reality we are being shoved about by our inner program. The psyche has become a set of predispositions and automatic response patterns which largely determine the quality of our interactions with reality. We automatically limit, select, organize and interpret our experience according to the demands of our self-project. Each of us is involved, in Castaneda's words, in a "personal construction of reality." Our inner world, then, becomes a representation of reality according to a personal order. It becomes an interlocking network of compensations for the unfortunate fact that we are not the omnipotent and immortal center of the universe we long to be. This interlocking network of compensations, writes Hubert Benoit,

> is like a special section cut in the volume of the universe... Every compensation is essentially constituted by an image involving my ego, by an image center around which is organized a multitude of satellite images... The essential character of a compensation is not that it should be agreeable to me, but that it should represent the universe to me in a perspective such that I am at the center of it.[7]

The chronic quality of this self-centeredness and the distance it creates between the person and reality indicates the common psychological wisdom behind, for example, the Christian's insistence on the "originality" of sin, the Buddhist's on the beginninglessness of ignorance, or the Muslim's on the recalcitrant quality of *ghaflah,* the forgetfulness of God.

We are suggesting, then, that in the course of human development, a network of psychological structures is built up by many and complex variations on the themes of affirmation and negation of one's will to be. Our long-term desires, aversions, sore spots, fixations—in other words, our deeply habituated predispositions—are crucial components of this network. They function as pathways along which our psychic energy automatically travels, and the result in consciousness is the endless associational chatter and emotive reactivity with which we are familiar. In other words, energy that would otherwise be manifested as the delight of open, receptive, and present-centered awareness is inexorably drawn to these structures and there disintegrates into the image-films and commentaries—the noise—that suffuses ordinary consciousness. As Charles Tart sees it, "there is a fluctuating but generally large drain on...awareness energy at all times by the multitude of automated, interacting structures whose operation constitutes personality."[8] The longer this process goes unchecked, the deeper the grooves of psychological habit are chiseled, and the more inclined we become to accept the dispersed states of our mind as perfectly normal.

Since all this is perhaps a bit abstract, let me offer a brief illustration. Suppose I was giving this paper before a live audience. I am hoping that it will be persuasive and well-received and that it will indicate my intellectual prowess and so on. If there is a favorable response at its end, my psyche will note it and be pleased. But it will not stop there. That affirmation of my being will kick off an associational chain, of which I may be only partly aware, which reels off a litany of what a clever and finely appointed fellow I am, painting my inner environment in rather bright colors. Like all highs, however, it will eventually stumble into the limits of the temporal plane and there begin its search for the next affirmation.

Similarly, if there is an unfavorable response, my psyche will have momentarily failed in its constant quest to be somebody. This will result in some degree of existential and emotional pain. But surely the drama will not stop there. The negation or diminishment of my being will ignite its own associational chain and I will be subjected to a command performance by the chorus of my contingencies.

Not that there is anything wrong with emotions as such. They are natural manifestations of real joy and real pain. But our imaginary associations prolong the emotive experience into spasm or cramp that afflicts our entire reception of and response to the world. At our worst, we simply move from cramp to cramp.

I have chosen an extreme example: speaking before an audience. But it seems that such associational firings that steal us from the real present and send us hurling through our private corridors of desire and anxiety occur constantly, even in our most trivial waking experience. The stream of experience incessantly activates those entrenched psychological structures which then produce a constant-running, imaginative-emotive film which not only comments on our incoming experience, but superimposes itself upon it, colors it, obscures it.

Now it seems to me that almost every aspect of traditional contemplative paths in some way contributes to shaking one out of the half-sleep that allows this state-of-affairs to preside. Our problem is habitual inattention, a form of unawareness that permits the automatized structures of the psyche to function unchecked.[9] As long as and to the degree to which we remain asleep, we continue to be slaves to psychological preconditions. And contemplative traditions unanimously agree that we are indeed asleep. The machinery built up by our psychological past runs by itself, disperses our attention down the lanes of our past or catapults it into the streets of our future, and largely determines our states of mind, indeed our lives.

The obvious antidote to such mental dispersion and the automated living to which it gives rise is, of course, attention. But before attention can suffuse our everyday lives, it must be trained intensely. And this, as I have been suggesting, is the common task of various contemplative practices. We have now reached a point when we must refine the concept of attention. For that which we ordinarily consider attention is, by contemplative standards, not truly deserving of the name. For example, you are at this moment following my argument, paying close attention to what you are reading/ hearing. Surely this is attention rather than inattention. The contemplative would agree. But he would add that this attention is discursive, multiplex, and largely passive. In this particular case, our words are doing the 'discursing' for your attention. If you turned away from this paper to work out a chain of reasoning or a verse of poetry, you would still do so largely in a mode of passive, discursive attention. You would be engaged in accepting and rejecting and sorting out what the mind presents. In less intellective and concentrative modes the phenomenon is still clearer. We may feel ourselves to be in attentive control, yet the mind takes us where it pleases. Julian Jaynes has argued, cogently we think, that ordinary thinking requires no attention whatsoever.[10] Ordinary attention, then, is hardly a state of autonomous vigilance. It is more accurate to say that attention is stimulated, conditioned, and led by mobilizations of energy along habit-pathways within our psyche, so that when it confronts its objects it is always faced, as it were, by a *fait accompli*.[11]

The mental posture of the contemplative, therefore, is distinct not only from inattention but from ordinary discursive attention as well. It is the cultivation of sustained, non-discursive, acutive attention which is, in fact, quite extraordinary. For there are many of us who in all our uncountable billions of mental moments and in all their variety, have never known a moment of truly active attention. Such a moment curtails the autonomous activities of ordinary psychological activity. If the reader doubts this, he or she may perform a simple experiment. Take up a 'speak-I-am-listening' attitude of acute attention toward the screen of consciousness standing close guard, as it were, at the place where the contents of consciousness are born. For as long as one is able to hold this posture of intense active attention, the inner dialogue and the flow of images will be stopped. As Benoit proposes,

> Our attention, when it functions in the active mode, is pure attention without manifested object. My mobilized energy is not perceptible in itself, but only in the effects of its disintegration, the images. But this disintegration occurs only when my attention operated in the passive mode; active attention forestalls this disintegration.[12]

Anyone who has ever attempted active attention as we have just described it finds, however, that it is difficult to maintain for any extended duration. The ubiquitous admonition in contemplative texts to somehow go beyond images, ideas, and all discursive thought involves one in the seemingly self-defeating task of trying to stop the mind with the mind. And so we find under the guidance of a teacher that this admonition against discursive thought is but a cavalry charge subsequently balanced by a far more subtle strategy, a second movement as it were. Given the fact the deep-seated habit patterns of the psyche will repeatedly overpower a still weak concentrative ability and assuming that the practitioner will repeatedly attempt to establish active, sustained attention, his constant companion in all of this is impartiality, equanimity, and non-reactive acceptance. When concentrated attention falters, one is asked to be a quiet, nonreactive witness to what has arisen. To do otherwise is to make meditation another aspect of the self-project to which one reacts with desire or aversion, thus multiplying the basic problem instead of undoing it. Now whatever emerges in the mind is observed and let go of without being elaborated upon or reacted to. Images, thoughts, and feelings arise due to the automatism of deeply-embedded psychological structures, *but their lure is not taken*. They are not allowed to steal attention and send it floundering down a stream of associations. One establishes and reestablishes concentrated attention, but when it is interrupted one learns to disidentify with the contents of consciousness and to maintain a choiceless, nonreactive awareness.

The theistic doctrines of grace and the dual Buddhist doctrines of no-self and dependent origination function beautifully in this context. In all contemplative traditions the aspirant is asked to exert his will to the utmost and periods of contemplation are no exception. Yet all contemplative traditions remind the aspirant in one way or another that the full solution to this predicament can never be his alone. The doctrines of grace and of no-self and dependent origination remind the aspirant that s/he is but a wave on an ocean of causes, wholly implicated in and subordinate to the Order of Things we call God or Dharma. To be nonreactively attentive is for theistic contemplatives to bring no new sinful self-willfullness to the practice of contemplation; for Buddhists it is to bring no new *karma* to a process designed to dissolve it. God and Dharma respond to these quiet overtures with the freeing force that is an aspect of their very nature.

On the posture of nonreactive attention, associational chains responsible for all the chatter in consciousness and our constant abduction into the past or future are now deprived of a chance to chain-react. The light of attention when directed to the beginnings of the associational process tends to forestall the automatic stimulation of other associational chains and thus to reduce imaginative-emotive noise. Tart suggests that:

> non-identification with stimuli prevents mental energy from being caught up in the automatic, habitual processes involved in maintaining the ordinary [state of consciousness]. Thus while awareness remains active, various psychological subsystems tend to drift to lower levels of activity…If one is successful in practicing non-attachment, the machine of the mind runs when stimulated but does not automatically grab attention/awareness so readily; attention/awareness remains available for volitional use.[13]

The systematic practice of attention within a traditional contemplative context would thus appear to short-circuit the automated process of imaginative-emotive reaction to experience dictated by our self-project. And it is precisely here that we must glimpse the extraordinary potential contemplative attention has for deep psychological transformation. Just as Freud compared his investigation of the unconscious to the draining of the Zuider Zee or a vast reclamation project, we may compare the practice of contemplative attention to a strategy of starvation. The automatized structures of consciousness need a constant diet of energy. But every moment available energy is consolidated in concentrated and nonreactive awareness is a moment when these automatized structures cannot replenish themselves. If the complexes do not grow more strongly solidified, they begin to weaken and dissolve. Of course, as these unconscious layers in which the ego-identity is rooted begin to be dissolved they assert themselves with all the more force. This is the stormy and dangerous part of the transformative work, and the battle to remain aware and nonreactive can take on tremendous proportions. Here the support of a two thousand year old tradition with its rich symbolism, its metaphysical and psychological maps, the accumulated experience of thousands of past spiritual wayfarers and the guidance of an experienced teacher—all are indispensable. In any case, when deprived of the nutriment and stimulation formerly afforded to them by our distracted states of mind, the automatized structures of the mind begin to lose their integrity, begin to disintegrate. Contemplative attention practiced over a long period of time uproot and dissolve even the most recalcitrant pockets of psychological automatism.

If the cleansing goes deep enough, even our old, cherished notions and images of God and ultimate reality will be called into question. For in these too has our ego been anchored. Because contemplative traditions call the mind or soul to know its true, formless Ground, they insist that the soul free itself from every particular symbolism upon which it has heretofore depended on the course of its journey. Contemplative attention is thus an extremely subtle iconoclasm that eventually penetrates to the innermost altars of the mind, sweeping out all the idols we have made.

To sum up: attention is the key to emptying the false self. And the false self is largely that set of habit patterns and identifications which involve us in inappropriate evaluations of selfhood and cut off from the experience of higher realities. But when we are rooted in a wisdom tradition and we take its Aim as our own all-pervading intention, then the long, slow process of contemplative attention begins to disassemble the old machine of the mind and to lighten its vagaries. Energy formerly bound in emotive spasms, ego defense, fantasy, and fear now becomes the very delight of present-centeredness and a reservoir for compassionate service. As the structures of the old man are *deautomatized*,[14] new structures are formed in alignment with the underlying intentionality of the aspirant. The purification of thought and the deautomatization of psychological structures leads to a new reticulation of those structures and, consequently, to the general mode of consciousness constellated by them. By emptying him/herself of the reactive patterns built up over time by the self-project, the contemplative discovers a new life of receptivity, internal freedom, and clarity. The creative possibilities of this emptiness show themselves in the Ulanovs' description of the disidentified ego who becomes

> free of unconscious identification with bits and pieces of his own personality and fragmentary parts of his world... The disidentified

ego can enter into any part of life with gusto...but is no longer unconsciously compelled to develop and support particular associations, intrigues, rituals of status...or certifications of possessions...The disidentified ego can take or leave things, enter into them and yet not be bound by them.[16]

In the words of St. John of the Cross, the soul becomes "free and empty even though it possesses."

Through the systematic practice of attention the mind acquires the new habit of spending less energy on the imaginative elaboration of desire and anxiety that haunt man's being-in-the-world. Ideas, images, and emotions still arise in the mind. But the contemplative mind, the emptying mind, is less easily caught up in spasmodic reactions to them, less easily yanked into the past or flung into the future by their reverberations and associations. They begin to be experienced in their purity and thus "leave no tracks," as the Zennists are fond of saying. The fear-and-desire bound natural man begins to wake up and to taste his primordial, ontic freedom. One is released into the Present, that intersection of time and eternity wherein Divinity dwells. And it is here in the Present that both the eye by which God and I see each other, and the heart which knows compassion for all beings, open wide.

NOTES

1 Arthur Waley, *The Way and Its Power* (New York: Random House, 1958), 43-50, 109-20.

2 Aryeh Kaplan, *Meditation and Kabbalah* (York Beach, Maine: Samuel Weiser, 1982), 1. See also Gershom Scholem, *Jewish Mysticism* (New York: Schocken Books, 1961), 34; cf. 101, 116, 139, 275-78. In a thirteenth-century text, Moses Maimonides speaks of focused as opposed to distracted attention as the way to cultivate the presence of God. Cf. *Guide of the Perplexed*, trans. Shlomo Pines (Chicago: University of Chicago Press, 1963), 620-23.

3 Thomas Keating, "Contemplative Prayer in the Christian Tradition," *America*, 8 April 1978, 278.

4 Dr. Javad Nurbakhsh, *In the Paradise of the Sufis* (New York: Khaniqahi-Nimatullahi, 1979), 20.

5 Ibid., 72.

6 Michael Washburn, "Observations Relevant to a Unified Theory of Meditation," in *Journal of Transpersonal Psychology* 10, no. 1, (1978), 59. *JTP* is the richest source of reflection I know of on these subjects. Contemplative disciplines (mainly Asian) are subjected to close psychological scrutiny yet without reductionism. Over the years I have found the contributions of Messrs. Washburn, Welwood, and Wilber particularly illuminating.

7 Hubert Benoit, *The Supreme Doctrine* (New York: Viking, 1959), 136.

8 Charles Tart, *States of Consciousness* (New York: E. P. Dutton, 1975), 23.

9 Not all automatisms are detrimental; in fact, many automatic bodily and mental functions are quite healthy and beneficial. It would be maddening to try to attend consciously to every movement made in the process of swimming, driving a car, walking, or any other simple motor activity. This is not to mention the near complete impossibility of doing so with our internal bodily functions. Moreover, we can count as a good that when we see the symbols $\frac{7+3}{5}$ we can automatically respond with "2" without consciously attending to each discrete step in the calculation. Many such automatisms are helpful time-and energy-saving devices, aspects of the body's instinctual wisdom or well-learned skills. The kinds of automatism we are speaking of throughout this paper are far less useful, consisting as they do of unnecessary, energy-wasting, imaginary elaborations and emotive assessments of experience.

10 Julian Jaynes, *The Origin of Consciousness in the Breakdown of the Bicameral Mind* (Boston: Houghton-Mifflin, 1976), 39ff.

11 Benoit, 147.

12 Ibid., 40.

13 Tart, 44.

14 My understanding of the process of deautomatization owes a great debt to Arthur Deikman's seminal piece, "Deautomatization and the Mystic Experience," in *Psychiatry* 29, no. 4.

15 Ann and Barry Ulanov, *Religion and the Unconscious* (Philadelphia: Westminster, 1975), 188-89.

Spiritual Discipline and the Hazards of Institutionalization

James Gaffney

The theme, "Spiritual Discipline and Ultimate Reality," has the advantages and the disadvantages of vagueness. Probably the advantages predominate in an ecumenical discussion, which can benefit us all by exhibiting enough variety of viewpoints, assumptions, and usages to arouse us from our dogmatic, or what is worse, doctrinaire slumbers. Nevertheless each of us must, I suppose, in the interest of discussion, transform the thematic phrase into something like a question to be answered or an hypothesis to be tested. And the broadest question the theme suggests would seem to be, what is the relationship (or what are the relationships, or some of the relationships) between spiritual discipline and ultimate reality? And to go anywhere from there, it is necessary to say something about the meaning (or meanings, or some of the meanings) of those two phrases.

A fair start may be provided by the standard dictionary definition of discipline as a transitive verb, meaning primarily to "bring under control, train to obedience and order."[1] This idea can be appropriately narrowed by invoking the primary definition of discipline as a noun meaning "mental and moral training." That definition dispenses us from including in our discussion strictly coercive or compulsive measures that might be employed to "bring under control," such as surgical, chemical, and electrical tamperings with our nervous systems, or those approaches to learning that pursue their effects, in Skinner's apt phrase, "beyond freedom and dignity."[2] It will also be worth noting, for later attention, that secondary meanings of these terms bring in significant connotation of severity or strenuousness, implying that the activity we call discipline is one that we expect to be vigorously resisted.

The dictionary may get us started also on the modifier "spiritual," defined as "of the spirit as opposed to matter; of the soul esp. as acted upon by God." Combining these accounts of English idiom we get a rough idea of what spiritual discipline spontaneously suggests to persons whose culture is expressed by that idiom. In order not to prolong this philological introduction, I shall merely affirm what I think, that very similar results are obtained when a similar inquiry is made about the nearest equivalent terms in other Western languages. That non-Western languages would fall so nicely into line I am inclined to doubt, but about that I am eager to learn and by no means competent to instruct.

Returning to the clues afforded by English lexicography, spiritual discipline primarily denotes a process of bringing order into the soul. With a strong connotation that this process requires some exertion. The additional connotation, that the term spiritual implies the soul's being under divine influence, suggests that our thematic phrase, "spiritual discipline and ultimate reality," expresses a connection that is already habitual in the culture that uses this language, and which has, throughout most of its history, taken "ultimate reality" to be a metaphysician's synonym for God.

Nevertheless, that connection is not unavoidable, and the first notable considerations of spiritual discipline that have been preserved in Western thought, and which have influenced nearly all subsequent ones, do not explicitly make it. Bringing the soul under control, or imposing order upon it, almost inevitably suggests the philosophy of Plato and of his master Socrates for whom philosophy and spiritual discipline are scarcely distinguishable notions. The most familiar accounts are presumably certain passages in the *Republic,* where we find ideas about the soul's order and discipline predicated on assumptions, taken to be commonsensical because implied in common language, about the soul's makeup. Although Plato was an uncompromising spiritualist, he did not suppose that the soul's distinctness from the body prevented its being influenced by it; we may recall that not only music, but also gymnastics, plays a major part in his curriculum for the soul's training, and that both genetics and nurture are blamed for its resistance to training.

But basic to Plato's interest was what we should nowadays call a psychological model comprising three factors, the "rational," the "spirited," and the "appetitive."[3] Since for Plato it is the proper relationship of those factors that constitute the soul's right order, fostering that relationship is what spiritual discipline is all about. Moreover, it is plain that for Plato the indication of a need for such discipline is identical with the evidence for the soul's having the composition he attributed to it. For to Plato it seemed undeniable that the springs of human conduct reveal their distinctness precisely by working against one another. This is brought out most graphically by the famous chariot metaphor, by which the soul's disorder is likened to the difficulty of getting two horses to function cooperatively as a chariot team.[4] Here rationality is likened to the charioteer, whose more recalcitrant steed especially, representing sensual craving, needs skillful management not excluding judicious application of the whip. In short, therefore, what spiritual discipline means for Plato is bringing the soul's unruly forces under the dominion of reason. How specifically this is to be accomplished is described in his detailed prescriptions both for education and for law.

Mention of law in this connection may remind us that Plato's psychological paradigm does additional duty as a political and sociological model. For in the state, as in the soul, he found three primary factors in need of order, and their harmony, in the one case as in the other, constitutes that hard-won state of well-being to which he gives the name of justice. Indeed, in a famous pedagogical maneuver, he transposes his whole investigation of justice in the soul from a psychological to a sociological plane, under the impression—or the pretext—that the state is the individual writ large.[5]

Ostensibly, it is merely a question of using the state as a convenient paradigm for analyzing the individual soul. But this process has consequences that far exceed its pedagogical intent. For in order to exploit the analogy it is necessary to match the main components of the individual soul with the components of political society. Since these components are themselves individual persons, each of the soul's function ingredients is likened to a department of society. There must, accordingly, be three main political sectors, each specializing in a function corresponding to one of the three main activities of the soul. And we know that Plato's ideal commonwealth turns out to be an organization of three very different types of persons, each of which is characterized by the disproportionate development of one of the soul's three principal dynamisms. The just society, like the just soul, is constituted by an harmonious ordering of potentially conflicting elements. And in the just society as in the just soul, this harmony depends on one factor's exercizing a control to which the others have been trained to submit. As in the soul, spirit and appetite must be brought to obey reason if the harmony of justice is to prevail, so in the state it is only when economic and military interests are induced to follow the rule of sages that political justice is achieved. What began as an account of spiritual discipline is thus transformed into the design of a social regimen.

But in this process a disconcerting thing has happened. The harmony of the individual soul has not merely been assimilated to that of the state, it has in considerable measure been sacrificed to it. The well-balanced individual, ruled by his own rationality has been systematically excluded from the two larger of society's three main divisions. Both the man of business and the man of war are precisely defined by the specific failures of their respective souls to realize that justice of soul which depends on the sovereignty of the soul's own reason. Spiritual discipline is not for them, and political discipline is to supply for their lack of it. They must indeed be ruled by reason, but not by their own reason. The rule of reason, and that spiritual discipline which enables reason to rule, have become the prerogative of an aristocratic minority. If ecclesiological metaphors may be applied to what is still at this point a strictly secular program of spiritual discipline, it may be said that a kind of philosophical clericalism has supervened upon what seemed at first to be the makings of a philosophical priesthood of all believers.

It is thus that Plato's account of spiritual discipline, as the means to establish justice in individual souls, is effectively combined with his unargued assumption that the vast majority of individual souls are simply not up to it. It is true that a kind of screening process is envisaged for selecting the spiritual elite during early stages of education, but the expected result of that process is not viewed hypothetically, and indeed any other outcome would be ruinous to the entire project of the Platonic utopia. By the same token, prospects of philosophically upward mobility in future generations are to be precluded by enforced eugenics. And finally, to assure general acquiesence in the gross inequalities of treatment essential to a political program based on such premises, Plato recommends with disarming simplicity "one of those necessary falsehoods," "just one royal lie," "an old Phoenician tale."[6] What follows is an exemplary myth of social control, a sanctimonious fiction designed to exploit religious credulity in the interest of uncritical subservience to a social ideology.

Here, for the first time, it may be said, however wryly, that "ultimate reality" comes into the argument that began as an account of "spiritual discipline." It comes in the form of a deliberate fabrication of civil religion, to be manipulated as propaganda for the maintenance of permanent rigidity in class structure. "Citizens," we shall say to them in our tale, "you are brothers, yet God has framed you differently."[7] And so the myth proceeds to inculcate a divine scheme of human inequality, belief in which may assure the steady supply of economic drudges and martial fanatics required by a recipe for perfect justice. "Enough," concludes Plato's Socrates to Glaucon, "of the fiction, which may now fly abroad upon the wings of rumour, while we arm our earth-born heroes, and lead them forth under the command of their rulers."[8]

Before turning to other, more positive aspects of Plato's account of the relationship between spiritual discipline and ultimate reality, it is well to ponder that crucial passage of thought whereby his account of spiritual discipline to achieve harmony of soul was transmuted into a blueprint for totalitarianism. For Plato, the politician manqué, very probably it was all quite deliberate, and yet it is curious how often the cultivation of personal ascetical ideals of spiritual self-mastery have spontaneously engendered forms of social organization based upon the many's unquestioning submission to the few. In Western religious life, as cenobitic monasticism rose on the foundations laid by solitary ascetics, it is fascinating to observe how rapidly and systematically all those qualities

105

of soul for whose sake the enterprise began were relegated to a decidedly secondary rank, well behind the all-encompassing virtue of obedience.[9] The socialization of spiritual discipline is a process abounding in ironies.

Nevertheless, whatever wholesome wariness such reflections may inspire, the socialization of spiritual discipline is, generally speaking, simply indispensable. For, evident as it may be to nearly everyone that the soul—or whatever one chooses to call it—contains uncomfortably conflicting forces, it is not so commonly evident how their conflicts should be coped with, or even that they can be coped with at all. There are self-educated geniuses of spiritual discipline as of other disciplines. But here as elsewhere, geniuses remain rarities and, for the most part, learning depends, at least incipiently, on teaching. Spiritual discipline depends normally on some kind and degree of spiritual discipleship. And since most teachers will themselves have been taught, and many disciples will teach others in their turn, spiritual discipline generates, and is sustained by, tradition.

Spiritual discipline is apt, therefore, to develop very much as other kinds of discipline do, begun with personal discovery, continued through the influence of one person upon another, and preserved by a tradition of such influence. As such traditions perdure, they acquire a certain regularity. One who has been taught and who teaches in turn is likely not only to transmit what he has learned but also to impart the way in which he learned it. One tends to teach not only what one has been taught, but as one has been taught. And one does so the more readily, the better satisfied one is with the way one was taught and the more eager one is to transmit what one has learned. As demand for the discipline grows greater, and disciples outnumber teachers, it becomes needful for the process of transmission to become in some degree standardized, for the influence of teacher upon learner to become increasingly formalized, for the entire undertaking to become progressively institutionalized.

It is an instance of what Newman described so effectively in his account of "The Rise and Progress of Universities": "Taking influence and law to be the two great principles of government, it is plain that, historically speaking, influence comes first, and then law... Universities are instances of the same course: they begin in influence, they end in system. At first, whatever good they may have done, has

106

been the work of persons, of personal exertions, of faith in persons, of personal attachments. Their professors have been a sort of missionaries and preachers, and have not only taught, but have won over or inflamed their hearers. As time has gone on it has been found out that personal influence does not last forever; that individuals get past their work, that they die, that they cannot always be depended on, that they change; that, if they are to be the exponents of a university, it will have no abidance, no steadiness; that it will be great and small again, and will inspire no trust. Accordingly, system has of necessity been superadded to individual action."[10]

The generalization Newman here extends from observing political life to analyzing the lives of universities evidently extends much farther. What began in sharings of thought, persist as schools of thought. Insights of sages and illuminations of prophets become in time the doctrine of a sect, the program of a party, the rules of an organization. In the process, profound changes are brought about precisely by the efforts intended to preserve from change. Influence gives way to system, faith to dogma, charisma to office, guidance to legislation, wisdom to ideology, friendship to membership. As with Plato, what begins as a conversation ends as a curriculum, and weary powers of private persuasion are relieved by tireless forces of public law.

I have described these phenomena rhetorically because their very familiarity make them require not argument but emphasis. Their occurrence is not likely to be denied, but it is likely to be forgotten or overlooked. They pertain to the outcome of a process that is in great measure unavoidable and that is by no means altogether undesirable. It is highly effective, and it is its very efficiency that makes overreliance upon it dangerous to spiritual discipline. For it tends to make the discipline of the spirit no longer a discipline by the spirit. The effects may be within the soul, but the causes are external to it. And a point can at last be reached where they are external to all souls. Built into a system and committed to an organization, the forces of spiritual discipline may pursue their work in ways that are virtually automatic and self-perpetuating, carried on by the careful contrivances of thoughtful men whose thoughts may have died with them while their devices work on by their own inertia.

No doubt the inertia of any such system eventually runs down unless it finds, at least sporadically, new impetus from more personal energies. But as long as it lasts, and that may be very long, it acquires a peculiar significance for those whose lives it most affects. For it becomes, for those who submit to its ministrations of spiritual discipline, the veritable author of what they perceive to be their spiritual lives. It provides the matrix in which they are sustained, the culture in which they are nourished. It loftily transcends them, yet embraces them intimately. It puts order into their lives by conforming them to its own order, leaving little to chance and still less to choice. It bestows peace by shutting out risk and turbulence. Its very inflexibility is experienced not as cramping or stifling confinement, but as security and relief, well-expressed in the words of Gerard Manley Hopkins attributed to a woman—of a kind commoner in his day than in ours, but by no means extinct—on entering the convent that was to be her "Heaven-Haven": "I have desired to go / Where springs not fail, / To fields where flies no sharp and sided hail / And a few lilies blow. // And I have asked to be / Where no storms come, / Where the green swell is in the havens dumb, / And out of the swing of the sea."[11] I remember years ago reading that poem to a class of college freshmen, and asking the students who had no previous acquaintance with it to suggest what they thought it referred to. I was completely unprepared for the unanimity of their suggestion, that it probably referred to—death! For all its irony, the reasonableness of that conjecture is evident the moment it is proposed, and it may evoke memories of the considerable use once made of funereal imagery in admitting neophytes to convents and monasteries, and in the initiatory rituals of many other spiritual associations.

The thoroughgoing institutionalization of spiritual discipline produces phenomena to which different sorts of people may react very differently. Undoubtedly Hopkins conceived as paradisal what to my students sounded merely sepulchral. An illustration of the same contrast is provided by the well-known essay, "What Makes a Life Significant?," in which William James described his sojourn at the famous utopian community of Chatauqua. "I went in curiosity for a day. I stayed for a week, held spell-bound by the charm and ease of everything, by the middle-class paradise, without a sin, without a victim, without a blot, without a tear. And yet, what was my own astonishment, on emerging into the dark and wicked world again, to catch myself quite unexpectedly saying, 'Ouf! What a relief!' "[12] The community James had visited represented a triumph of socialized spiritual discipline, and that triumph had not been gained without great struggle. Yet the very completeness of its success, expunging all traces of struggle, produced in a sympathetic observer a sense rather of lassitude than of tranquility. As James expressed his afterthoughts, "The ideal was so completely victorious already that no sign of any previous battle remained, the place just resting on its oars... Such absence of human nature *in extremis* anywhere seemed, then, a sufficient explanation for Chatauqua's flatness and lack of zest..."[13]

Reflections of a related kind may be suggested by the fact that Christian monasticism found it necessary to call attention and assign a name to a new species of vice, found peculiarly common among its members. The Greek word from which its name derives means literally a freedom from trouble, or stress, but what the moral psychologists of monastic asceticism meant by *acedia* was not a blissfully untroubled state, but a condition of crushing spiritual boredom. Medieval moralists like Thomas Aquinas described it as "the torpor of a mind neglectful of getting good things started," and regarded it as a profound joylessness of spirit.[14] No doubt our contemporary psychologists could propose instructive labels and diagnoses of their own, but it is noteworthy that it was the monastic environment, during its most thriving epoch in Western religion, that found these symptoms so endemic as to demand a new entry in the classical catalogues of vice.

It is not religion as such that produces this torpid disposition or the conditions that foster it. It is that process whereby, under whatever auspices, secular or sacred, spiritual discipline becomes entrusted to social agencies that have systematized and traditionalized their methods to the point where they can and do grind on as impersonal routines. The symptoms of *acedia* are recorded not only by monastic observers, but by behavioral scientists studying the workings of so-called "total institutions," devoted to imposing a supposedly salubrious order on apparently ill-controlled lives. I recall that when Erving Goffman's fascinating study of such institutions, *Asylums,* was published, among the readers who most valued its analysis were, not psychiatrists or penologists, but Roman Catholic religious, especially nuns, concerned about the extent to which their own community regimens had approximated the model of "total institutions," and fostered behavior disquietingly similar to what that book described.[15]

We are thus again reminded that certain forms and functions of religion are among the important contributors to such social arrangements. And it may also be observed that religion may have a passive as well as an active relationship to such arrangements. For insofar as the kind of spiritual discipline I have been referring to is urgently sought, and believed to be satisfactorily provided by a kind of self-surrender to an institution that virtually imposes it, that institution enlarges not its power only, but its significance as well. By a peculiar paradox, the more impersonally and, as it were, automatically it does its work, the more it tends to become personified as an object of trust and loyalty, and even of deepest trust and deepest loyalty. Spiritual discipline, in its most intensely socialized forms, may in this way virtually create ultimate reality for their own adherents. How often has a monastery, religious order, cult, sect, or church become, for all practical purposes, the terminal object of its members' faith, hope, and love? No doubt this is part of the truth contained in the increasingly popular assumption that society is, in some sense or other, the real basis and proper referent of all our talk about God. It is especially when institutions become credited with omnicompetence that their apotheosis is likely to occur, and if they happen to have been in the first place religious institutions, this development has to be either resisted or accommodated theologically. The alternatives were more than usually plain in the Protestant by the term ecclesiolatry. Since that time talking about the institutional church in terms appropriate to divinity has generally sounded all right to Catholics, and all wrong to other Christians.

So far, the connections I have made between spiritual discipline and ultimate reality have been of a rather ironic kind, envisaging the latter as a more or less fictitious product of the former. And I have suggested that it is the socialization of spiritual discipline which, carried to a certain degree of technical completeness, provides the conditions necessary for this development.

In writing down these remarks it eventually occurred to me, and should have occurred to me sooner, that the kind of social arrangement I was thinking of has a great deal in common with what Henri Bergson described as "closed society," and regarded as one of his celebrated "two sources of morality and religion."[16] Only, whereas Bergson took these social phenomena as his starting point, I have wished to suggest, following Plato's hint in the *Republic*, that they may themselves be a product of the quest for spiritual discipline, which thereby becomes a mediate source of morality and religion. It has also occurred to me that salient characteristics of this sort of social development are closely related to what Kenneth Kirk, in his classic Bampton Lectures, described as the principal recurrent aberrations of Christianity's pursuit of that kind of union with ultimate reality it believes to be possible in this life.[17] In the first of those lectures, entitled "The Vision of God and the Problem of Discipline," Kirk analyzed that problem as having three main component aspects, called respectively "the problem of institutionalism," "the problem of formalism," and "the problem of rigorism." I think those terms are sufficiently self-explanatory to exhibit the general resemblance of what Kirk meant by "the problem of discipline" to what I have suggested are typical consequences of the institutionalization of spiritual discipline.

If Plato is among the primary sources of persistent Western assumptions about how spiritual discipline is to be understood and pursued, he is equally a primary source of Western ideas about the nature and the accessibility of ultimate reality. One of these conceptions is closely connected with the account of spiritual discipline presented in the *Republic*, and it is elaborated in that same work. It represents the crowning achievement of that reason whose liberation from sensual constraints is the very goal of spiritual discipline. It is based upon Plato's distinctive epistemology, and constitutes a kind of intellectual mysticism whose progressive transcendence of material phenomena leads finally to direct awareness of those pure ideas which alone constitute authentic reality. The famous allegory of the cave is probably the most memorable account of this Platonic way to ultimate reality.[18] It is an account that is likely to seem rather trivially related to the political design of the book that contains it, and yet it does presuppose the initial description of order in the soul and its subsequent transposition into prescription for order in the state. It is an exclusive prerogative of the ideal ruling class, in whom alone reason reigns supreme, qualifying its members both for the knowledge of ultimate reality and for the wielding of ultimate authority.

The unlikelihood of successfully combining the contemplative life with the tasks of government was a lesson Plato appears to have learned through his own painful and humiliating failure to make the *Republic* a political reality. By the time he wrote the *Theaetetus*, Plato had drastically reconceived the philosopher's life as one for which politics was beneath notice, and which, to devotees of politics, could only appear ludicrous. The would-be philosopher king was transmuted into the prototype of the wise fool, stumbling through the corridors of power, reassured by his very awkwardness, at once an object of derision and a salutary sign of contradiction. No longer the confident architect of a perfect city, his pursuit of ultimate reality has become unashamedly a flight from the world. There is no longer any panacea, only present detachment and the prospect of eventual escape. "Evils, Theodorus, can never pass away; for there must always remain something which is antagonistic to good. Having no place among the gods in heaven, of necessity they hover around the mortal nature, and this earthly sphere. Wherefore we ought to fly away from earth to heaven as quickly as we can; and to fly away is to become like God, as far as this is possible: and to become like him is to become holy, just, and wise."[19]

Spiritual discipline remains, for Plato, the first necessity, but it is no longer the elementary curriculum of a civil servant. More nearly it is the purgative way of a contemplative life whose dominant values are no longer political but eschatological and mystical. The totalitarian utopia has vanished from sight, and the lover of wisdom is complacently caricatured as the most intensely individual of men, having here no lasting city and addressing his compatriots in accents more reminiscent of prophets than of kings. "There are two patterns eternally set before them; the one blessed and divine, the other godless and wretched: but they do not see them or perceive that in their utter folly and infatuation they are growing like the one and unlike the other, by reason of their evil deeds; and the penalty is, that they lead a life answering to the pattern which they are growing like. And if we tell them, that unless they depart from their cunning, the place of innocence will not receive them after death; and that here on earth they will live ever in the likeness of their own evil selves, and with evil friends—when they hear this they, in their superior cunning, will seem to be listening to the talk of idiots...There is, however, one peculiarity in their case: when they begin to reason in private about their dislike of philosophy, if they have the courage to hear the argument out, and do not run away, they grow at last strangely discontented with themselves..."[20]

One easily recognizes in this greatly altered description of the lover of wisdom the lineaments of what would become an ideal type for the philosophic sect of the Cynics, whose resemblances to and probable influence upon early Christian asceticism has become a subject of increasing attention.[21] And in a broader sense one may see it as foreshadowing the persistent tension in the history of Christian spirituality between trends towards social integration and towards social detachment. James Martineau has pointed out how suggestive is Plato's *Republic* of the highly institutionalized forms of Christian religion developed especially by Roman Catholicism.[22] But it should not be forgotten that, in a different vein, Plato also anticipates very different developments, of a strikingly reactionary kind in Christian sectarian and reform movements.

Plato's influence, especially as mediated by neo-Platonism, on Western mysticism can scarcely be overestimated, especially in view of the almost total lack of encouragement given to mysticism by the Bible. Moreover, Plato's remarkable presentation in the *Symposium* of a mystical ascent founded not on knowledge as such, but on love, enabled Platonic influence to be exerted on both of the two main orientations of Christian mysticism.[23] At the same time, the Platonic conception of spiritual discipline established the classic design of Western asceticism, secular as well as religious, but with, as I have wished to suggest, curiously different consequences depending on how that discipline was related to the organization of society.

NOTES

1 *The Concise Oxford Dictionary of Current English* (Oxford: Clarendon, 1964).

2 B. F. Skinner, *Beyond Freedom and Dignity* (New York: Knopf, 1971).

3 *The Dialogues of Plato,* trans. B. Jowett (New York: Random House, 1920), 1:704.

4 Ibid., 257.

5 Ibid., 631.

6 Ibid., 679.

7 Ibid.

8 Ibid., 680.

9 *Obedience* (London: Blackfriars, 1953), pt. 2.

10 John Henry Newman, *Essays and Sketches* (Westport, Conn.: Greenwood, 1970), 2:315.

11 *Poems and Prose of Gerard Manley Hopkins* (Harmondsworth: Penguin, 1953), 5.

12 William James, *Talks to Teachers on Psychology and to Students on Some of Life's Ideals* (New York: Norton, 1958), 173.

13 Ibid., 174.

14 Thomas Aquinas, *Summa Theologiae* (Turin: Marietti, 1952), IIa IIae, 35, 1.

15 Erving Goffman, *Asylums: Essays on the Social Situation of Mental Patients and Other Inmates* (Chicago: Aldine, 1961).

16 Henri Bergson, *The Two Sources of Morality and Religion* (Notre Dame, Ind.: University of Notre Dame Press, 1977), 26.

17 Kenneth Kirk, *The Vision of God* (London: Longmans, 1932), 3.

18 *The Dialogues of Plato,* 1:773.

19 Ibid., 2:178.

20 Ibid., 2:179.

21 A. J. Malherbe, "Cynics," in *The Interpreter's Dictionary of the Bible, Supplementary Volume* (Nashville: Abingdon, 1976), 201.

22 James Martineau, *Types of Ethical Theory* (Oxford: Clarendon, 1886), 1:82.

23 *The Dialogues of Plato,* 1:334.

III

ULTIMATE
REALITY
AND SPIRITUAL
DISCIPLINE
IN A SECULAR
WORLD

Spiritual Disciplines and Teilhard de Chardin's Understanding of Spirituality

Ursula King

*I*n a recent editorial the well-known British philosopher Dorothy Emmet deplored the fact that contemporary theologians tend to concentrate their efforts on discussing little rather than really big questions, which matter most of all. She writes:

> Theologians, go on increasingly in an effectual way. Their ideas are losing their impact, and one no longer feels that there is anything one can *learn* from them. They tend to take refuge in studies of their past history, but, as *present* thought theology is high and dry, because it is no longer fed by the springs which used to feed it from science, philosophy and the mystical life...The *religious* interest and concern is much more alive...but it is not met by the ways in which professional philosophers and theologians try to interpret it.[1]

However, many signs in the present world indicate a genuine hunger for things of the spirit whilst there also reigns widespread confusion as to what the practice of spirituality may entail in concrete terms. What spiritual disciplines are available to us today, what inspiring examples are being offered? Many writers on spirituality seem to stress the cultivation of the inner life in a rather evasive way, implying a considerable withdrawal from the contemporary world and its problems, a spiritual discipline little fed by the springs of science, philosophy, and the mystical life of which Dorothy Emmet speaks. It does not nearly seem enough to merely revive spiritual and mystical disciplines of the past, to cultivate the life of prayer, meditation, and worship, or to develop exclusively the resources of inwardness. On the contrary, we need to reconsider the practice of spiritual disciplines *in the light of contemporary experience,* so that we may find practical guidelines to live by in an increasingly complex and confusing world. Not simply guidelines for the individual to pursue an inward spiritual quest, but guidelines to participate fully in the building of secular society in the late twentieth century, guidelines relating to the interdependence of person and community, individual and society, and guidelines to create a truly peaceful world at the global level. Spiritual disciplines must help us to develop integration and wholeness which can truly become the raising leaven of our daily work and world.

Much thinking about spirituality might be called "soft thinking" because it is not subjected to either hard analysis or firmly constructed synthesis. It tends to be subjective, individualistic, inspirational, and visionary without having undergone the acid test of critical reflection. Yet in the present state of self-reflective consciousness this critical test has to be applied, for we live in a period of true crisis, demanding decisive choices about the future of the human community and all persons within it.

It seems that in contemporary discussions about the spiritual life the reflections of Teilhard de Chardin are rarely given much attention. Teilhard's own understanding and practice of spirituality can perhaps best be summarized as a "cosmic-christic mysticism" or a "pan-christic mysticism."[2] His concrete interweaving of the mystical and the practical, the passive and the active, the theoretical and the applied throughout the vicissitudes of his own life provide an inspiring example of lived Christian spirituality in the contemporary world. For this reason, studies of Teilhard's own spirituality can be thought-provoking, since the inspirational force of his concretely lived example has been little explored so far.[3] However, we are less concerned with this practical aspect here than with the attempt to give critical attention to his thought on spirituality.

Teihard's thinking proceeded from the matrix of mystical experience without which it cannot be fully understood. But his thinking was equally informed and controlled by the rigorous discipline of scientific training and laborious fieldwork, requiring the arduous piecing together of fragments of facts to provide evidence for a hypothesis or theory with which to push further the frontiers of our consciousness of the real. The method at work here is a dialectic of analysis and synthesis brought to bear on the entire range of human experience from the infinitesimal small to the infinitesimal great and the infinitesimal complex. This synthesis of vision unfolds at its most complex and complete in Teilhard's main work, *The Phenomenon of Man,* but it is too complex there, too condensed and abstract to make all the elements of his argument and analysis fully apparent to the reader. Also, the English title is a mistranslation of the French, *Le Phénomène Humain,* for Teilhard speaks neither about the phenomenon of "man" in a generic sense nor in the restricted sense of "male." In his phenomenology based on observation, reflection, and interpretation, he wanted to explore the human phenomenon in all its amplitude from the sources to the summit of its development, as part of the cosmic flux and dynamic of the creative transformation of matter into spirit. Some of our contemporaries find this canvas too large, too complex, and too frightening, fearing as they do that the individual person might be lost to sight in this vast vision of evolutionary development. But Teilhard saw with lucid clarity that it is imperative to ask what it means to be human today and what specifically singles out the 'human' in the cosmic evolution of life and consciousness.

In his view the evolution of the human phenomenon cannot be dissociated from the phenomenon of religion and mysticism. In fact, he uses the term "mysticism" far more often than the term "spirituality." This is already a first hint that a rightly understood and practiced mysticism holds an absolutely central place in his understanding of spirituality.[4] Elements of Teilhard's thought on spirituality are scattered throughout many of his writings. However, they find a particularly clear expression in the essays contained in the two volumes on *Activation of Energy* (1963) and *Human Energy* (1969). The latter comprises an essay explicitly devoted to the discussion of "The Phenomenon of Spirituality" (*Human Energy,* 93-112) which we shall use as a basic source to highlight Teilhard's particular understanding of spirituality.

The Phenomenon of Spirituality

Written in 1937, only a year before he began working on *The Phenomenon of Man*, this essay proposes a *theory* about the phenomenon of the spirit within evolution which to Teilhard appears to be a theory "as *true* as any large scale physical hypothesis can be" (p. 112). "Besides the phenomenon of heat, light and the rest studied by physics, there is, just as real and *natural,* the *phenomenon of spirituality*" (p. 93). This is certainly an unusual, if not to say novel, way of looking at spirituality, easily open to criticism from natural scientists, traditional philosophers and theologians alike.

The phenomenon of the spirit has always attracted the attention of human beings thinking about themselves, engaged in the exercise of conscious self-reflection. In fact, Teilhard asserts that this phenomenon of spirit

> has rightly attracted man's attention more than any other. We are coincidental with it. We feel from within. It is the very thread of which the other phenomena are woven for us. It is the thing we know best in the world since we are itself, and it is for us everything. (P. 93)

Yet Teilhard also points out that, in spite of the natural givenness of "this fundamental element" of the spirit, there seems to exist no adequate understanding of its nature. In the past, two fundamentally different viewpoints can be discerned. One contains all the spiritual philosophies for which spirit is really a "meta-phenomenon," something so special and so high that it could not possibly be confused with the earthly and material forces which it animates. Incomprehensibly associated with them, it impregnates them but does not mix with them. There is a world of souls and a world of bodies" (p. 93).

In contrast to this, the second viewpoint, in ascendancy since the nineteenth century but by no means restricted to the modern era, considers the spirit as an "epi-phenomenon," something of secondary and passing importance; a view according to which

> spirit seems something so small and frail that it becomes accidental and secondary. In face of the vast material energies to which it adds absolutely nothing that can be weighed or measured, the "fact of consciousness" can be regarded as negligible. (P. 93)

Teilhard was in no way concerned to distinguish between the many different varieties of spiritualist-idealist philosophies on one hand and empirical-materialist ones on the other, nor did he inquire into historical-geographical and socio-cultural distribution of these different schools of thought. In a very simple, schematic manner he contrasts these two fundamentally opposite ways of understanding the spirit as either a "meta-phenomenon" or an "epi-phenomenon" with his own understanding which, again, is not unique to him but historically and contemporarily shared by others. He describes this as

> a third view-point towards which a new physical science and a new philosophy seem to be converging at the present day: that is to say that spirit is neither super-imposed nor accessory to the cosmos, but that it quite simply represents the higher state assumed in and around us by the primal and indefinable thing that we call, for want of a better name, the "stuff of the universe"...
> Spirit is neither a meta- nor an epi-phenomenon; it is *the* phenomenon. (P. 94)

This passage may be compared with the discussion in *The Phenomenon of Man* where the meaning of the human phenomenon within the process of evolution is presented as *the* phenomenon rather than a meta- or an epi-phenomenon. As regards the understanding of spirituality, the third viewpoint presented here is not unlike Teilhard's description of the *"via tertia"* in his schematic treatment of the different mysticisms.[5] The first, vertical way is the seeking of God to the exclusion of everything else, whether world, work, society, the body. The second way, the horizontal, is the total immersion in the world and its development, in its matter, so to speak, at the loss of any spiritual or transcendent concern. The *"via tertia"* or third way, by contrast, represents neither a vertical nor a horizontal line but a diagonal one which indicates a basic thrust in spirituality and mysticism whereby spirit comes into being and the spirit of God is found through a creative transformation of matter, world, work, and society.

In a short space the essay on "The Phenomenon of Spirituality" demonstrates Teilhard's basic approach, his method of analysis and synthesis, his use of dialectic, as well as his attempts to extend the boundaries of scientific argument by using the concepts and tools of scientific debate for a subject not normally studied within the purview of science. It is for others to consider whether this implies that Teilhard's remained "scientistic," too narrowly constrained by the codes of the scientific community of his day, or whether he made a first attempt to explode the all too narrow confines of traditional science, an attempt pursued now with much greater thrust and confidence by many more scientists of our own day.

In order to establish the value of his third viewpoint regarding the phenomenon of spirituality, Teilhard appeals to the argument of "coherence" employed by modern science. He wishes to establish the truth of his thesis about spirituality by trying to show that his viewpoint more coherently organizes or harmonizes a larger body of facts regarding our experience, thoughts, and actions in the contemporary world.

The evidence for this argument is tightly structured under the three headings of "Spiritualization," "Personalization," and "Moral Application." It would take too long to analyze his argument step by step, but I would like to pick out the salient features of each section. In "Spiritualization" he emphasizes the cosmic roots and dimensions of the spirit. Taken as a whole, the dimensions of the spirit "are the dimensions of the universe itself" (p. 95), and "the phenomenon of the spirit is coextensive with the very evolution of the earth" (p. 98). Contrary to the customary way of looking at spirit and spirituality primarily from an individual and personal point of view, Teilhard first assumes a cosmic and collective perspective, emphasizing their global dimension. For him, "the phenomenon of spirit is not a divided mass; it displays a general manner of being, a collective state peculiar to our world" which is defined by a certain tension of consciousness on the surface of the earth, an "animated covering of our planet" for which Teilhard coined the term "noosphere." The phenomenon of the spirit has to be examined within a time-perspective, in terms of its past, present, and future. In other words, the phenomenon of spirit is linked to growth in complexity and consciousness; it is affected by a profound dynamic and a process of transformation. For Teilhard, the true name of spirit is "spiritualization," a dynamic process linked to increasing interiorization, the growth of consciousness in its movement from the unconscious to the conscious, and from the conscious to the self-conscious, leading to a "cosmic *change of state*" (p. 97). Teilhard believes that this perspective allows him to link the evolution of spirit and matter in such a way that it overcomes their traditional contradiction, stressed in an exclusive way by either materialists or spiritualists.

The growth of the spirit is linked to the historical expansion of consciousness on earth as well as to its increased concentration or "interiorization" within the individual person. Thus, at its most intimate, it is linked with a process of "Personalization" to which the second part of the essay is devoted. In this densely packed section, Teilhard's thoughts about the process of centering, the image of the center and the sphere, and his philosophy of creative union through the unification of multiple elements into a complex All which is a person, are all briefly alluded to. "The phenomenon of spirit has entered into a higher and decisive phase by becoming the phenomenon of man" (p. 102). Looked at phenomenologically, we encounter a vast pluralism in the world around us, characterized by various forms or elements of consciousness (or unconsciousness); the question now arises how to understand and interpret the existence of this plurality and fragmentation. Was there a primal unity of things, one reality which has been broken up into fragmentary consciousness*es* or, on the contrary, can we imagine that these elements will "join other like fragments in the building of a super-conscious" (p. 103)? Teilhard adopts the latter point of view. He sees the center of a person being enhanced through union with others. This process of unification and convergence culminates in union with the spirit of God or the All, elsewhere also called Christ Omega. Here he simply states:

> As regards the final nature of the spirit into which all spirituality converges, that is to say all the personality in the world, we see that its supreme simplicity contains a prodigious complexity. In that spirit...all the elements into which the personal consciousness of the world appeared in the beginning to be broken up...are carried to their maximum individual differentiation by maximum union with the All...

> As regards the direction of our present activity, we observe that, to complete ourselves, we must pass into a greater than ourselves. Survival and also "super-life" await us in the direction of a growing consciousness and love of the universal. All our action

should be organized—that is to say our morality should be shaped—towards reaching (and at the same time bringing into being) this pole. (P. 105)

The third section, entitled "Moral Application," tries to spell out some of the implications of this perspective. Here Teilhard contrasts the old "morality of balance" with a new "morality of movement." Instead of being a jurist trying to preserve and protect the individual and the balance of society, the moralist should become "the technician and engineer of the spiritual energies of the world" whose task is "to develop, by awakening and convergence, the individual riches of the earth" (p. 106).

Teilhard speaks of "the present crisis in morality" (p. 110). Whilst deliberately refraining from a "critique of religions," he emphasizes that it is necessary for the religions to change in order to meet the new needs of today (p. 110). Again in summary form he lists three principles which define the value of human action according to a morality of movement. He writes:

(1) *Only* finally good is what makes for the growth of the spirit on earth.
(2) Good (at least basically and partially) is *everything* that brings a spiritual growth to the world.
(3) Finally *best* is what assures their highest development to the spiritual powers of the earth. (P. 107f.)

He applies these principles to a number of examples, especially money morality and the morality of love. The morality of balance is characterized as a "closed morality," whereas the morality of movement is an "open morality" inclined towards the future, in the direction of great consciousness, and ultimately in pursuit of a God conceived as a God of cosmic synthesis as well as a supremely personal God. The cosmic genesis of the spirit (he describes "the development of consciousness as *the* essential phenomenon of nature," p. 105) is linked to "a God to be realized by effort, and yet a personal God to be submitted to in love" (p. 109). "The time has passed in which God could simply impose Himself on us from without, as master and owner of the estate. Henceforth the world will only kneel before the organic center of its evolution" (p. 110).

Thus the morality of movement modifies or rather completes

our ideas of goodness and perfection. Teilhard speaks of "the powerlessness of moralities of balance to govern the earth," the vain attempt "to maintain social and international order by the limitation of force." What we need is a change of state, a morality of movement and love, a "transformation which will bring the universe from the material to the spiritual state" (p. 111f.). In fact, "What we are all more or less lacking at this moment is a new definition of holiness" (p. 110).

Teilhard is surely not alone in saying this, but he said it earlier than most. He reflected about spirituality both in theory and in practice, yet his complex and rich thought is at times clothed in such abstract, if not to say lifeless, language possessing all the dryness of a scientific memoir, that it is difficult for many readers to see what he wants to say.

His ideas about the growth of the spirit and the phenomenon of spirituality in the development of the world are presented as a hypothesis, a theory. The hypothesis of a cosmos "in spiritual transformation" (p. 110) explains for him best of all the features and behavior of the world around us. But beyond the explanatory power of this theory he also thinks that further proof for it can be obtained by direct observation. This proof is available in the experience of the mystics and their love of God. Without further analysis, his essay simply concludes with the assertion:

> If it is true, as we have been led to imagine, that cosmic developments of consciousness depend on the existence of a higher and independent center of personality, there must be a means without leaving the empirical field, of recognizing around us, in the personalized zones of the universe, some psychic effect (radiation or attraction) specifically connected with the operation of this center and consequently revealing its positive existence.
>
> The definitive discovery of the phenomenon of the spirit is bound up with the analysis (which science will one day finally undertake) of the "mystical phenomenon," that is of the love of God. (P. 112)

I think this is an important essay, especially when one considers its date, but it has not been given the attention it deserves.[6] Looking at it from contemporary thinking about spirituality, I would like to single out significant elements in Teilhard's understanding and relate them to practical considerations. Within the overall evolutionary framework of his thought the dynamic, process-character of spirituality as growing spiritualization in both the individual as well as society provides the basic framework for his thinking. Within this framework, three interrelating perspectives can help us to situate the practice of spirituality: (1) Spirituality and time; (2)Spirituality and energy; (3) Spirituality and development.

Spirituality and Time

Teilhard's thinking is shaped by the dynamic of the time-process and the directionality of time moving from the past to the future. In this perspective there is greater emphasis on the potential of development than on the question of origin. There is also a sharp awareness of the acceleration of time, clearly apparent in the increase of inventions and social changes and the intensification of shared thinking made possible through the growth in communications. Unlike some authors who consider spirituality as operating in a timeless perspective, being essentially of the same kind and quality at all times and places, Teilhard saw the modern experience of time as itself affecting the practice of spirituality. Thus, a revival of past spiritualities, whether Christian, Buddhist, or Islamic, which is not also a new creation, will not be enough. Spirituality must neither be time- nor place-evasive by divorcing itself through segregation and contemplation from the problems of the "real" world. To be involved in true "soul-making," to use an expression of Keats, the knowledge, experience, and sensibility of our age have to be taken into account. Certain virtues, and also certain spiritual traditions, consider the spiritual quest as something which concerns only the individual and his or her self-realization. For Teilhard, on the contrary, the problem of spirituality is not only linked to the stages of the life-cycle development of the individual psyche but also the evolution of society and humankind as a whole. Spirituality is a phenomenon of universal extension closely interwoven with the development of the human phenomenon in all its amplitude. In other works, the evolution of consciousness, of social structure, and of spirituality are closely interrelated.

It is a vain effort to think that past spiritualities can be transplanted across time and cultures without being changed in the process, or without being affected by the complexification of contemporary social developments and thinking. Teilhard felt that we were at the threshold of a new critical step in the development of human evolution, a breakthrough from the individual to a social phase of consciousness. The American theologian Ewert H. Cousins has called this "the second axial period" after Jaspers' term of the "first axial period."[7] Whereas the first period, between the sixth and fifth century B.C., produced a breakthrough to individual, self-reflective consciousness, this second axial period is characterized by the emergence of global consciousness. Cousins understands this global development in two senses: it is global in that it encompasses the entire human community and all its historical experience around the globe; it is also global in that it is a consciousness recovering its rootedness in the earth. Teilhard fully valued the human being's rootedness in nature; he also stressed the urgency of moral choices for building the human community now, so as not to let its development run riot and thereby destroy life on our planet.

Spirituality and Energy

Thinking about the future of human development, Teilhard was at an early stage conscious of the problem of energy resources, but conceived of it in much wider terms than it is usually understood. He expressed his surprise and concern over the fact that many thousands of engineers, scientists, and technicians are preoccupied with the available quantity of the world's material energy resources, its stocks of coal, oil, and uranium, whereas no one seems to worry about the availability of the spiritually moral, mental, and psychic energy resources which supply the deepest springs for human action. Who surveys and takes stock of these resources, who cares to feed our "zest for life," to animate our taste for growth and development, our need for action so that we shall not succumb to the very real danger of indifference, boredom, and the lack of a love for life?

Teilhard considered that the world religions possessed irreplaceable spiritual energy resources, but he did not divorce their spiritualities from concrete material and social development. In terms of our material culture, our technological and scientific know-how, we can to some extent already see a global oneness of external civilization, but the forces of external unification alone are not enough. Most of all we need a common mind and spirit which can weld humankind into a closer-knit community. Teilhard saw the forces of convergence, of coming more closely together, clearly at work in the realm of material and social developments. He linked these developments with the convergence of mental and psychic developments and also spoke of the closer convergence of world religions and their distinct spiritualities. Convergence is not an automatic process, however; it requires critical reflection, decisive moral choices and definite action. Although Teilhard looked at the different spiritualities only in a very schematic, one might even say superficial, way, he stressed the need to approach the problem of spirituality today in a *global, cross-cultural,* and *convergent* perspective whereby Western and Eastern religions have to come into much closer contact. What is called interreligious encounter or dialogue must not be limited to getting to know one another or remain at the simple level of sharing one's experiences; convergence also requires a process of mutual critical reflection which can act as a catalyst by bringing out the distinctive element of each religious tradition within a global religious heritage. Theologically, very little detailed work has been done on the convergence of religious and spiritual traditions.[8] Much that is being published on the encounter of religions belongs to a naively syncretistic perspective without looking at spiritual energy resources in terms of globally convergent developments. Several writers have praised the creative originality of Teilhard's views of convergence. Yet in the light of contemporary experience, their limitations have to be pointed out, as Ewert Cousins has done with great incisiveness. He writes:

> Although Teilhard provided a brilliant theory for understanding the convergence of religions, I believe that his own application of the theory to specific religions was limited. In his personal reaction to the religions he encountered in the Orient and in his theoretical speculations on them, he seems to lack the very complexification of consciousness that is characteristic of this period in the evolution of religious consciousness. I believe that the central element in this new complexified religious consciousness is sympathy or empathy for the values of other religions. For example, the Christian does not look on the other religion merely

from his own theological perspective; rather he enters into the very structure of consciousness of the other religion and grasps its distinctive value from *its* own perspective. From this perspective he also views his own tradition, both sympathetically and critically. Then he returns to his Christian consciousness, but now enriched by his own horizons and with the spiritual energies that he has activated by a center to center union with the other mode of consciousness.

In the present generations of Christian theologians, this empathetic religious consciousness is appearing in a way not found in Teilhard himself or the theologians of his time.[9]

Teilhard emphasized that the most powerful energy for the unification of the human community and the centering of the individual person is the energy of love. Love has its roots in cosmic evolution but it ascends to the summit of the spirit. It is the "unitive element" which brings everything together from the smallest "within" in matter to the highest personal union. Teilhard tried to trace the evolution of love. He saw it as an all-pervading cosmic principle, an untamed force which has its roots deep in matter; its matrix is both the earth and the body. Thus, human sexuality is one of the most powerful forces to shape, and also to distort, human experience. All too often spirituality has been pursued in separation from and in denial of sexuality, whereas Teilhard stresses the need for the transformation and sublimation of the powers of sexuality. The human sense of the earth and the sense of the body are not divorced from the sense and experience of the spirit. From its roots in the earth and the body, love can lead to the height and transcendence of the spirit, and therefore love is our most sacred energy-resource, the very lifeblood of further human and spiritual evolution. Rooted in matter, love is an all-transforming spiritual energy. We must summon and harness its power as we have harnessed the powers of wind and water, of atoms and genes, in order to build a future worth living, a future which will extend rather than diminish our capacity of being human.

As with the perspective of convergence, Teilhard's vision of love in its concrete rootedness and transforming force is a powerful one without being wholly satisfactory in the light of contemporary experience. In some passages, Teilhard called the unitive element that is love—covering such diverse meanings as interatomic attraction, human love, and the love of God—"the eternal feminine." In fact, he devoted an early essay (1918) to this theme. He tried to elucidate the meaning of human sexual differentiation and the mutual attraction between the two sexes for the understanding and practice of spirituality. But his treatment, and even more H. de Lubac's commentary on "The Eternal Feminine," seem to me to fall short of the very integration they seek.[10] The "feminine" as a principle of unification and love is here imperceptibly and too uncritically equated with "woman" as an actual sexual being, whilst the concrete attitude to and expectations about woman's image and roles are still too much determined by traditional ascetic theology and its male celibate representatives. Here again, contemporary experience, especially as reflected in the feminist movement, has gone further in its search for an integral spirituality and a richer understanding of love.

This is a criticism of a particular element in the intellectual expression and construction of Teilhard's vision, not of the fundamental thrust and dynamic of the vision as a whole. Teilhard himself was a person filled with love, love for the world and its development (he dedicated the *Divine Milieu* "to those who love the world"), love for his church and order, and deepest of all, the fire of love for "the ever greater Christ." It is not without reason that the symbol of fire, standing for the warmth and radiance of love and light as well as for the fusion and transformation of the elements, is so frequently found in his writings. Fire can both transform and destroy. Thus one might speak of the fire of the noosphere, the supreme, transforming power of love which alone can create a true human community and provide it with its strongest bonds. The fire of love may be the only energy capable of extinguishing the threat of another fire, namely, that of universal conflagration and destruction.

Spirituality and Development

Teilhard's ideas about the concrete role and power of the energies of love are central to his understanding of the human phenomenon and the place of spirituality within it. Another name for evolution at the social level is development, but all too often development is only seen as an economic problem or as a problem of wealth and justice, the distribution of resources and the balance of power. Teilhard's inspiring words about "building the earth" can provide a strong inspirational force for this kind of development, but his question about the spiritual energy resources available today and his vision of the convergence of spiritualities also pose the question of how far we have thought of the spiritual dimensions of development. How far may the question of the inner development of human beings also become an issue of justice and concern for us in the future? The Russian philosopher Berdyaev rightly pointed out long ago that the problem of labor, of industrial relations in modern society, has so far not been tackled by traditional spirituality nor, as mentioned before, has the problem of sexual activity within the context of current developments in medicine and genetics. Berdyaev describes the revival of inwardness as a truly revolutionary act in relation to the outer world; it may prove to be a revolt against determinism, a spiritual permeation of the world which will transfigure it. But this would not be achieved by a withdrawal into inwardness alone without paying full attention to the requirements of the developments of society. If we were truly able creatively to combine the contemplative and the active mode, not in terms of the separation of people, but in terms of alternating phases in the daily rhythm of our lives, if we could learn to combine the spiritual disciplines and insights of the mystics with full participation in secular society, perhaps this would truly be the birth of a new religion, the development of Christianity to its limits and beyond itself, the development of what Teilhard also called "a new mysticism," a mysticism of action which would give us that new understanding of holiness so much needed today.

To emphasize the need for spirituality is not to plead for a false and evasive "spiritualization." A critical approach to the spiritual heritage of Western and Eastern religious traditions can and must ask how far spirituality has not been divorced from the earth, from society, from the body, from sexuality. Has it not often meant the exclusive search of the transcendent, of the spirit at the rejection of matter, particularly by ascetics and monastics? Many spiritualities include strong antifeminist tendencies, since the spiritual quest has in the past often been the prerogative of men pursuing a spiritual ideal at the rejection and exclusion of women. How far have past spiritualties existed in a vacuum of comfort and privilege, mainly accessible to a social and intellectual elite? How far has the pursuit of a spiritual ideal produced situations of emotional and intellectual invulnerability, of spiritual sentimentality, instead of being an animating force penetrating, illuminating, and transforming the real problems of concrete life, the life lived and labored by the multitude of women and men in this world?

When Teilhard reflected on the evolution of spirituality, he was in search of such a force of integration, a spirituality which can creatively relate the different aspects of reality and experience to each other rather than separate and divide them into dichotomies of spirit/matter, mind/body, heaven/earth, East/West, etc.[11] From the vantage point of our own day which has experienced further inner and outer developments, we can see the particular constraints of the situation from which Teilhard was speaking—as an exile in the Far East living at the margin of new developments, as a censured priest living in the closed atmosphere of the pre-Council Roman church, as a European living among colonial expatriates in the Far East, as a Western Christian looking at Eastern religions from the outside rather than the inside, as a man writing about women from a rather one-sided point of view which predates the current feminist consciousness and is in tension with his own goal of finding a harmonious balance in human relationships.

But Teilhard tried more than most to develop a concretely rooted spirituality, rooted in the experience of the earth and its peoples, rooted in nature, body, and community. The general principle of his spirituality, as of his understanding of the human phenomenon as a whole, is the emphasis on *creative transformation* which can operate at all levels, transforming our work, our thoughts, our prayer, our society, our world. On his vast canvas of the cosmic emergence of the human phenomenon he outlined in strong brushstrokes the genesis and rise of the spirit. Analyzing the structural relationship between spirit and matter, he emphasized the preeminence and sovereignty of the spirit, pointing to its growth and transformation as well as its transformative powers. Drawing on powerful symbols and formative personal experience, he saw that the center of spirituality must be animated by the dynamics of love. The traditional concept of love is too static, too "spiritualized" and divorced from natural passion in which all love, including the love of God, must be rooted. Teilhard spoke of "the transformation of love" whereby love is undergoing a change of state. This love is the only energy capable of transforming human society. Towards the end of his life he was fascinated with developing a comprehensive program for the study of "human energetics," closely related to what he once described as his particular vocation, namely, "the strategic defense of the 'noosphere'." Probing the full meaning of this new word of Teilhard's one must remember that the noosphere, the specifically human layer covering the earth, is not only a sphere of conscious reflection and invention but also the sphere of union between souls, the sphere of true love. It is interesting to note that the Greek *nous* on which "noosphere" is based, does not denote the ordinary mind with its faculty of reasoning, but a faculty of direct, intuitive vision, a spiritual faculty which in its operation transcends the multiplicity of discursive reasoning and overcomes the subject-object differentiation in a vision of unity. For the Greeks, *nous* was the spiritual intellect which primarily serves as the instrument of self-transcendence.[12] Given this meaning of *nous,* one can immediately see that we have to go further than analytical-critical reflection in our understanding of the noosphere. The growth of the noosphere is closely related to the rise and expansion of consciousness, but at the center and heart of the noosphere, at the center of the human, lies the radically transforming power of spirituality with the source of all energy residing in the fire of love and union. This fire is burning most vividly in the life of the mystics and saints, the seers of all ages and climes. Teilhard strongly criticized a one-sided, evasive mysticism; but, rightly understood, the mystic is the true animator of the world:

> Seeing the mystic immobile, crucified or rapt in prayer, some may perhaps think that his activity is in abeyance or has left this earth: they are mistaken. Nothing in this world is more intensely alive and active than purity and prayer, which hang like an unmoving light between the universe and God. Through their serene transparency flow the waves of creative power charged with natural virtue and with grace.[13]

Like many before him, Teilhard sang the praises of the powers of love which deepens our development as a person and is equally necessary for the development of society:

Love has always been carefully eliminated from realist and positivist concepts of the world; but sooner or later we shall have to acknowledge that it is the fundamental impulse of Life, or, if you prefer, the one natural medium in which the rising course of evolution can proceed. With love omitted there is truly nothing ahead of us except the forbidding prospect of standardization and enslavement—the doom of ants and termites. It is through love and within love that we must look for the deepening of our deepest self, in the life-giving coming together of humankind. Love is the free and imaginative outpouring of the spirit over all unexplored paths. It links those who love in bonds that unite but do not confound, causing them to discover in their mutual contact and exaltation capable, incomparably more than any arrogance of solitude, of arousing in the heart of their being all that they possess of uniqueness and creative power.[14]

He sees the dynamic of love as one of the most distinctive elements of Christianity. At the end of *The Phenomenon of Man* Teilhard looks at "The Christian Phenomenon" in human evolution. He there discusses the existence value, the quality, the growth of love, and describes Christian love as "a specifically new state of consciousness." He goes on to say:

Christian love is incomprehensible to those who have not experienced it. That the infinite and the intangible can be lovable, or that the human heart can beat with genuine charity for a fellow-being, seems impossible to many people I know—in fact almost monstrous. But whether it be founded on an illusion or not, how can we doubt that such a sentiment exists, and even in great intensity? We have only to note crudely the results it produces unceasingly all around us. Is it not a positive fact that thousands of mystics, for twenty centuries, have drawn from its flame a passionate fervor that outstrips by far in brightness and purity the urge and devotion of any human love? Is it not a fact, that if the love of God were extinguished in the souls of the faithful, the enormous edifice of rites, of hierarchy and of doctrines that comprises the Church would instantly revert to the dust from which it rose?[15]

Teilhard's view of spiritual disciplines and practical spirituality is not based on facile activism and presentism which discounts all contemplation, all interiority, all tradition. On the contrary, in order to shape the future and develop the human phenomenon further, he emphasizes the need to explore our roots more deeply and expand the dynamic zone of love, fed and energized by the irreplaceable insights of the great religious traditions.

To return to the perceptive comment by Dorothy Emmet quoted at the beginning, the problem of spiritual disciplines and practical spirituality is one of the really big questions facing us today. This question invites and demands critical reflection and a creative use of the theological imagination, all the more so as the religious sense is actively alive and religious awareness is being sharpened and undergoing a profound process of transformation. Teilhard de Chardin's mysticism, a mysticism dynamically directed toward action, can contribute a great deal towards focusing our awareness on the need for spiritual disciplines and evolving an adequate spirituality for the present and future as it is not first and foremost a "mysticism of knowing," as one author has called it,[16] but more than anything else a "mysticism of loving," a mysticism of the dynamic, all-transforming fire of love which permeates all realities and sets the noosphere aflame.[17]

Although Teilhard de Chardin's views have met with criticisms, based more often than not on insufficient knowledge of his works, his inspiring vision and critical reflections can make a substantial contribution to our emerging world civilization and can help to shape a much needed global spirituality which may rightly be called a "New Genesis."[18]

NOTES

1 Dorothy Emmet, "Editorial," *Theoria to Theory* 14, no. 4 (1981), 269.

2 See J. Lyons, *The Cosmic Christ in Origen and Teilhard de Chardin: A Comparative Study* (Oxford: Oxford University Press, 1982).

3 See H. de Lubac, *The Religion of Teilhard de Chardin* (London: Collins, 1967); T. Corbishley, *The Spirituality of Teilhard de Chardin* (London: Collins, Fontana Library, 1971); R. Faricy, *All Things in Christ: Teilhard de Chardin's Spirituality* (London: Collins, Font Paperbacks, 1981); *idem, Christian Faith and my Everyday Life: The Spiritual Doctrine of Teilhard de Chardin* (Slough: St. Paul's Publications, 1981).

4 Teilhard's understanding of different mysticisms is analyzed in U. King, *Towards A New Mysticism: Teilhard de Chardin and Eastern Religions* (London: Collins, 1980).

5 For a discussion of the *via tertia,* see U. King, 200-204.

6 Except for Corbishley, 7-16.

7 E. H. Cousins, "Teilhard de Chardin and the Religious Phenomenon" (paper presented at the International UNESCO Symposium on the Occasion of the Centenary of the Birth of Teilhard de Chardin, Paris, 16-18 September 1981).

8 The only detailed study I know of is R. E. Whitson's book, *The Coming Convergence of World Religions* (New York: Newman Press, 1971).

9 Cousins, 9-10.

10 See H. de Lubac, *The Eternal Feminine: A Study on the Text of Teilhard de Chardin* (London: Collins, 1971).

11 In another cultural and religious context Sri Aurobindo has looked for such integration in his "integral yoga." Critical comparisons of Aurobindo's and Teilhard de Chardin's respective understanding of spiritual disciplines would be a worthwhile field for research. For existing comparisons see R. C. Zaehner, *Evolution in Religion: A Study in Sri Aurobindo and Pierre Teilhard de Chardin* (Oxford: Clarendon, 1971); and K. D. Sethna, *The Spirituality of the Future: A Search Apropos R. C. Zaehner's Study in Sri Aurobindo and Teilhard de Chardin* (Toronto: Fairleigh Dickinson University Press, 1981).

12 These ideas are based on notes taken at a lecture by Archimandrite Kallistos Ware on "The Human Person in Greek Mystical Theology" (London, 14 September 1981).

13 P. Teilhard de Chardin, *Writings in Time of War* (London: Collins, 1968), 144.

14 "The Grand Option," see P. Teilhard de Chardin, *The Future of Man* (London: Collins, 1965), 54-55.

15 P. Teilhard de Chardin, *The Phenomenon of Man* (London: Collins, 1966), 295-96.

16 See T. M. King, *Teilhard's Mysticism of Knowing* (New York: Seabury, 1981).

17 One can represent Teilhard's understanding of spirituality and mysticism diagrammatically:

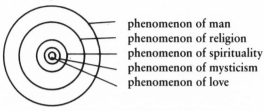

phenomenon of man
phenomenon of religion
phenomenon of spirituality
phenomenon of mysticism
phenomenon of love

Each phenomenon represents a further stage of concentration and intensification; each possesses a center which radiates outwards through the entire sphere and thereby activates and transforms all other phenomena in turn. Ideally, one would need a three-dimensional representation of this. The diagram represents a further development of that found in U. King, 216.

18 For the great outlines of this theme see R. Muller's inspiring book *New Genesis: Shaping a Global Spirituality* (New York: Doubleday, 1982).

Spiritual Discipline as the Actualization of the Heart of God

Dagfinn Aslid

There are good reasons to think twice today before making any claims about the nature of "Ultimate Reality." In modern ears the very term has a rather preposterous ring: contemporary minimalistic philosophies have tended to dismiss metaphysics altogether, and a widespread nihilistic relativism and its disenchantment with traditional spiritual disciplines no longer permit us to take for granted any meaning intended by our use of the term "God." When my daughter, at the age of nine, after her evening prayer asks, "But, daddy, how can you *prove* that God exists?," she is no longer prepared to acquiesce in biblical literalism; and when my finest moral admonitions are followed by a candid, "But it's so *boring* to be good!," the challenge of secularism takes on very intimate dimensions—it no longer is one that can be lightly dismissed.

Intentionally, the present essay does not take its primary point of departure in abstract or general principles. Instead, I have elected to begin with the particular, the concrete: the faith, the vision and values of the Unification Church. Even so, the doctrines and practices in question are subject to my own theological imagination, formed, as it is, by my Lutheran upbringing, my adventures in the counterculture of the sixties, and, for the last five years, by exposure to Whitehead's metaphysics.

Further, I have come to believe that the particular way in which an emerging Unification theology may contribute to our pluralistic age will be found in the persuasion of its integrative synergy rather than in the proclamation of a new doctrine.[1] However, let it be clear that a penchant toward aesthetics and holistic modes of thought is in no way intended as intellectual licence, or, as it were, a demise of logic. Rather, I see it as a response to the widespread quest for a certain intimacy and enchantment evident today not only in the field of theology but in the broader areas of science and humanities. It may well be that Unification themes sound a sharp dissonance with modern critical scholarship—but the basic criteria for viability, namely, coherency and plausibility, remain relevant and important in Unification thought even though these often are transposed into an Eastern key.

To dismiss, *a priori,* all and any inquiry into the nature of ultimate reality is, in effect, only to make oneself more vulnerable to a tacit metaphysics inevitably present in the very act of consciousness, even the mere business of living. There is no metaphysical virginity, only metaphysical naiveté or illiteracy. Philosophy serves a valuable, sobering function in forcing us to a rational scrutiny of our terms. Since we have no choice but to draw on the "house of language" for the conceptual tools by means of which we construe our sense of reality, the fundamental symbols and root metaphors inevitably form our very identity and values. Accordingly, when we choose to use the term "God" to name ultimate reality it is only to be expected that the structure of our existence is intimately correlated with the way we construe the nature of God. In terms of praxis, we inevitably find that the image of Divinity closely coheres with spiritual discipline. In what follows we shall see that Unification spirituality is no exception.

In most theologies, the "Heart of God" is not, strictly speaking, a metaphysical category—it is rather taken in a devotional, evocative sense, and most frequently used in a pietistic rather than in a cognitive sense. In Unification theology, however, "Heart" is affirmed as a proper metaphysical ultimate; it is indeed the one pivotal concept that lends intelligibility and coherence to the whole scheme.[2] To place "Heart" at the center and origin of reality has led the Unificationists to affirm a fundamental mensurability of all entities: relationality and experience become categories prior to substance and consciousness. Thus, the primordial intuition in Unification thought that roots the conception of ultimate reality is the "combinability" of all things.[3] The vision is one of a world where all creatures, be they natural, human, or divine are constituted in such a way that they together function as an organism. Put in Process language, we would say that entities are constituted by their experiences and relationships, rather than that they are substances that "have" experiences and relationships.[4]

Where the doctrine of God is concerned, the Unificationist is hesitant to affirm the traditional "metaphysical compliments" —God's omnipotence, omniscience, aseity, immutability. In particular, the insistence on aseity and immutability as essential attributes of ultimate reality is seen as a rather unfortunate heritage from Greek metaphysics that sometimes has tended to distort the more relational biblical paradigms. At least, a deity which has the attributes of complete aseity and immutability can, by definition, have no experience of, and therefore no love for, the creatures in any but the most paradoxical sense. Further, I would argue that "absolute totalitarian power" is a contradiction in terms: God's total power over us becomes a pseudo-notion if and when "we" are, in effect, degraded to mere automata. This is what A. N. Whitehead had in mind when he wrote, "the Church gave unto God the attributes which belonged exclusively to Caesar."[5] And I really don't think Christian piety intends each "Praise the Lord!" to echo "What worms *we* are!"

Unification spirituality thus resonates most strongly with those trends in Christian and other religious orientations which look for the love of God not "up above, or somewhere else, but here on earth."[6] On this view, the natural world retains a sacred value and significance due to the ubiquity of God's Heart in the co-constitution of all things. And, importantly, this vision cuts against the disenchantment of the world that, in turn, delivers all earthly treasures to unscrupulous exploitation in the hands of technocrats. Once the natural order is bereft of intrinsic value there are nothing but pragmatic restraints put on our use of it.

Since the main thrust of Christian spiritual disciplines has been guided by a predominant valuation of "higher realms" over against "the world," it has, in practice, been difficult for traditional theology to grant anything but an anemic embrace of

"Mother Earth," (and so, also, anything but an *ad hoc* rationale for ecology). Again, I do not think these otherworldly spiritualities are really scripturally founded—they are, rather, perversions of a more holistic and wholesome vision.

Let us now consider the Korean roots of the Unification movement in this regard. It is often pointed out that Korean autochthonous spiritualities are solidly rooted in, and affirming of, the natural world.[7] For instance, the foundational Tangun myth eloquently portrays the desire of gods for intimacy and participation with the human and the natural. The Unification view locates the fullness of existence, and the richest potential for growth, in human rather than in angelic existence. This view does not dismiss the world as "a veil of tears," but assumes a radical sense of responsibility for making the world fit for divine cohabitation. Very perceptibly, Richard Rubenstein has suggested that "insofar as the Rev. Moon is not cut off from the sources of inspiration present in indigenous Korean religious culture, he may be able to infuse his movement with a spirit of inspiration that is no longer possible in the secularizing and disenchanted West."[8]

A few remarks are in order here to clarify the nature and function of the ultimacy of God in Unification theology. In particular, we need to address the question of the availability of a God who displays the very real needs for intimacy and the candid vulnerability evident in the Unification view. Some may argue that such a God, subject to the contingencies of the world, is religiously not available, and therefore no "God" at all.

Again, I will draw on Whiteheadian conceptual tools to develop and refine the basic Unification intuitions. To begin with, if we conceive of God in terms of bi-polar theism we see that there is no logical contradiction in saying that God is both absolute and relative.[9] On the Primordial side God is the ultimate source of cosmic order, law, and principle.[10] Importantly, the ultimate source of this eternal structuring of reality is God's unchanging Heart. Thus, at the root of Creation lies God's yearning to realize the actual experience of love in and with the creatures.[11] In other words, God's ultimate, eternal, and unchanging will is to actualize this primordial vision of the kingdom of heaven on earth. In the original act of creation God freely established the metaphysical structures of reality in such a way that they are supremely fitted for tingency.[12] In Whiteheadian terms, *that* the Divine purpose and the primordial structures (forms of definiteness) for its actualization shall be actualized is absolutely determined; *how* these are actualized and concretized is, by definition, relative and undetermined.[13] This, then, is why the fullness of existence is not sought in the abstract, but in the concrete, the *actualization* of the Divine Heart. This metaphysical vision requires that spiritual discipline not be an ascetic ascension to "Higher Spheres," but rather a striving towards the maximum of synergy between the Divine Purpose and the quality of our actual living response, in the here and now, as free creative agents.

On this view, the human and the Divine co-mingle in the creative process of "incarnating" the Divine Heart. Or, to put it more strongly, God's will and love are only actual to the extent that we live in significant resonance with the Divine principles that are intrinsic to the created order, much as the healthy and enjoyable functioning of our bodies is subject to organic and biological principles. Of course, the notion that all natural entities are intimately interrelated in the ecological system is a popular one in our generation. The Unification Principle intends to provide a truly ecological view of ultimate reality in its exploration of the manner in which spiritual and physical dimensions are cooperative throughout creation.[14] More specifically, this view is developed (in terms of spiritual discipline) in the *Divine Principle* under the topic "The Three Blessings,"[15] which deals with the progressive actualization of Heart on the intrapersonal, interpersonal, and universal levels, leading up to the fulfillment of the ideal of creation in which "God would enjoy utmost happiness by feeling His essential character and form through the world of His creation, which consists of (human beings) and all things in harmonious oneness."[16] Granted, this is in many ways a rather idealistic view. However, it is if not the achievement, at least the intention of Unification Thought to offer a proposition that can satisfy the criteria of logical coherency and scientific plausibility. Evidence of this intention can be seen, I believe, in the open scholarly dialogues in which the Unification Church freely submits its theology to critique. Sobering as these encounters have been at times, they have served the invaluable function of saving the movement from isolation in an intellectual ghetto which has given less fortunate alternative religions a rather unhealthy protective anesthesia against ravenous scholarship.

The Unification affirmation of essential sympathy between the natural, the human, and the divine accords an ultimate function to the human element as "the mediator and the center of harmony of the universe."[17] This may appear rather arbitrarily anthropocentric and calls for some clarification.[18]

An organismic view of reality calls for harmony as the important criterion for "rightness." The ultimate source of this harmony, as seen above, is the Heart of God. It is only natural, therefore, that the *Divine Principle* employs metaphors from artistic activity, even of parenting, to describe the most central aspects of both Divine and human life. True, Unification ontology bears an important parallel to the Whiteheadian "Creativity," even to the Buddhist "Emptiness," when it speaks of "Universal Prime Force" as, in itself, an ultimately neutral, nondirectional source of existence. However, when actualized, Universal Prime Force is inevitably polarized by some aspect of heart and purpose: there can be no neutral actual entity. In the organismic hierarchy all entities are co-constitutive of one another; the *value* is here determined by the function served by an entity in contributing to, and ordering, the various dimensions of the whole environment.

The Unification dogma of the centrality of human existence rests on the assumption that we were "created in God's image," that is, given a full capacity for sharing substantially in the Divine Heart. The practice of spiritual discipline is directed at the cultivation of sensitivity to, and receptivity of, God's Heart—a direction shared, I believe, by a majority if not all spiritual discipline: what matters, ultimately, is the quality of experience.

Taking its cue in the biblical narratives, the created order is seen as the optimal environment for the realization, through orderly growth, of the divine parent/child relationship in human experience. In turn, the quality of the human contribution makes it analogous to an absolutely vital biological organ, like the heart, or the brain, without which the created order cannot properly function, or to use the language of Paul, due to our failure to live as sons and daughters of God, "the whole creation has been groaning in travail together until now" (Rom. 8:22).

Without dwelling on the details of the human fall and the

origin of evil and suffering that came to fill the world in place of the intended enchantment, let us simply acknowledge that existence, at least here on planet earth, appears lamentable. The Unification God is no more free to retreat *an sich* than parents are when their children are tormented. Evil, as we know it, can by no means be trivialized in light of some higher spiritual principle or necessity: the fall is an ultimate tragedy, a very real violation of God's will and desire. And, again, brute force or manipulation are just as inadequate means in the hands of God as in any human parent: there is no relief for God's pain until we freely elect to change our ways.

Insofar as the Unificationist argues that God's nature is made intelligible in creation (cf. Rom. 1:20) it is indeed a natural theology. As noted, there is a pronounced reluctance to acquiesce in the assumption that God is *so* far above us, and *so* different from us that we really cannot make any statements whatsoever about the Divine Character. On the contrary, Unificationists argue that since love seeks understanding, God must be understandable, in loving. Also (in a somewhat Confucianist manner) all things are seen as containing a certain principle of rightness, a Law of Heaven, if you will, which is intelligible to the human mind as it is sensitized through spiritual discipline. It should be noted, however, that although God's Heart and His principles are accessible to human understanding, they are not exhaustively so. Some aspects of God must always surpass human understanding, which remains limited. However, the claim is made that God's essential *character* can be known.

Now a word on the Unification mode of knowledge. Although Unification thought does not intend to compromise rational cogency, its view of ultimate reality as Heart naturally leads to a primary emphasis on experience, and a relative subordination of discursive consciousness. The affirmation of the artistic (in Unification jargon, "heartistic") dimensions in God's activity affirms, in particular, the aesthetic dimensions in cognition: things and events are intelligible in their intimacy rather than in their "strict objectivity." With W. I. Thompson, we would argue that scholarship stands to gain by making the passage from *Wissenschaft* to *Wissenkunst*.[19]

The Unification view is clearly pan-psychic: all entities are characterized by a mental as well as a physical pole, and as such all are, at least potentially, co-constituents of human experience. The actualization of "The Three Blessings" as the fulfillment of spiritual discipline and the gradual perfection of the human potential is essentially the progressively inclusive experience of, and resonance to, the whole of reality. This "polar" ontology strikes a balance between dualism and monism: reality is engendered in the give and take of polarities. And so there can be no separate actuality of the spiritual and the physical, no "knowing God" apart from "living with God." Or, to express it in Oriental terms, there can be no dualism between a universal principle of "propriety" (Li) and an ultimate material principle (Chi),[20] or, as in the epistemology of Wang Yang Ming, there can be no separation of knowing and doing.[21]

Since Descartes, much of the Western discourse on ultimate reality has tended to equivocate on the rational and the real, with the ensuing scholarly hypertrophy of the intellect. Rather than a romantic swing of the pendulum toward indulgence in the emotional and sensuous dimensions of experience, I would suggest that we need to engage in a creative struggle with the key meaning of "rationality." And, once again, here we must carefully choose our conceptual tools. For instance, the major part of Western philosophies assumes a substantialist metaphysics and a logic of objectification—the traditional discourse is on "things," "being," and "subjects knowing objects." The common intuition, partly due to the very structure of Western languages, begins with a dichotomy of the knower and the known: ask a Westerner about "ultimate reality" and watch the finger point "up and out there."

One might say that the Unification movement sounds its distinctive key for spirituality in proposing a distinctive synergy in its lifestyle and ideals between sensuous intimacy and heavenly enchantment. Just as an otherworldly spirituality would be anemic and devoid of ultimate value without its physical pole, so also would sensuous experience be trivial when isolated from all spirituality. For instance, regarding the important sexual dimensions of human lives, the sexual act in itself rapidly becomes boring when focused on itself apart from the relational qualities of the interpersonal relationship.[22] Again, in the language of antiquity, the Unification movement strives for the delicate (and precarious) balance between the Dionysian and Apollonian lifestyles. There is a candid embrace of sensuality, but yet an uncompromising commitment to the marriage of the physical pole to a principle of rightness and immanent Divine purpose to be actualized in all domains of life—social, economic, political, etc.

It is quite understandable that, given this point of departure for spiritual discipline, living tradition has tended to assimilate and replace doctrine. Indeed, the main collection of the sayings of Reverend Moon significantly bears the title "The Way of Tradition."[23] In this respect, Thomas McGowan has correctly noted the affinities between the ideas of Horace Bushnell and the Unification vision.[24] Both put heavy emphasis on the formative efficacy of familial life, stressing the organic bonds that give identity to the growing child, as it were, by osmosis. The paradigm of religious conversion is here replaced by a spirituality of religious nurture. I should expect that most members of the Unification movement thus would affirm the essential function and importance of Reverend and Mrs. Moon as "True Parents" not so much as one of giving the "true doctrine," but as shaping the true way of life. "Moonies" accordingly are preeminently intent on instantiating and establishing the New Tradition, and only in a derivative sense interested in doctrinal orthodoxy. This, of course, is one reason why academic and critical discussions of Unification theology can be so freely undertaken, with little or no sense of "threat" to the identity and faith of members of this alternative religion.

Today's theologians, groomed, as they most often are in the critical milieu of contemporary scholarship, often express surprise, if not frank outrage, when first encountering the apparently "precritical" elements in Unification thought. In many ways they are quite right in pointing out the needs for a more responsible biblical hermeneutic, for attention to the logical consistency in concepts and arguments, and, not least, to historical accuracy. As any emerging system of thought, Unification theology is yet rough and unpolished, and largely intuitional. In fact, these criticisms have been of invaluable worth (especially during the last five years when the movement has been particularly active in ecumenical dialogue) and have enriched Unification sensitivities and raised its awareness to such important contemporary issues as feminist and liberation theologies.

Thus, it is not at all the Unification intention to dismiss the contributions of historical-critical and rational scrutiny of religion and of religious language. These are surely necessary, lest we sink into the quagmire of superstition. The point I wish to make next is that the Unification vision and style of consciousness join important contemporary vector in contemporary cultural and religious trends in attempting to do justice to the fullness of human experience and, especially, to those most intimate elements that, by definition, are prior to and constitutive of any rational clarity of which we may pride ourselves.

Where our most intimate convictions are concerned, none of us lives by pure reason; rather, we are "such stuff as dreams are made of." The richness of our lives depends in a very real sense on the richness and evocative power of the symbolic tools by means of which we spin our images of reality. The virtue of any symbol-system, constitutive of any faith, religious or otherwise, should be assessed not only in terms of its comprehensiveness and coherency in general, but more specifically with regard to the quality of life and zest it generates and sustains. As William Dean points out, the orientation of theology has largely ignored the latter in an exclusive emphasis on *meaning*.[25] A God exhaustively analyzed by an army of eggheads naturally has little religious zest to offer, and, conversely, a Deity shrouded in pious ineffability supports but hollow religious sentiments. Historically, the most powerful and vital religions have been those that offer the possibility for a synergy between heart and intellect in a symbol-system apt to assimilate the greatest assortment of human experience and thus effectively to polarize life with mythic energy. The more disenchanted and reductionistic trends in Western scholarship ignore this mythopoeic function in their zeal for dialectical acuteness and "scientific" evidence.

However, our time shows many signs of a "re-enchantment" of the world, indeed, even of the world of scholars. For instance, in theology as in biblical studies there may be noticed significant tendencies toward ways to affirm the more intimate and aesthetic dimensions: the "theology of story," the newer literary criticism along with feminism, liberation theology, not to mention the hosts of New Age groups. Increasingly, those trends find proponents on the cutting edge of intellectual life. Be it the radical theology of a Harvey Cox, the musings of a Sam Keen, the esoteric vision of

William Thompson, or the mythic universe of a Campbell or a Progoff or a Hillman, the drive is indeed toward a spirituality of enchantment.

Outside the narrow field of religion there is also evidence that our culture may be in the process of assimilating more holistic and ecological paradigms. The change may not be as dramatic as an "Aquarian Conspiracy" may lead us to believe, but theories that only ten years ago were cursorily dismissed as hopelessly esoteric are now increasingly the subject of "serious" research. For better or worse, the very nature of the mass media has ushered in a "neo-mythology." Just consider the astounding resonance to science fiction, like *Star Wars*, with its tacit and overt religious overtones. And if we cry that these golden calves of modernity are grotesque parodies of the sacred we have no one but ourselves to blame; when we create a visionary vacuum by neglecting the cultivation of the evocative riches of our religious traditions, when we let them perish in archaic styles of expression and outdated cosmologies, then the muses on Rodeo Drive, Beverly Hills, are only too pleased to exploit the void. When theologians and religious leaders neglect the mythopoeic task, they must not be surprised to find religious ultimates and religious spirituality dismissed as intolerably boring, and duly replaced. Many of today's alternative religions ground their appeal precisely on the strength of their story and vision. With regard to the Unification movement, Frank Flinn has argued very aptly that the *Divine Principle*, in its function as theological epic, as a *mythos* for post-modernity, "presents a consistent and motivating symbolic structure for the adherents of the Unification Church."[26]

It is particularly with regard to the resurgence of the aesthetic dimensions in religion that I have found the thought of Whitehead most helpful in providing a rational foundation for what otherwise often has remained on a "gut level." Whitehead argues that rational judgment is at times rightly "eclipsed by aesthetic delight,"[27] or, to use one of his widely quoted passages, that "it is more important that a proposition be interesting than that it be true."[28] The Unification apology for the cognitive value of its *mythos* and symbol-system may best be developed, however, from the remark that continues the latter quotation in *Adventures of Ideas*, namely, that "a true proposition is more apt to be interesting than a false one." This faith in the coherence of truth and aesthetic appeal lends viability also to the Unification vision and hope that the right and proper way of life will eventually prevail (the kingdom of heaven on earth) because it is also the most appealing, and natural, as well as the most reasonable:

> The final principle of religion is that there is a wisdom in the nature of things, from which flow our direction of practice, and our possibility of the theoretical analysis of fact.[29]

No discussion of Unification spirituality is complete without mention of the central role played by providential history: spiritual discipline is in practice always oriented towards participation in the providence of restoration. Here, some aspects of Unification lifestyle that otherwise might be hard to understand find their rationale in the principle of indemnity. Naturally, the term "indemnity" is apt to be misunderstood due to its legalistic connotations in the English language. As it is used in talk of Unification spirituality, however, it takes on a somewhat more positive and constructive meaning. Indemnity then becomes a means of grace in that it becomes a means to restore and actualize the living presence of God's Heart in and with humanity. Admittedly, how and why this occurs in particular instances is contingent upon the actual course and present state of salvation history—and Unification *Heilsgeschichte* is as detailed and intricate as can be.

But the basic scenario which informs the "Principle of Restoration through Indemnity" is quite straightforward.[30] In the Unification doctrine of the fall, the first generation of humankind took a wrong course in neglecting to actualize God's Heart by their premature and self-centered love relationship. Accordingly, God's Ideal was never alive in the world of strife and suffering that followed. Evil came to flourish as a parasite on the essential goodness of the created order, but, nevertheless, this "sweet putrefaction" is as tenacious as a malignant cancer in the organism. Naturally, the function of indemnity in spiritual discipline is to provide a meaningful way to heal the hateful and unhealthy misuse of God's gifts.

In some respects then, the Unification God is a tragic figure, suffering numerous setbacks in the course of salvation history.

However, He is not a God who will ever stand resourceless. In literary terms, the theological epic displays, not the fateful decline towards disaster, but rather what Susanne Langer has called the "comic rhythm"—the episodic victories of "a brainy opportunism in face of an essentially dreadful universe."[31]

Since human cooperation is absolutely needed for the fulfillment of God's will, it follows that history is not predestined, but openended and contingent upon the human response to God's call. God's power is primarily of an evocative nature—it is never imposed in a macho manner by brute force, but "dwells upon the tender elements in the world, which slowly and in quietness operate by love."[32] Again, *that* God's Heart be eventually somehow fulfilled is determined, but *how* and *when* this happens is contingent on human freedom. The graceful aspect of indemnity may be understood as the giving of a way, a direction without which there could be no willing whatsoever.

I shall end in an autobiographical key. During my years as a musician in Paris I sometimes dared imagine Divinity as a Dixieland bandleader and ourselves as members of the band. And so I knew very well that without tuned instruments, and with musicians unable to follow chord progressions and join in rhythm, all we get is a mean cacophony and a frustrated *maestro*. However, with musicians sensitive to one another and all to the subtle cues of the lead I had tasted the effervescent creativity and artistic joy when things finally came tight and the music soared. For all its triviality, I think there is something to be learned about spiritual discipline from this metaphor. If nothing else, it affirms a measure of playfulness and zest and community—and that is not a bad place to begin.

NOTES

1 The term "synergy" is borrowed from physics, and refers to the "cooperative action of discrete agencies such that the total effect is greater in sum of the two effects taken independently" (*Webster's Seventh New Collegiate Dictionary*, 894). The use of the term refers to the aptitude of the Unification movement to absorb and assimilate a variety of religious traditions all while avoiding the pitfalls of syncretism.

2 Many Unification concepts become problematic when taken out of their Korean context. The English language is sometimes inadequate in rendering the rich overtones of the original meaning. In the case of 심정 , this term may also be rendered as "to be profound," "full of significance," "pregnant with meaning," "mental," "psychological," "psychical." *Dong-A's New Concise Korean-English Dictionary* (Seoul, 1971), 841.

3 *Unification Thought* (New York: Unification Thought Institute, 1973), 15.

4 To those familiar with the thought of Alfred North Whitehead, it will become obvious that my development and presentation of Unification views are heavily influenced by his metaphysics. In my opinion, this is a legitimate "translation" of a system of thought that, in its original form, is not yet fully responsive to the demands of critical scholarship. It is, however, *one* of many other possible developments of the Unification vision—but the one that I have found the more convincing. Naturally, Whitehead himself is, by many less speculatively inclined scholars, seen as somewhat of a philosophical *bête noire*.

5 Alfred North Whitehead, *Process and Reality,* corrected ed., ed. David R. Griffin (New York: Macmillan, 1978), 342.

6 Sun Myung Moon, *The Way of Tradition* (New York: Holy Spirit Association for the Unification of World Christianity [HSA-UWC], 1980), 1:265.

7 *A Handbook of Korea* (Seoul: Korean Overseas Information Service, 1979), 169.

8 Richard Rubenstein, "Radical Secularization, the Modern Age and the New Religions," in *Ten Theologians Respond to the Unification Church*, ed. Herbert Richardson (New York: Unification Theological Seminary, 1981), 101.

9 For some further explanation of the term "bipolar" (sometimes "dipolar") cf. John B. Cobb, Jr. and D. R. Griffin, *Process Theology: An Introductory Exposition* (Philadelphia: Westminster, 1976), 47, 135.

10 Ibid., 28, 43, 141; also, 48, 59, 62, 109, 125.

11 To speak of God's "yearning" may sound offensively anthropocentric to some. On the Unification view, due to the essential commensurability between the Divine life and the human, such language does find some metaphysical justification.

12 Cobb and Griffin, 48, 62, 109, 122, 135, 141-42.

13 In regard to the relative stress and importance given, respectively to the Primordial and Consequent natures of God, Process thinkers are divided.

14 For the development of an ecological view of reality I am indebted to John Cobb and Charles Birch, *The Liberation of Life* (Cambridge: Cambridge University Press, 1981).

15 *Divine Principle* (Washington, D.C.: HSA-UWC, 1973), 42-46.

16 Ibid., 45.

17 Ibid., 59.

18 Christian theologies have traditionally drawn on the Johannine logos on this point.

19 William I. Thompson, *Passages About Earth* (New York: Harper & Row, 1973), intro. and chap. 3.

20 Cf. Frits Vos, *Die Religionen Koreas* (Stuttgart: Kohlhammer, 1977), 166-68.

21 Wang Yang Ming was a Chinese contemporary with Martin Luther.

22 Cf. George Leonard, *The End of Sex* (Los Angeles: G. P. Tarcher, 1983); also Peggy Taylor's interview with Leonard, "High Monogamy, The Ultimate Sexual Adventure," *New Age* 8, no. 7 (Feb. 1983), 30.

23 Sun Myung Moon, *The Way of Tradition*, 4 vols. (New York: HSA-UWC, 1980-82).

24 Thomas McGowan, "Horace Bushnell and the Unification Movement: A Comparison of Theologies," in Richardson, 19-40.

25 William Dean, "Theology and Boredom," in *Religion and Life* 47 (Spring 1978), 109-18.

26 Frank Flinn, "The New Religions and the Second Naiveté: Beyond Demystification and Demythologization" in Richardson, 58ff.

27 Whitehead, *Process and Reality*, 185.

28 Ibid., 259; cf. also his *Adventures of Ideas* (New York: Macmillan, 1933), 244.

29 Alfred North Whitehead, *Religion in the Making* (New York: New American Library, Meridian Books, 1974), 137-38.

30 *Divine Principle*, 221-39.

31 Suzanne Langer, *Feeling and Form* (New York: Scribner's, 1953), 331.

32 Whitehead, *Process and Reality*, 343.

God Is Reality: Metaphysical Knowledge and Spiritual Realization

Seyyed Hossein Nasr

To attain knowledge of Ultimate Reality, which is metaphysical knowledge *par excellence,* is not only a possibility for man, but human intelligence may be said to have its *raison d'être* in the attainment of that knowledge and man himself can be defined as the being created for the consciousness of the Absolute and awareness of God as Reality. Man in his present terrestrial nature (or what Christianity calls fallen man, and particularly modern man, who is no longer protected by the merciful guidance of tradition) has forgotten who he is. He has lost awareness of his primordial nature or what Islam calls *al-fiṭrah.* An inversion has taken place within him which has atrophied the power of his intelligence and veiled the eye of his heart by which he can "see" God as Reality and what appears as reality to the eyes of fallen man as relativity and veil.[1]

In fallen man the center has in a sense become the periphery and the periphery the center. The solvent heart from which flows the spring of Divine Knowledge has become frozen and solidified, while the adamantine mind, which should reflect the light of the Divine Sun like a clear, cut diamond, has become solvent like a flowing stream of unending images and thoughts impossible to control and opaque to the illuminating rays of the Intellect. The deepest yearnings of the soul (which should be towards the center or the heart, interiorized toward that locus wherein resides the "Throne of Divine Mercy," to quote the Islamic doctrine) have become externalized so that man seeks avidly through never-ending outward dissipation the peace that resides in that "kingdom of God which is within you." Meanwhile, those radiations of mercy and generosity, which in the case of the spiritual man flow outward to fill the surrounding ambience with grace and light, are turned inside toward the ego to further strengthen its shell and fire its passions.

To regain the state of that man who can know Ultimate Reality (in the sense of realized knowledge) there must be spiritual discipline and a grace, both of which can in fact issue in a valid way only from a living, orthodox tradition possessing a Divine Origin and roots which are sunk deeply into the spiritual ground of all terrestrial existence, and not from concoctions made up for the marketplace by purblind leaders of the blind. Spiritual discipline, with all the different modes that it possesses in various traditions, possesses this universal goal of the remolding of man in such a way that he becomes himself and gains that primordial perfection wherein he realizes God as Reality or the Absolute as Ultimate Reality. Spiritual discipline, which is not to be equated with religious and moral discipline, is dispensed only by a qualified master for the sake of spiritual realization. If religious and moral discipline, which is for all human beings, enables man to be saved, spiritual discipline, meant for those capable of following its demands and requirements, allows him to be delivered from the bondage of limitative existence and to gain principal knowledge whose highest mode is the knowledge of the Principle as such.[2]

There is in man something that must contract and die; something that must expand and overflow the boundaries of his limited existence; and finally a substance which can know the Ultimate Reality and "become" one with It because it is already a spark of Divinity and was in reality never separated from Ultimate Reality. It is that spiritual heart which is not only the "Throne of the Compassionate" according to the Quranic dictum "The Heart of the Faithful is the Throne of the Compassionate" (*galb al-mu'in 'arsh al-raḥmān*), but also the "instrument of knowledge" *by which* that reality is known. That is why the Sufi who knows God as Reality is called "he who knows *by* God" (*al-'ārif bi'Llāh*). The path of spiritual realization can be summarized, therefore, in the three grand stages of contraction, expansion, and union, the modes differing according to the particular techniques and methods of the path in question.

The path can also be summarized in the famous stages of the alchemical process, alchemy itself being a science of the soul with a symbolic language to describe the stages of the cure of the soul from its imperfections, the process being *solve et coagula*. Before gold, that is, the incorruptible perfect metal which symbolizes the soul of the saint, is made, that which is coagulated and solidified in the base metal must be melted and dissolved. The element which must be dissolved is the hardened heart; it must be melted so that the spring of Divine Knowledge can flow from it. And what must be "coagulated," hardened, and crystallized or stilled is the ever moving mind which, because of the incessant flow of thoughts and images within it, is incapable of reflecting the knowledge of the heart upon the mental plane.

In any case, spiritual discipline and realization are necessary for the attainment of a realized knowledge of Ultimate Reality, although it must be remembered that since human intelligence was made for such a knowledge, an intuition of metaphysical knowledge is always possible; for the wind doth blow where it listeth. In a traditional world, moreover, the fruit of spiritual realization in a sense flows beyond the boundary of those immediately concerned and the presence of both revelation and intellectual intuition prevent channels of knowledge from becoming limited to the external senses and the ratiocination based upon data drawn from them. In the traditional world, reality is still related to Divinity, in contrast to the situation which one observes in the modern world, where what appears as reality is depleted of the sense of the sacred.

The sensualist and empirical epistemology, which has dominated the horizon of Western man in the modern period, has succeeded in reducing reality to the world experienced by the external senses hence removing the concepts of "reality" as a category pertaining to God. The consequence of this change in the very meaning of "reality" has been nothing less than catastrophic, reducing God and in fact all spiritual realms of being to the category of the abstract and finally to the unreal. At the base of the loss of the sense of the reality of God by modern man in his daily life lies the philosophical error of reducing the idea of reality to that of the externally experienced world, of altering the idea of realism in its early medieval sense to the connotation it has gained in modern schools of philosophy. Cut off from the twin sources of metaphysical knowledge, namely, revelation and intellection,[3] and also deprived of that spiritual discipline and inner spiritual experience which makes possible the concrete realization of higher levels of being, modern man has been confined to such a truncated and limited aspect of reality that of necessity he has lost sight of God as Reality. Also, even if he continues to have faith in the Divinity, the conception of the Divinity as Reality does not at all accord with that empirically determined world view[4] within which he lives and whose premises he accepts unwittingly or often unconsciously.

It is possible for man to gain knowledge of God and to come to know Him as Reality because of the very nature of human intelligence which was made to know the Absolute as such. But to gain this knowledge it is necessary to have access to those twin sources of metaphysical knowledge and certitude, namely, revelation and intellection. Moreover, the second is accessible to man in his present state only by virtue of the first, while the fruit of wisdom which it bears lies at the heart of revelation and also resides at the center of man's own being. To reach the inner man (or the heart which is the seat of the intellect through the grace issuing from revelation) and to reach the heart of revelation (by means of the penetrating rays of this sanctified intellect) enables man to gain an adequate metaphysical knowledge of God as Ultimate Reality and, in the light of this knowledge, an awareness of relativity as relativity or more precisely as veil.

It can be said that not only modern man does not possess an adequate doctrine of God as Reality in its absolute sense, but also that because of this lack of knowledge he is deprived of an adequate understanding of relativity as veil. To conceive the Absolute in relative terms is also to absolutize the relative in some sense. To remove from God the attribute of reality is also to fail to see the world as only partial reality, as a veil which at once hides and manifests, the veil which as *al-ḥijāb* in Islam or *māyā* in Hinduism plays such a basic role in Oriental metaphysics.

Moreover, it is necessary to mention that whereas an adequate metaphysical doctrine pertaining to God as Reality can be found in traditional Christian metaphysics as seen in the works of such masters as Erigena, St. Bonaventure, and St. Thomas, the doctrine of the veil is more implicit and less clearly stated even in traditional schools in the West than it is in either Islam or Hinduism, although there are certainly allusions to it in the works of such sages as Meister Eckhart. The reformulation of an adequate metaphysical doctrine concerning the nature of God in a contemporary language requires therefore not only a doctrine concerning God as Ultimate Reality or the absolutely Real but also the doctrine of cosmic illusion, the veil, that creative power which at once manifests the Divine Principle as relativity and veils the Principle through that very manifestation which is none other than the veil, so that a Sufi could address God as "O Thou who hidest Thyself by that which is none other than Thee."

God as Ultimate Reality is not only the Supreme Person but also the source of all that is, hence at once Supra-Being and Being, God as Person and the Godhead or Infinite Essence of which Being is the first determination. Both He or She and It and yet beyond all pronominial categories, God as Ultimate Reality is the Essence which is the origin of all forms, the Substance compared to which all else is accident, the One who alone is and who stands even above the category of being as usually understood.

God as Reality is at once absolute and infinite, and goodness or perfection. In Himself He is the Absolute which partakes of no relativity in His Essence. The Divine Essence cannot but be absolute and one. All other considerations must belong to the order of relativity, to a level below that of the Essence. To assert that God is one is to assert His absoluteness and to envisage Him in Himself, as such. The Divine Order partakes of relativity in the sense that there is Divine Relativity or Multiplicity which is included in the Divine Nature, but this relativity does not reach the abode of the Divine Essence. God in His Essence cannot but be One, cannot but be the Absolute.[5]

God as Reality is also infinite, *the* Infinite, as this term is to be understood metaphysically and not mathematically. Ultimate reality contains the source of all cosmic possibilities and in fact all possibilities as such, even the metacosmic. God is Infinite not only in the sense that no limit can be set upon Him, but also in the sense that He as ultimate reality contains all possibilities. Metaphysically, He is the All-Possibility.[6] When the Bible states that with God all things are possible or the Quran asserts that God has power over all things, these scriptural statements must not be understood only in the usual theological sense of alluding to God's infinite power. They also refer to God's nature as the All-Possibility and confirm in another language the Quranic verse: "In His hands is to be found the dominion (*malakūt*) of all things." That is, the essential reality of all things is to be found in the Divine Nature. It is perhaps useful to recall that the words "possibility," "puissance," and "potentiality" are from the same root. To say that God is the All-Powerful, the All-Potent is also to say that He is the All-Possibility.

The understanding of the Divine Infinity is so essential to an adequate doctrine of the nature of God that its neglect has been the main cause for the philosophical objections to the religious idea of God as goodness and perfection, the source of all that is good and at the same time creator of an imperfect world. No problem has been as troublesome to Western man's understanding of God as presented in the mainstream of Christian theology than the famous problem of theodicy, that is, the question of the creation of a world in which there is evil by a Creator who is good. The lack of a complete metaphysical doctrine in the modern West has brought about the eclipse of the doctrine of Divine Infinity and the grades of manifestion or levels of being, with the help of which it is possible to understand perfectly well why a world in which there is evil has its origin in God who is pure goodness.

Here it is necessary to add that there would in fact be no agnostics around if only one were able to teach metaphysics to everyone. One cannot expect everyone to comprehend metaphysics any more than one could expect everyone to understand physics or mathematics. But strangely enough, whereas modern man accepts the discoveries of physics on faith and is willing to undergo the necessary training to master the subject in case he wishes to understand physics himself, unlike the traditional man of faith he does not extend this faith to the fruits of metaphysical knowledge. Without willing to undergo the necessary discipline, which in the case of traditional metaphysics and in contrast to modern science includes moral and spiritual considerations, modern man expects to understand metaphysics immediately, without any preparation. If he fails to comprehend, then he rejects the very possibility of that knowledge which alone can solve the antinomonies and apparent contradictions of the problem of theodicy and evil, and he does not even accept the revealed truth on the basis of faith, as was the case of traditional man who usually possessed a greater awareness of his own limitations than does his modern counterpart.

In any case, the doctrine of the Divine Infinity makes it possible to understand why there is a world which is limited and imperfect. The Divine contains all possibilities including the possibility of its own negation without which it would not be infinite. But this possibility implies a projection towards nothingness which, however, is never reached. This projection constitutes the world, or rather the many worlds standing below their Divine Origin. Since only God is good, this projection or elongation means of necessity separation from the source of goodness and hence the appearance of evil which is a kind of "crystallization of nothingness," real on its own level of existence but an illusion before God who alone is Reality as such. The root of the world resides in the infinity of the Divine Nature.

The metaphysical doctrine of God as absolute and infinite is contained in an explicit fashion in the Quranic chapter called "Unity" or Sincerity, al-Tawḥīd or al-Ikhlāṣ (CXIII), which according to Muslims summarizes the Islamic doctrine of God concerning the Divine Nature. The chapter is as follows:

In the Name of God - Most Merciful, Most Compassionate
Say: He is God, the One (al-aḥad)!
God, the eternal Refuge (al-ṣamad)!
He begetteth not nor was He begotten.
And there is none like unto Him.

The "Say" (qul) already refers to the source of manifestation in the Divine Principle, to the Logos which is at once the Divine Instrument of Manifestation and the source of manifestation in the Divine Order. He (huwa) is the Divine Essence, God in Himself, God as such or in His suchness. Al-aḥad attests not only to God's oneness but also to His absoluteness. God is one because He is absolute and absolute because he is one, *al-aḥadiyyah* or quality of oneness implying both meanings in Arabic. *Al-ṣamad,* a most difficult term to render in English, implies eternal fullness or richness; it refers to the Divine Infinity, to God the All-Possibility. The last two verses emphasize the truth that God in His Essence is both above all relations and all comparisons. The chapter as a whole is therefore the revealed and scriptural counterpart of the metaphysical doctrine of the Divine Nature as absolute and infinite, this knowledge also being revealed in the sense that it issues from that inner revelation which is the intellect.[7]

There is, however, one more statement in this Quranic chapter with which in fact the other chapters of the Quran also open and which refers to the third aspect of the Divine Nature referred to above, namely, goodness. God is not only absolute and infinite, but also goodness and perfection. To use the Quranic terminology, He is *al-raḥmah*, mercy in Himself, and as such cannot but manifest Himself. The expansive or creative power of the Divinity, which "breathing upon the Divine Possibilities" manifests the world, issues from this fundamental aspect of the Divine Nature as goodness or mercy. That is why the Sufis consider the very substance of the universe to be nothing other than the "Breath of the Compassionate" *(nafas al-raḥmān).*[8] If God is both absolute and infinite, goodness or mercy also reside in His very Nature for as Ibn ʿArabī has said, "Mercy pertains to the essence of the Absolute because the latter is by essence 'Bounteous'."[9] To reinstate the integral metaphysical doctrine of the Divine Nature in the contemporary world, it is necessary to go beyond the relativities of various orders to gain access to a doctrine of God as that Reality which is absolute and infinite, and goodness, perfection, and mercy.

Such a vision requires not only an adequate knowledge of the Principle as absolute but also an adequate grasp of the meaning of relativity, of levels of existence, of the relatively real and even of the "relatively absolute," an elliptical term which far from being contradictory contains an indispensable key for the understanding of the science of God. To use the mutually exclusive categories of Creator and created as is done theologically is to fall into certain dichotomies which can only be bridged over by an act of faith in the absence of which there is created skepticism concerning the very tenets of revealed religion. To begin with the world as reality, as is done by most of modern philosophy, is to reach an even more dangerous impasse which of necessity leads to nihilism and skepticism by reducing God to an abstraction, to the "unreal," and philosophy itself to the discussion of more or less trivial questions or to providing clever answers for ill-posed problems.

To avoid such impasses, it is essential to revive the doctrine of the veil as already alluded to above and to rediscover the traditional teaching about the gradation of reality or of being. To understand God as Reality, it is necessary to understand that there are levels of reality and not only reality as an empirically definable psychophysical continuum "out there." The world is real to the extent that it reveals God who alone is Real. But the world is also unreal to the extent that it hides and veils God as Reality. Only the saint who sees God everywhere can claim that that "everywhere" is real.

Moreover, a particular object is not real in only one sense of the term but partakes of levels of reality from being an opaque object, an "it" as understood in modern science which is its face as *māyā* in the sense of illusion, to its being a theophany, a reflection of Divine Presence and a witness to the Divine *māyā* which is none other than Divine Creativity.[10] To understand God as Reality is also to grasp the world as unreality, not nothingness pure and simple but as relative reality. It is to be saved from that central error of false attribution which issues from our ignorance and which causes our attributing reality to the illusory, and as a consequence the character of illusion to that which is Reality as such and which ultimately is alone Real.

To reinstate the doctrine of God as Reality is, needless to say, impossible without a change in the way we envisage the question and possibility of knowledge. As long as the prevalent empiricism or its complementary rationalism continue to reign or are replaced by that irrationalism which has erupted against nineteenth century European philosophy from below, there is no possibility to grasp the validity of that traditional wisdom, or that *sophia perennis*, which has always seen God as Reality and the world as a dream from which the sage awakens through realization and forgetful man through death. To grasp this doctrine, the traditional sapiential perspective based on the possibility of principial knowledge from the twin sources of the intellect and revelation must be reinstated along with the metaphysics which is the fruit of this way of knowing.[11]

In the light of this fact, the role of traditional Islamic wisdom, or what the Quran calls *al-ḥikmah*, becomes clear in this contemporary discussion on the nature of God. As a religion based completely on the doctrine of the oneness of God, a religion in which God is seen as both Reality and Truth, the Arabic term *al-ḥaqīqah* meaning both, and *al-Ḥaqq*, which is related to *haqīqah*, being a Name of God, Islamic wisdom can play an important role in enabling modern man to rediscover that plenary doctrine of the nature of God, a doctrine whose loss has led to the unprecedented skepticism and relativism which characterize the modern world. Islam is able to achieve this goal not only because of the nature of the Quranic revelation based as it is in an uncompromising manner upon the doctrine of Divine Unity, but also because it has preserved intact to this day its sapiential tradition which guards the absoluteness of God and His Transcendence while hearing in the song of the bird and smelling in the perfume of the rose the sound and breath of the Beloved, which contemplates on the very veil of creaturely existence the Face of God.

Furthermore, not only has Islam preserved its sapiential tradition, but it has kept intact, despite the vicissitudes of time and turmoils of history, the spiritual disciplines necessary for the attainment of that knowledge which the sapiential tradition carries within its heart. The various paths within Sufism, as well as certain esoteric and spiritual disciplines found within Shi'ism, still dispense methods of meditation, prayer, invocation, and other disciplines which make the knowledge of the One not only a theoretical possibility but an actual and ever-present reality.

According to Islam's own teachings, this doctrine of Unity and the vision of the One as being at once Ultimate Reality and Truth is not unique to Islam, but lies at the heart of all revelations whatever be the actual possibility of attaining such a knowledge in other traditions in their present-day condition. But as the last echo of the Primordial Word upon the stage of human history during this present cycle of terrestrial existence, Islam still reverberates in a particularly vivid manner to that eternal melody of Divine Unity, recalling man to his perennial vocation as witness on earth to that Reality which is at once absolute, and infinite, and boundless goodness or mercy.

NOTES

1 See S. H. Nasr, *Sufi Essays* (New York: State University Press, 1975), esp. chap. 6.

2 Properly speaking, spiritual discipline belongs to the inner or esoteric dimension of religion, and religious discipline to the exoteric, which is also indispensible for those who aspire to follow the esoteric path. See. F. Schuon, *The Transcendent Unity of Religions* (New York: Harper & Row, 1973).

3 Throughout this discussion the intellect is distinguished rigorously from reason which is its mental reflection. See Nasr, *Knowledge and the Sacred,* (New York: Crossroad, 1981), chaps. 5 and 6. For a synthesis of the traditional doctrine of the intellect as it pertains to epistemology see F. Schuon, *From the Divine to the Human,* trans. G. Polit and D. Lambert (Bloomington, Ind.: Word Wisdom, 1981), 5-35.

4 Although modern rationalism is in many ways opposed to empiricism, as far as the present discussion is concerned, it is nothing more than a complement of empiricism because it, too, has to rely finally upon only the evidence of the senses or the limitations of the mental plane as a result of its denial of both intellection and revelation. See F. Schuon, *Logic and Transcendence,* trans. P. Townsend (New York: Harper & Row, 1975), 7-55.

5 It is not only possible for man to know God as the Absolute, but it is only the Absolute that can be known absolutely. Human intelligence was made to know the Absolute as such and no amount of "anti-metaphysical cleansing of language" by various types of positivists can remove from intelligence this power to know God as Reality and this Reality as the Absolute. If the use of human language to express such metaphysical assertions has become meaningless to many modern philosophers, it is not because of the shortcoming of such a language or the impossibility of making metaphysical assertions, but because such assertions become meaningless the moment human intelligence is cut from its own roots and made subservient to the dictates of a purely sensualist and empirical epistemology.

6 This doctrine has been expounded in an incomparable manner in the metaphysical works of F. Schuon who has brought the metaphysical term "*Toute-possibilité*" into current usage. See especially his "The Problem of Possibility," in *From The Divine to the Human,* 43-56, in which the difficult and at the same time cardinal metaphysical concept of possibility is discussed. For a general introduction to the works of this singularly neglected figure see S. H. Nasr, *The Writings of Frithjof Schuon: A Basic Reader* (New York: Crossroad, 1983).

7 This inner revelation cannot, however, become operative except by virtue of that external revelation which provides for it an objective cadre and enables it to be spiritually efficacious. If there are exceptions, they are there to "prove the rule."

8 This doctrine has found its classical formulation in the *Wisdom of the Prophets* or the *Bezel of Wisdom (Fuṣūṣ al-ḥikam)* of Muhyī al-Dīn ibn 'Arabī. See the translation of R. W. J. Austin (New York: Paulist, 1980). See also T. Izutsu, *A Comparative Study of the Key Philosophical Concepts in Sufism and*

Taoism (Princeton: Princeton University Press, 1983), chap. 9; H. Corbin, *Creative Imagination in the Sufism of Ibn 'Arabī*, trans. R. Mannheim (Princeton: Princeton University Press, 1969), pt. 1; T. Burckhardt, *Introduction to Sufi Doctrine*, trans. D. M. Matheson (London: Thorstons, 1976), 58ff.; and S. H. Nasr, *Science and Civilization in Islam* (Cambridge: Harvard University Press, 1968), 344ff.

9 From the *Fuṣūṣ*, quoted in Izutsu, 110.

10 A. K. Coomaraswamy in fact translated māyā as "Divine Creativity," while Schuon has rendered it as "Divine Play." On *māyā* and veil see Schuon, "The Mystery of the Veil," in his *Esoterism as Principle and as Way*, trans. W. Stoddart (London: Perennial Books, 1981), 47-64; and "*Māyā*," in his *Light on the Ancient Worlds*, trans. Lord Northbourne (London: Perennial Books, 1965), 89-98.

11 See Nasr, *Knowledge and the Sacred*, chaps. 2-4.

IV

SPIRITUAL
DISCIPLINES
IN PURSUIT
OF ULTIMATE
REALITY

Art as Spiritual Discipline in the Lives and Thought of Rabindranath Tagore and Sri Aurobindo Ghose

William Cenkner

eligion and art coalesce in the spiritual disciplines of Rabindranath Tagore and Sri Aurobindo Ghose. Creation of literature for Tagore is not didactic but a *sādhanā*, a spiritual discipline uniting a person to the world of nature, developing greater knowledge, and opening one to the realization of the spirit. For Sri Aurobindo art is similar to yoga because both share the same goals: namely, to become more and more conscious. For both personalities the end of art is the realization of the spirit. Yet Tagore and Aurobindo are far too innovative to be poets in a classical Vedic sense. This study examines these contemporary Indians as individuals whose art can be understood as spiritual discipline. It further demonstrates how aesthetic and spiritual disciplines are similar through an examination of the creative and aesthetic imagination.

Aesthetic Discipline as Spiritual Discipline in the Life of Tagore

Tagore's aesthetic sensibility emerges from the order of feelings. The aesthetic sense is understood within the life of the emotions. He writes: "Creative expressions attain their perfect form through emotions modulated."[1] Early in his poetic development, he spoke of his work in terms of feelings that seek form. In a poem from the volume *Utsarga,* he writes: "Feeling seeks to embody itself in

Form, / and Form abandons itself to Feeling."[2] Tagore draws a distinction between sense and sensibility: the senses regulate and register, so to speak, the perception, but sensibility discovers relationship. Aesthetic sensibility is a relational capacity opening to a new vision which reasoning and intellect articulate. For Tagore, literature holds the transformative possibility of turning the objective world into a subjective world of feelings and emotions. We know something because we feel it. A whole new world, he writes, is perceived "when it comes within the range of our emotions."[3] "Our emotions," moreover, "are the gastric juices which transform the world of appearance into the more intimate world of sentiments."[4] The aesthetic sensibility, in this case feelings and emotions, calls for ritualization. In what follows it will be shown how Tagore used ritual, as conceived by Mircea Eliade, to give constant form to the aesthetic sense.

What was Tagore's yoga? He awoke early each morning and awaited the new day in meditative silence. Meditation which began and ended his day could be considered his yoga in a somewhat classical sense. More significantly though, Tagore's yoga consists in that activity making possible either meditation and silence, or years of productive writing and creativity, or a life of social involvement. His yoga is the discovery and extension of relationships, and in this sense he gives a contemporary meaning to yoga. In the *Religion of Man* he writes: "We can make truth ours by actively modulating its inter-relations. This is the work of art; for reality is not based in the substance of things but in the principle of relationship."[5] The artist thus seeks unity within himself and with the greater world. Where this unity is not deeply felt, there can be no great form of art. The artist establishes harmonious relationship with all things with which he deals. Creativity exists when the artist integrates relationships within his own life and within the greater world. "All our knowledge of things is knowing them in their relation to the Universe, in that relation which is truth," writes Tagore.[6] To know things in their relatedness, he thinks, is to know the truth of things which in all its relatedness passes through the consciousness of the artist and transforms that consciousness. As the relationality between the world and the artist becomes more conscious, the individual is thought to encounter a wider and deeper experience of reality. The activity underscoring all of

Tagore's life is the search and discovery of relationships, the extension and integration of such relationships, and the transformative encounter with them. This work, his most concrete yoga, is expressed in a prolific manner in poetry: this is the ritualization of his aesthetic sensibility.

This account of Tagore's work accepts the presupposition that myth and ritual give structure not only to spiritual discipline, but also to the aesthetic personality and its creativity. The act of creation is a ritual process.[7] Again Eliade's notion of ritual is applicable, since, for example, in the aesthetic act there is transcendence of ordinary time and space. There is a return to a primordial moment of experience and expression, and matter is sacralized to the degree that it is experienced as hierophanous or numinous. Both aesthetic and spiritual discipline are also sustained by myth. An image or story or metaphor sustains the ritual process, holding it within the order of the concrete, the order of praxis.

How do myth and ritual function in the life of the aesthetic person? Tagore's aesthetic sensibility expresses itself in poetry, drama, fiction, essay, letters, and painting. He spent twelve hours each day pursuing some form of literary activity. Tagore, of course, is primarily a poet. Indeed, from his first verse at age five or six to his death at eighty, he daily wrote poetry. Through the ritualization of poetry he achieves his more profound experiences of the human, the cosmic, and the numinous. Effective ritual is repetitive, returning one to new time and space, to a primordial moment perhaps, to an experience of the ordinary in an extraordinary and hierophanous way. Consistent writing of poetry, when viewed as a ritual process, may be seen as the means for the transformation of consciousness. Writing poetry is a creative experience, and it becomes religious experience when the poet achieves ego-transcendency, nonattachment, transformation, and integration of new vision.

It is somewhat more difficult to surmise what functioned as Tagore's controlling myth, that image contextualizing the writing of his poetry. Since his basic discipline is the discovery and extension of relationships, he seems to have looked upon his life as a vast journey, for the "road" theme is an important motif in his writing, and he often spoke of himself as a wanderer, a sojourner. Tagore observes that he is not called to the householder's life but to that of the wanderer.[8] It is my contention that Tagore's journey into

immensity is his myth, his story, the controlling image that is ritualized through poetry. He is a journeyman, a quester for immensity through the aesthetic life. His aesthetic sensibilities, emotions
and feelings, are pitted into the journey toward fullness. *Bhumā*
(fullness) is generally recognized as the goal of Tagore's life and
the goal of all human life, according to him. The actual experience of his journey into fullness or immensity constitutes his personal myth. Within the more general image of his journey into
fullness, he seeks interrelationships with the world of nature, the
human world, the sacred world, and finally the solitary and
silent world of immensity. No one set of relationships ever satisfies
him. He hurries from one world to another with rapidity and impa-
tience. No one *rasa* (sentiment) characterizes Tagore's poetry,
because no one set of relationships ever brings an end to his journey
into immensity. The reason his poetry is not always God-centered
is that he discovers the face of beauty and mystery everywhere.

Myth functions as *śakti* (the instigator, vitalizer, power) in the
ritual process. Nature, the human and sacred planes, the world of
stillness—all function as *śakti* within the myth of his journey.
What he discovers with the myth is a world of vast relationships,
all vital and alive and giving birth to new worlds of relationships.

Thus, the aesthetic discipline of Tagore is a spiritual discipline.
His aesthetic sense gives rise to the yoga of discovering and extending
relationships, a yoga caught within the gigantic myth of a journey
into immensity that is articulated in the ritual act of writing poetry.

Aesthetic Discipline as Spiritual Discipline
in the Life of Aurobindo

Sri Aurobindo's aesthetic sensibility emerges from what he
calls the illumined and intuitive mind. While for Tagore emotions are the source for the artist's harmonization with the world,
for Aurobindo it is a higher form of mind that gives expression to
aesthetic life. The aesthetic person, he thinks, is a gnostic being. The
aesthetic faculties lead to intellectual being but ultimately go
beyond it. The Sanskrit word for poet is *kavi,* one who sees or
discloses. In *The Future Poetry* he speaks of the poet's power as an
"inner seeing and sense,"[9] a vision which is the peculiar power of
the poet.[10] In *Savitri* he describes poetic psychology as "intuitive
knowledge leaping into speech..."[11] The aesthetic sensibility, in

172

this case illumined mind and vision, once again calls for ritualization. How did Aurobindo give this form to his mental vision?

What was his yoga? Although he wrote volumes on the nature
of yoga, along with hundreds of letters to his disciples concerning
the practice of yoga, it is difficult to point to Aurobindo's personal
discipline. He wrote for twelve hours each day, followed by six
hours of reflective walking within his secluded quarters. Aurobindo's
yoga would seem to be that activity of mind resulting in creative
writing and advancing personal transformation. This yoga is in fact
his surrender and an aspiration for the divine life, rather than a
fixed method for the development of consciousness, and in this way
he separates himself from Patanjali's classic formulation.[12] There
is neither a specific method nor a distinguishing mark to Aurobindo's
yoga. He saw the usefulness of both classical forms of yoga but did
not think that such practices were absolutely necessary. Only aspiration and self-surrender receive consistency in his own life. For
effective aspiration and surrender, the mind and heart, he thought,
must be concentrated sufficiently in order to call upon the power
of *śakti* to transform consciousness. Concentration, of course, is
needed to condition consciousness for effective surrender and aspiration, but aspiration is an act of receptivity, and surrender is an act
of self-giving.[13] Aurobindo believes that if one is able to surrender,
"no other *tapasya* (spiritual observance) is needed."[14] To be united
to divine consciousness and to experience its descent are paramount.
All aspects of the human person must aspire to divine life and
surrender to the divine consciousness, including physical being,
vital being, mental being, even psychic being. Once aspiration and
surrender reach a type of completion, the activity of divine life
begins to unfold within the human person.

Aurobindo's most concrete yoga, aspiration and surrender,
however, is expressed in his ritual of writing, especially in his
poetry, although his writing comprises poetry, philosophy, essay,
and letters, by the early 1920s he had already completed his great
philosophical and yogic treatises; his philosophical writing,
moreover, did not commence until several years following his
retreat to Pondicherry. Poetry is the single form of writing that
sustained him from youth through his mature years as an ascetic and
mystic. Aurobindo wrote publishable verse at nineteen, and by the
time he secluded himself in Pondicherry, he had already com-

pleted a large number of short poems, translations from Kalidasa and Bhartrihari, two narrative poems in blank verse, and an initial version of the epic poem *Savitri*. In the first fifteen years in India, following his education in England, he wrote close to 25,000 lines of verse. From 1926 onward, following his psychic transformation, Aurobindo repeatedly worked on the epic poem *Savitri*. Thus, although he understood himself as a yogi, a psychic personality, the most predominant work of his yogic and psychic personality was the creation of poetry.

If writing poetry is Aurobindo's ritualization of yoga, surrender and aspiration to divine life, what is the controlling myth that gives him a sustained image for his psychic journey into gnostic being? *Savitri* itself functioned as his myth. He himself has written that "I used *Savitri* as a means of Ascension,"[15] and Diane Apostolos-Cappadona has recently brilliantly demonstrated how *Savitri* must be understood as Aurobindo's personal and spiritual myth.[16] He did not write *Savitri* for others but for himself alone, for he observes, "What I am trying to do everywhere in the poem is to express exactly something seen, something felt or experienced... *Savitri* is the record of a seeing, of an experience which is not of a common kind and is often far from what the general human mind sees and experiences."[17] The initial version of *Savitri,* it seems, was written around the turn of the century and recast eight or ten times in the following fifty years. It received three substantive revisions in the course of those years, each revision corresponding to the triple transformation Aurobindo experienced in his own life. This is the only such work that he so revised.[18] The fact is that the myth of *Savitri,* taken from the general lines of a story in the *Mahābhārata,* remained foremost in Aurobindo's imagination and consciousness for over fifty years. It is the story that he consistently lived.

In Aurobindo's use of the *Mahābhārata* myth, Aswapathy requests a boon in the form of a child as a reward for his yogic efforts; a female child is born, a manifestation of the goddess, Savitri, and she discovers her true nature through her own practice of yoga. She and her husband, whom she saves from death, opt not for eternal bliss through their self-realization but to return to earth in order to bring about the transformation of humanity and earth itself. Aswapathy has frequently been interpreted as a representation of Aurobindo and this may be true in the first version of the epic poem. But the self-realization that both Savitri and her husband experience parallels the growth in consciousness of Aurobindo and his spiritual collaborator, the Mother of the Sri Aurobindo Ashram, before November of 1926, when he had undergone what he calls his second transformation. If so, this may well correspond to the second version of the poem. Finally, Savitri working for the transformation of earth and humanity shows the history of Aurobindo and the Mother following the transformation of 1926. This final moment corresponds not to the total epic as it comes to us in the third version, but at least to parts of it. What begins as a myth of not more than twenty lines in the original *Mahābhārata* ends up as 23,800 lines of verse. The poem thus reflects the odyssey of Aurobindo's life and the life of the poem is itself also the spiritual ascent of its author. Writing the poem facilitated surrender and aspiration, most literally his yogic activity, by giving structure and image to surrender and aspiration. The poem functions in his life as *śakti,* the instigator, the vitalizer, the inner-power of his spiritual journey.

Once again an aesthetic discipline can be said to be a spiritual discipline. Aurobindo's aesthetic sense gives rise to the discovery of a yoga caught within the majestic myth of Savitri and articulated in the ritual act of writing poetry. The most repetitive ritual act in Aurobindo's life is writing poetry with a consciousness of aspiration and surrender, while his most sustained mythic image is the Savitri legend. The poet gave to *Savitri* the subtitle, *A Legend and a Symbol;* and the first drafts are indeed legend, but when the later versions were written, *Savitri* functions as a living symbol into divine life. In this sense Aurobindo's poetry is a *mantra,* a constant prayer discovering divine life. Thus aesthetic experience is converted into prayer.

The Similarity of Aesthetic and Yogic Disciplines

That aesthetic and yogic discipline are somewhat similar can be seen in what poetic creativity achieves. Since for Tagore art is "man's world of reality in which he is revealed to himself in his own light,"[19] his journey into fullness/immensity is a yogic process of self-discovery. He writes that "the true meaning of living is outliving, it is ever growing out of itself."[20] Both yoga, in its sense of a spiritual discipline, and aesthetic discipline may bring about a disengagement from the limitations of the empirical self. Self-transcendency and nonattachment are aspects of typical yogic and aesthetic experiences. Aurobindo's spirituality draws upon all aspects of one's self—physical, vital, mental, spiritual, and psychic—not merely to achieve an integral personality but to transcend the limitations of ego and the unactualized dimensions of one's being. Self-transcendency and nonattachment are the core of Aurobindo's discipline, because effective surrender and aspiration attain such goals.

If an aesthetic discipline is comparable to a yogic or spiritual discipline, the discipline must involve at significant moments a reintegration of the self and effect spiritual transformation. Aurobindo's yoga is called *purna* (integral) yoga because integration serves a primary function. Transformation of the old by the new makes integration possible on a new and higher level of reality. For example, one's physical being is first transformed by the discovery of one's vital being and the two are then raised into a higher synthesis and integration. Integration establishes the gnostic being in Aurobindo's spirituality.

There is little doubt that transformation took place in Tagore's life at many moments. Yet Tagore did not consider himself a mystic; he, in fact, denied it. His cosmic experience as a youth on Sudder Street, his severe loss of family through death at the turn of the century, resulting in the ecstatic and God-centered *Gitanjali* trilogy, are signs of progressive change in life. Transformation may be traced further into his adult life as he became the world traveler and painter, when death, longing, and immortality appear as more common themes. Stages of passage in the moods and manners of Tagore are evident. The difference between Tagore and Aurobindo, at this point, is that the former has no conscious principle of integration operative in his philosophy or in his *sādhana,* whereas the latter does. This type of integration taking place in Tagore's life was accomplished more unconsciously. Nonetheless, when integration is not consciously sought, it lacks clarity. The differences between Tagore and Aurobindo on this point determine why the former achieves in both theory and fact a humanized being as the goal of the spiritual life, while the latter achieves also in theory and fact a more gnostic being.

The aesthetic process engages myth and ritual. Aurobindo's

myth of Savitri is singular and specific; Tagore's myth of journey into immensity is general and universal, drawing upon diverse images. What unites these two poets is their commitment to the world, the belief that the world is false unless it manifests spirit. They lived their myths through a profound experience of the world and the greater cosmos. Their approach to the world is modulated by the way their myths function in consciousness. Tagore not only discovers his myth in human experience, but he also lives it out in the world of *māyā* (illusion) because his aesthetic sensibilities are feelings and emotions. Aurobindo gathers his myth from the poetic imagination of India and lives it out in the world of consciousness because his aesthetic sensibilities are the higher and illumined mind.

Aesthetic and yogic disciplines eventually achieve some degree of self-transcendency, nonattachment, transformation, and integration. In the process an aesthetic act becomes a religious or sacred act.

The Role of the Aesthetic Imagination in Tagore's Spiritual Discipline

Aesthetic life is a form of religious life if the aesthetic imagination carries with it ritual power and effectiveness. For Tagore the aesthetic product does not result from ordinary perception, that is from the dyadic relation of a subject perceiving an object, but from imaginative expression, that is from a triadic relation of the subject perceiving an object and constructing a new object in imagination. The new object may be expressive or constitutive of reality as experienced by the artist.[21] Tagore speaks of the imagination as "the faculty that brings the mind the vision of one's greater being."[22]

In dealing with Tagore's understanding of the aesthetic imagination, one could, for the sake of exploration, conceive of two levels: the expressive imagination and the constitutive imagination. Although they are complementary and holistic in operation, they may be separated for the purpose of discussion. In both cases the ritual process may occur: significant repetitive acts bearing reality; new perceptions of time and space, height and depth; the greater sacralization of the world; and most significantly a *kenosis* or emptying/death of the old self with a type of *plerosis* or filling/creation of a new self.

The expressive imagination for Tagore perceives and expresses aspects of reality as they present themselves to consciousness. This may either include perceptions from the world of nature, certainly common within Tagore's horizons, or the world of the human and the poet's understanding of personal man, or the sacred as it presents itself in personal and theistic terms.[23] The imagination operates, as previously explained, from aesthetic feelings and emotions. Tagore observes that "...to attain cosmic consciousness we have to unite our feelings with this all pervasive feeling. In fact the only true human progress is coincidental with this widening of the range of feeling."[24] Early in his career, he spoke of feeling seeking form in the creative process, but in his mature years he decided that form abandons itself to feeling. If such is the case, Tagore as an artist and spiritual personality is not an imitator but a creator of reality.

Tagore perceives a universe of lines and colors and the rhythm and harmony that lead to the building of the creative image. What makes this level of imagination truly expressive and aesthetic is that it cannot be reduced to a pictorial or literal image. On the other hand, what makes the expressive imagination religious, involving a ritual process, is the repetitive aspect extending or even transcending the self. The imagination may also envision a new center of personal life. Yet, there is no evidence that this level of imagination elicits a definitive transformation of the self. Imagination is still subject to the constraints of time and space; in terms of the ritual acts of the imagination, they are still punctuating time in an important but not a transformative way. In brief, the expressive imagination is partitive, moving from new image to new image, from one new perception to another, with no serious integration and, consequently, no perceptible transformation. Ritual is present because the repetitive nature of the aesthetic process brings about a gradual *kenosis,* a purgation of the original self. Can this be established from Tagore's creativity? Yes. The poet surpasses the realistic image, the pictorial and literal interpretation of previous self-understanding. The expressive imagination thus offers a hint of future and radical transformation. A ritual process presents itself as an initiation, a breakdown of the past and a break-in of the future, through new ecstatic images and the rejection of previous images. All is sporadic at this level of perception and imagination, and the durative aspects of time and space, self and new-self are only suggested.

The second level, the constitutive imagination, perceives and expresses aspects of reality as they present themselves to both consciousness and the unconscious/supraconscious planes of existence. This may include material from the conscious world; but, more pointedly, perception engages the unfathomable dimensions of the cosmos and the human passage. Durative experience replaces ordinary time and space horizons; the world is not only the context for *ecstasis* but also *enstasis;* the old self is not only diminished but a new being, imperceptibly, seeks release. This suggests that transformation has become more definitive. At this level of creativity, the imagination begins to control the artist, and, in this manner, is constitutive of reality. For Tagore this is the aesthetic act which especially contributes to spiritual life. The interpretation of this moment will differ, but it must be maintained that the constitutive imagination does not result from a free, unwielding, and unconscious urge. The unconscious and *mysterium* are positive and creative forces. They present new reality. They fill, as a powerful *plerosis,* the purified self with new power and meaning.

The above can be demonstrated more easily from Tagore's works themselves than from his own articulation of the creative process. Even so, Tagore says that art has its impulse "in the subsoil of consciousness, where things that are of life are nourished in the dark,"[25] and that "the work of creation goes on unconsciously."[26] A greater freedom is evidenced in Tagore's paintings and drawings as a consequence of being created from this level of imagination. He had no preconceived subject for his paintings as he did for his poems and prose. A new aesthetic process takes place on this level of imagination, in which the artist's own feelings and emotions do not necessarily relate to a world of conscious objects and their relationships, but the feeling-states unleash hidden forces from the unconscious but now expressed in some aesthetic manner. The imagination is, in fact, probing the subconscious or the supraconscious world and bringing it into creative dialectic with the conscious world. The artist thus establishes reality with his words and images and the constitutive imagination perceives and expresses durative time and space beyond particular horizons, universal and holistic reality, and similar states of experience.

Tagore's conception of universal man is generated by the constitutive imagination, but his vision of supreme man is realized by the constitutive imagination, not necessarily created by it. The creative imagination, as a ritual process, brings about an initiation into completeness. But since the initiatory process is iconoclastic, transcending typical images and discovering new images, new visions, and a new world, Tagore's paintings, as Stella Kramrisch observes, are not works of art as much as "records of the process of art."[27] Holistic vision and experience result from the ritual process. In this way the ritualization of Tagore's journey into immensity finally impinges upon ultimacy.

The Role of Aesthetic Imagination in Aurobindo's Spiritual Discipline

Aurobindo's ascent to divine life would also seem primarily to be the work of the aesthetic imagination. Poetry, as an act of the creative imagination, is set within an evolutionary scheme of reality. Aurobindo writes:

> Poetry, like everything else, evolves... [It is] the poetic impulse, a highly charged force of expression of the mind and soul of man, therefore, in trying to follow out the line of evolution, it is the development of the line of evolution, it is the development of the psychological motive and power, it is the kind of feeling, vision, mentality which is seeking in it for its word and idea and form and beauty, and it is the power of the soul through which it finds expression or the levels of mind from which it speaks which we must distinguish to get a right idea of the progress of poetry.[28]

Just as there are levels of progressive mind in Aurobindo's theory, so too there are ascending stages of imagination as prelude to gnosis and mystical poetry.[29] The objective imagination is the mere act of perception in which some form is elicited; corresponding to this is the subjective imagination in which the form brings forth an emotive and cognitive response. These levels do not draw upon the aesthetic sense. A higher level, called the regulative imagination, is a stage that may be aesthetic, because it delights in the beauty of image, sound, and rhythm, and has the capacity to represent. It is termed regulative because it accepts form as normative and operates within the strict boundaries of form. Finally there is still a higher imagination that Aurobindo calls poetic. It has the capacity to express a new vision of reality because it proceeds from heightened perception. The poet, for Aurobindo, is always a creator of new reality. He views every poetic act as constitutive of reality. The poetic imagination perceives and exists within the universal and not the particular. New vision and new image are expressed in concrete name and form. The highest level of imagination for Aurobindo, however, is the creative imagination. It presupposes the earlier stages and differs from poetic imagination insofar as the latter intermittently exists within the experience of the universal, while the creative imagination subsists in a condition of universal life, which is being, consciousness, and truth as cosmic perdurance.[30] This is the life divine, certainly a yogic consciousness, but attainable by relatively few poets and artists. The creative imagination not only brings one to self-transcendence and nonattachment, since, presumably, these are accomplished by the poetic imagination, but also evolves radical transformation and integration.

Poetic and yogic consciousness are clearly identified in the thought of Aurobindo:

> He is the Maker and the world he made,
> He is the vision and he is the seer;
> He is himself the actor and the act,
> He is himself the knower and the known,
> He is himself the dreamer and the dream.[31]

If yogic and poetic consciousness are comparable, Aurobindo's system must speak to the psychic transformations of the yogi and how these condition poetic expressions. In the ascent toward integral personality, Aurobindo speaks of four grades of spiritual transformation wherein consciousness is raised from Higher Mind to Illumined Mind to Intuition and, finally, to what he calls Overmind. These are called overhead planes because they influence the mental, the vital, and the physical dimensions of personal life. Aurobindo's poetic criticism speaks of an overhead consciousness—a cosmic awareness—which may be detected in a poetic work. The poet perceives and expresses from these overhead planes. He writes:

> The Higher Thought has a strong tread often with bare unsandalled feet and moves in a clear-cut light: a divine power, measure, dignity is its most frequent character. The outflow of the Illumined Mind comes in a flood brilliant with revealing words or a light of crowding images, sometimes surcharged with its burden of revelations, sometimes with a luminous sweep. The Intuition is usually a lightening flash showing up a single spot or plot of ground or scene with an entire and miraculous completeness of vision to the surprised ecstasy of the inner eye; its rhythm has a decisive inevitable sound which leaves nothing essential unheard, but very commonly is embodied in a single stroke.[32]

Thus all overhead poetry does not come from Overmind, and in fact much of *Savitri* is written from the Illumined and Intuitive Mind. Aurobindo does not equate the Overmind with the aesthetic because Overmind is concerned with a reality other than beauty, namely truth and knowledge. When Overmind speaks through poetry, as it infrequently does, truth is its essential quality. Nonetheless, the aesthetic, spiritually based, is involved in all overhead expressions because it is not limited to the rules and canons of art. "It sees a universal and an eternal beauty while it takes up and transforms all that is limited and particular," writes Aurobindo.[33] The higher levels of consciousness open to universality, not merely fleeting perceptions but an enduring state out of which one experiences and expresses.

In speaking of *Savitri* as a means of mental and spiritual ascension, Aurobindo observes: "In fact *Savitri* has not been regarded by me as a poem to be written and finished, but as a field of experimentation to see how far poetry could be written from one's own yogic consciousness and how that could be made creative."[34] The poem was originally written from lower levels of poetic, mental, and psychic intelligence, but Aurobindo tells us that finally Higher Mind, Illumined and Intuitive Mind, intervened. As the poem now reads, "there is a general Overmind influence, I believe, sometimes coming fully through, sometimes coloring the poetry of the other higher planes fused together, sometimes lifting any one of these higher planes to its highest or the psychic, poetic intelligence or vital towards them."[35]

To be fair to Aurobindo's implied cosmology, reference must be made to the role of the divine in the creative process. The divine as Consciousness-Force is continually manifesting itself into world. Aurobindo raises the point in an attempt to distinguish the creative poet from the uncreative poet: "He is a medium for the creative Force which acts through him; it uses or picks up anything stored up in his mind from his inner life or his memories or impressions of outer life and things, anything it can or cares to make use of and this it molds and turns to its purposes."[36] He goes on to say that the creative Force either dominates the poet or it operates in a mutual and dialectic fashion drawing upon the genius of the poet, raising the poetic potential. Aurobindo experiences this. The poetic and creative imagination opens to the creative Force and the active life of the poet.

The focal point of poetry as ritual process in Aurobindo is that the divine breaks into the consciousness of the artist. Aurobindo's theory of aesthetics speaks of creativity from a divinely infused consciousness. Poetry as ritual also brings one into encounter with the creative Force manifested in the world. Consequently, the poet's *sādhana* advances not only one's personal ascent but also conditions one for the divine descent into human life.

Art as a Spiritual Discipline

Tagore and Aurobindo meet on common ground as poets who assimilate the aesthetic as a spiritual discipline. The aesthetic impulse is a thrust for realization; the aesthetic act is a concrete step to realization. Neither are imitators of the Indian aesthetic tradition, especially that of Abhinavagupta in particular, because each is more concerned with universalizing cosmic and worldly consciousness than with consciousness of the self.

They separate considerably in their embrace of the aesthetic as a spiritual discipline, since for Tagore the aesthetic faculties surpass the intellect, while for Aurobindo the aesthetic is an intellectual act. Dialectical experience leads Aurobindo in the upward ascent and the descent of the divine; no such dialectic is present in Tagore's almost exclusive intuitive disposition. The most apparent difference between them is the goal of spiritual discipline. Aesthetic life does not evolve beyond the conception of the universal man according to Tagore, but for Aurobindo the spiritual process leads ultimately to gnostic being, a complete change of the human species. Tagore could not envision a future so beyond the world of *māyā*, since it was not part of his experience. Finally, Tagore looks upon the fullness of the aesthetic-self as a total-self, while Aurobindo speaks of the integral-self, a new but yet transitional being in the divine life as more complete.

Spiritual discipline for each is his aesthetic life. Aesthetic discipline frees the creative imagination, constituting reality and impinging upon ultimate reality. This may be spiritual discipline in a still traditional Indian sense but certainly not a path of classical yoga. Poetry for both is a contemplative act. Their *sādhana* brings them, in different ways and depths, into the mystery of the ultimate. Their conceptions of ultimate reality result from aesthetic life within the compass of the creative imagination. The geography of the imagination is as important as the psychic technologies of these poets. Even Aurobindo's architectonic ascent of inquiry and gnosis, in its majestic sweep, falls under the pall of the aesthetic imagination.

NOTES

1 Rabindranath Tagore, *Thoughts from Rabindranath Tagore* (London: Macmillan, 1927), 162.

2 Rabindranath Tagore, *Utsarga,* Poem 17, in V. S. Naravane, *Modern Indian Thought* (Bombay: Asia Publishing House, 1964), 123-24.

3 Rabindranath Tagore, *On Art and Aesthetics: A Selection of Lectures, Essays and Letters* (Calcutta: Orient Longmans, 1971), 18.

4 Ibid.

5 Rabindranath Tagore *The Religion of Man* (Boston: Beacon, 1961), 133.

6 Rabindranath Tagore *Creative Unity* (London: Macmillan, Indian Edition, 1962), 6.

7 This concept and some of the following perceptions on ritual and art come from Diana Apostolos-Cappadona, "To Create a New Universe: Mircea Eliade on Modern Art," *Cross Currents* 32, no. 4 (1983), 408-19. I thank the author for permission to draw upon her work.

8 In 1916 Tagore wrote to his daughter Miru: "I have clearly realized that God has not created me for a householder's life. I suppose that is why, from my very childhood, I have been wandering about and have never been able to establish a home anywhere." R. Tagore, *Chithipatra,* bk. 4, (Santineketan: Visva Bharati, 1934), 10.

9 Sri Aurobindo, *The Future Poetry and Letters on Art, Literature and Poetry,* Sri Aurobindo Birth Centenary Library, vol. 9 (Pondicherry: Sri Aurobindo Ashram, 1972), 14. For further discussion cf. K. D. Sethna, *Sri Aurobindo-The Poet* (Pondicherry: Sri Aurobindo International Centre of Education, 1970), 203f.

10 Ibid.

11 Sri Aurobindo, *Savitri,* 435, quoted in Sethna, *Sri Aurobindo-The Poet,* 219.

12 William Cenkner, *The Hindu Personality in Education: Gandhi, Tagore, Aurobindo* (Delhi: Manohar, 1976), 156f.

13 Diana Apostolos-Cappadona, "Poetry as Yoga: The Spiritual Ascent of Sri Aurobindo," *Horizons* 7, no. 2 (1980), 275.

14 Sri Aurobindo, *Letters of Sri Aurobindo* (Pondicherry: Sri Aurobindo Ashram, 4th ser.), quoted in Narayan Prasad, *Life in Sri Aurobindo Ashram,* 2d ed. (Pondicherry: Sri Aurobindo Ashram, 1968), 90.

15 Sri Aurobindo, *Savitri,* Sri Aurobindo Birth Centenary Library, vol. 29 (Pondicherry: Sri Aurobindo Ashram, 1972), 727.

16 I refer to one of the most significant works in recent Aurobindo studies: Diana Apostolos-Cappadona, "Poetry as Yoga: The Spiritual Ascent of Sri Aurobindo," *Horizons* 7, no. 2 (1980), 265-84.

17 Sri Aurobindo, *Savitri,* Centenary Library, 794.

18 John Collins, "Savitri: Poetic Expression of Spiritual Experience," in *Six*

Pillars: Introductions to the Major Works of Sri Aurobindo, ed. Robert A. McDermott (Chambersburg: Wilson Books, 1974), 11.

19 Rabindranath Tagore, "Message of Farewell to Canada," *Visva-Bharati Bulletin,* no. 14 (November 1929), 66.

20 Rabindranath Tagore, *Thoughts from Rabindranath Tagore* (London: Macmillan, 1933), 37.

21 William Cenkner, "Rabindranath Tagore and the Aesthetic Imagination," *Visva-Bharati Journal of Philosophy* 10, no. 2, 1980 (1973), 42-60. Also, William Cenkner, "Tagore and the Aesthetic Imagination," *Rabindranath Tagore: American Interpretations,* ed. Ira G. Zepp, Jr. (Calcutta: Writer's Workshop, 1981), 55-77.

22 Rabindranath Tagore, *The Religion of Man,* 134.

23 William Cenkner, "Tagore and Aesthetic Man," *International Philosophical Quarterly* 13, no. 2 (June 1973), 229-41.

24 Rabindranath Tagore, "The Relation of the Universe and the Individual," *Modern Review* (Calcutta) 14, no. 1 (July 1913), 5.

25 Rabindranath Tagore, *On Art and Aesthetics,* 12.

26 Rabindtanath Tagore, *A Flight of Swans, Poems from Balaka,* 2d ed., trans. Aurobindo Bose (London: John Murray, 1962), 40. Cf. Diana Apostolos-Cappadona, "Imagination in the Aesthetic of Rabindranath Tagore," *Journal of Studies in Mysticism* 2, no. 1 (1979), 35-57.

27 Stella Kramrisch, "The Drawings of R. Tagore," *The Visva-Bharati Quarterly* 7, pts. 1 & 2 (1941), 117f.

28 Sri Aurobindo, *The Future Poetry,* quoted in Sisirkumar Ghose, *The Poetry of Sri Aurobindo* (Calcutta: Chatuskone Private Ltd., 1969), 45.

29 Sri Aurobindo, *The Future Poetry,* Centenary Library, 24f.

30 Ibid., 168.

31 Sri Aurobindo, *Savitri,* Centenary Library, 61.

32 Ibid., 806.

33 Ibid., 743.

34 Ibid., 727-28.

35 Ibid., 729.

36 Sri Aurobindo, *The Future Poetry,* Centenary Library, 328.

The Spiritual Exercises of St. Ignatius: A Model For Today

Ruth Tiffany Barnhouse

U ntil relatively recently, the Spiritual Exercises of St. Ignatius had fallen into desuetude, were hardly known outside the Jesuit Order, and even there many felt their power had waned. Things have changed in the last thirty years, particularly since the Second Vatican Council. The revival of interest in the Exercises has also been stimulated by depth psychology, comparative religion, and a general rise of serious, informed attention to human interiority. For this audience I need not expand on my belief that this and all other signs of the contemporary rise of interest and attention to personal, life-changing religion have also received impetus from the divine plane, however much sociologists may choose to explain it as a recurrent historical response to times of great cultural upheaval and uncertainty.

On first reading the Exercises might seem hopelessly provincial, appealing only to those with Roman Catholic sensibilities, and even then limited by the antique style of their metaphors and theology. Ignatius of Loyola, a sixteenth-century Spanish nobleman, was a soldier until his conversion at about the age of thirty, and a military viewpoint pervades his writing. But I shall attempt to show that deeper examination, illuminated by the profusion of scholarship and experience devoted to the subject in recent years, reveals the Exercises he composed to have unexpected possibilities for a thoroughly modern application.

Ignatius believed that some version of the Exercises was suitable for everyone, lay people as well as religious. He did not want an elitist system which had no application to the general public. Because of his own experience before conversion, he was fully aware of the paucity of good spiritual training available to lay people who had no vocation to the ordered religious life. Yet the spiritual needs of ordinary people were obvious, and so he designed his system to be accessible to them. He also recognized that there were certain psychological and intellectual capacities essential to those who were to go through the standard version of the Exercises. This calls for a thirty-day period of retreat, during which five or six hours a day of prayer, reflection and scripture study are combined with at least one session per day with the spiritual director. Not everyone is ready for such an intense experience, even if they are so situated in life that they can afford to set aside the necessary month. But Ignatius believed that there was no one who could not benefit from a modified version, and gave detailed directions for various adaptations to particular circumstances.

Although he had had mystical experiences, Ignatius was also an intellectual. This is not a common combination. I see him as temperamentally not unlike St. Paul. Neither was of the usual psychological type for such experience, but this led to the happy result that their highly developed thinking function enabled them to communicate something about the results which is far more comprehensible to the ordinary person than most reports from mystics. These are often subjective and personalized, metaphorical to the point of obscurity. But Paul and Ignatius have both left usable records of their spiritual journey in clear, propositional thought. Ignatius, however, recognizing that those wishing to use his system would vary greatly both in temperament and capacity, wrote his book for the use of spiritual directors, not for the exercitants themselves. This makes it possible for him to be extremely direct not only about the pitfalls, but also about the adaptations required to suit the condition of particular exercitants.

The Exercises, Preliminary Observations

These are best described in Ignatius' own words:

Four Weeks are assigned to the Exercises given below. This corresponds to the four parts into which they are divided, namely: the first part, which is devoted to the consideration and contemplation of sin; the second part, which is taken up with the life of Christ our Lord up to Palm Sunday inclusive; the third part, which treats of the passion of Christ our Lord; the fourth part, which deals with the Resurrection and Ascension; to this are appended Three Methods of Prayer. (Sec. 4).

Although this description seems extremely concrete, the actual method used permits ample flexibility. Ignatius himself introduced much of this, but more has been developed by modern interpreters. Prior to the beginning of the Exercises themselves, there is brief introductory material. At the end, after the Fourth Week, there are given the "Rules for the Discernment of Spirits," and other addenda. Each section is numbered, and the references in what follows are to those numbers.[1]

The first twenty-two sections give general directions, and describe the attitude which the director should bring to the work:

> The one who explains to another the method and order of meditating or contemplating should narrate accurately the facts of the contemplation or meditation. Let him adhere to the points, and add only a short or summary explanation. The reason for this is that when one in meditating takes the solid foundation of facts, and goes over it and reflects on it for himself, he may find something that makes them a little clearer or better understood. This may arise either from his own reasoning, or from the grace of God enlightening his mind. Now this produces greater spiritual relish and fruit than if one in giving the Exercises had explained and developed the meaning at great length. For it is not knowledge that fills and satisfies the soul, but the intimate understanding and relish of the truth. (Sec. 2).

This shows considerable psychological insight, and is similar to the instructions a psychiatric supervisor might give to a trainee about not making "premature interpretations."

The Title section reads: "Which have as their purpose the conquest of self and the regulation of one's life in such a way that no decision is made under the influence of any inordinate attachment" (par. 21). The purpose is spiritual freedom. Inordinate attachments are attitudes which tie persons to those things or ideas which hold back their progress. Guidance is therefore given for self-mastery and conquest of the "selfish" self.

The word "self" in English is difficult, particularly when one tries to interpret how it is used by various spiritual masters. The "selfish" self is located in the ego of psychiatric theory, and may include what Jung calls the *persona*. This "self" must be mastered, perhaps even obliterated, if spiritual growth is to take place. But there is another self, the one capitalized by Jung in his archetype of the Self, which I take to correspond to the *imago dei* in which we are created. This is the truest self, the finding and nourishing of which is the aim of all systems of spiritual advancement.

The retreat is further designed to give extended opportunity for spiritual direction in one's prayer; to provide a time when, because of the abundant graces of a loving God, one can discern how to bring harmony into one's life. The conditions for an experience of personalized revelation are fostered, a revelation strong enough to free the exercitant from disordered attachments or affections, so that appropriate life decisions can be made.

Many people reading Ignatius' language for the first time, or through various kinds of personal filters, think that he is proposing a life of difficult and unpleasant self-denial. Not so. The term "Exercises" is apt, since the actual intention is to produce persons who are freer, more whole, more independent, more mature—in short, all of whose natural good qualities are enhanced because freed from the factors which were preventing them from full flourishing before the Exercises were undertaken. The only kind of self-denial envisaged, in the usual simplistic meaning of that term, is that of postponing or abandoning some immediate gratifications for the sake of more distant, more valued goals. But then, that is a very good general definition of maturity. It is true that in order to secure this result the director, of course with the prior free consent of the exercitants, makes them engage in serious, often painful, regular self-examination, whether they happen to feel like it at the time or not. But the goal is more mature, far freer individuals. In this respect, there is an obvious similarity to intensive psychotherapy or analysis.

The Presupposition is also important: "To assure better cooperation between the one who is giving the exercises and the exercitant, and more beneficial results for both..." (sec. 22). It is understood that the director is also learning, growing, and benefitting from the interaction. Thus, the relationship is not, as many have misperceived, one between an all-powerful director and a passive exercitant, but an opportunity for mutual growth. This rests on Ignatius' understanding that God does not speak exactly the same way to any two people:

> The director of the Exercises ought not to urge the exercitant more to...one state of life or way of living than to another...the director...as a balance at equilibrium, without leaning to one side or the other, should permit the Creator to deal directly with the creature, and the creature directly with his Creator and Lord. (Sec. 15).

It is true that Ignatius envisaged a considerably narrower range of possible ways in which the Creator might deal with his creatures than the range we now see. But he did make that essential point. Interesting experiments with this are now going forward. Although I am not Roman Catholic, my Jesuit director did not hesitate to take me through the Exercises. He had also worked with a Jewish exercitant, and even with an atheist. (He, as have many others, viewed atheism as a transitional stage between two modes of faith.) Although Ignatius' own sense of permissible range is far smaller than ours and seems reactionary and constricted, at the time he wrote, his ideas were perceived as extremely liberal and contributed to the difficulty he and his followers had with the Inquisition.

In the same vein he goes on to say that

> It is necessary to suppose that every good Christian is more ready to put a good interpretation on another's statement than to condemn it as false... If an orthodox construction cannot be put on a proposition, the one who made it should be asked how he understands it. (Sec. 22)

Or, loosely rendered, listen with an open mind and heart. He was opening the door to the introduction of new ideas which he believed could enhance and build on orthodox doctrine. Unlike many of his contemporaries, he did not believe that the new was automatically heretical.

The well-known supremacy of the Jesuits as scholars and teachers is one way in which this spirit of their founder shows its influence. But it shows in other ways as well. Jesuits may not like or agree with those with whom they are engaged in discussion, but will always feel that they have learned something, and this is an active enjoyment. They have an unusual capacity to stick to the issue during discussions, not taking disagreements personally, or defensively jockeying for a position of superiority during the argument. There is no idea that even the most orthodox or conservative among them will not examine. This peculiar openness has often been misinterpreted as heterodoxy, and has contributed to the fact that by the rest of the Roman church they have frequently been viewed as heretics, potential if not overt.

Two of the original band of Ignatius' followers were missionaries to China. After spending many years at the Emperor's court, they finally devised what became known as the Chinese Rite. This was an attempt to put the truths of Christianity in a form consonant with the Chinese cultural heritage. Unfortunately, the Dominicans got wind of it, and their unfavorable opinion of this radical approach prevailed in the Vatican. The Rite was suppressed. With regret one realizes that if that had not happened, the entire history of Christian missionary effort might have been different. It was the first time, but not the last, that the Jesuits attempted to implement an excellent idea whose time had not yet come. The important point is that all of this is the direct result of the spirit of the Ignatian Exercises.

The Principle and Foundation. (Sec. 23)

The Four Weeks of the Exercises are preceded by the Principle and Foundation. This section is extremely short in the text, nor is it accompanied by any directions. At first reading, it appears to be a rather austere statement of unimpeachable orthodoxy. Closer inspection shows it to be remarkably profound, not only theologically but psychologically. The way in which Ignatius himself used it shows that the deeper implications were intentional. Until a prospective exercitant could demonstrate that the inner meaning of the Principle and Foundation had been assimilated, he was not allowed to proceed with the Four Weeks. Ignatius was prepared to wait patiently in this propaedeutic phase for as long as it might take—in one case nearly three years! I shall quote it in full:

> (1) Man is created to praise, reverence, and serve God our Lord, and by this means to save his soul. (2) The other things on the face of the earth are created for man to help him in attaining the end for which he is created. Hence, man is to make use of them in as far as they help him in the attainment of his end, and he must rid himself of them in as far as they prove a hindrance to him. (3) Therefore, we must make ourselves indifferent to all created things, as far as we are allowed free choice and are not under any prohibition. Consequently, as far as we are concerned, we should not prefer health to sickness, riches to poverty, honor to dishonor, a long life to a short life. The same holds for all other things. (4) Our one desire and choice should be what is more conducive to the end for which we are created. (Sec. 23)

The deeper meaning of this apparently simple statement has been most excellently put in contemporary language by Robert Doherty, S. J. Excerpts from his paraphrase follow:

> (1) The affirmation of human creaturehood: we have been from the very start recipients of God's creative love...We express our innermost meaning as persons by responding to this love of God in our "history."...A sense of fear and a sense of security from an awareness of what my life in and with God means. The immanence of God.[2]

The central *experience* is that of *knowing* that one is a child of God. Until one has had that experience, it is not possible to go through the later, often frightening, stages of the Exercises since the sense of basic trust is absent. An attempt to proceed without that sense can only lead to superficiality in the later phases, leaving important aspects of one's life untouched. In some cases it can make progress altogether impossible. The experienced director will be able to assess accurately the true stance of the exercitant in respect to this clause.

Father Doherty goes on to explicate the third and fourth clauses as follows:

(3) We can become "indifferent" or detached, radically free, only when we have a deep awareness that we are loved human beings. Being is entrusted to us as a challenge, a summons. We are ever involved in change...It is in the exercise of freedom that we become free...It is the Spirit freeing man in these relationships. (4) Finally, we have to go beyond passive indifference and acceptance; we have to commit ourselves to achieving the "more" of life.

This points to deep convictions which the exercitant may not achieve until the completion of the Exercises. But the work cannot be begun until the exercitant can truly believe that the kind of freedom envisaged as the ultimate fruit of the work is possible— not just in theory for someone else, but for himself. It is relatively easy to assent to such ideas in principle. But many people secretly imagine that while *others* may be saved, they themselves are either too bad or too insignificant. Further, many are not altogether sure that they wish to entrust themselves so fully to God's direction as to surrender what appears to be control of their own life. It is the clarification and dissolution of such reservations which constitute the *experience* of the Principle and Foundation.

Explanation of Terms

Since Ignatius wrote, many words have acquired new and different connotations; in addition, he used some words idiosyncratically. Therefore, it will be helpful to explain some of these usages.

The word *matter* is used throughout to mean something like "subject matter." The particular scripture passage, idea, thought, dream, or fantasy which has been chosen for a meditation is its *matter*, and is conceived in quite concrete terms. The word *points* is used to cover the ways in which Ignatius suggests that the *matter* be handled so that nothing is overlooked. In each exercise he suggests *points* of this kind.

He also speaks of the "three powers of the soul"—memory, reason, and will. These powers are to be applied in each prayer period as follows: memory is used to bring the *matter* before one in contemplation; reason, which includes understanding, is to add detail. For most modern persons the word *will* is tainted with discomfort and austerity; will power is usually understood as forcing oneself to do something painful or difficult, something which goes contrary to one's natural emotions. For Ignatius, the meaning is different. *Will* helps one to focus on the *matter* so that the natural emotions associated with it may be aroused, not overcome. He knew that no real progress could be made through the intellect alone, and saw the use of *will* as overcoming such imbalance.

Ignatius also speaks frequently about what *movement* is to be expected in the Exercises. Only if there is total involvement, if something affectively real is happening interiorly, can *movement* or lasting change be expected to occur. When there is no *movement*, the prayer is characterized by dry repetitiousness and intellectualization, attitudes and dispositions remaining unchanged. There is some similarity between this use of the word *movement* and the way modern psychotherapists use the word *insight*, though Ignatius' *movement* necessarily engages more of the psyche than is always the case with therapeutic insight.

The Preparatory Prayers, Preludes, and Colloquies which form part of each Exercise contain detailed instructions for the use of the imagination. These help the exercitant to become uniquely involved in each mystery, evoking personal desires in space/time reality, calling on individual experiences and insights. Of particular interest are two techniques called *composition of place* and *application of the senses*. If one is praying a particular scripture passage its specific physical aspects are to be imagined. This does imagining a three-dimensional play with oneself as one of the participants in the scene. For instance, if the *matter* of meditation were the wedding at Cana, a first-century village party should be imagined in detail. To achieve this *composition of place* does not call for historical accuracy, but for the exercitant's own telling image however anachronistic. So far as possible, all five *senses* are to be *applied* in each exercise. Again using the wedding at Cana as the *matter*, the exercitant should in imagination drink some of the wine, and otherwise participate in the festivities. When this degree of realism has been secured, one is ready for the Colloquy. Here one conducts a conversation with one or more of the characters in the scripture passage or other *matter* of meditation—Our Lord, the Blessed Virgin, or other person. Ignatius' way of describing this is vivid:

The colloquy is made by speaking exactly as one friend speaks to another, or as a servant speaks to a master, now asking him for a favor, now blaming him for some misdeed, now making known his affairs to him, and seeking advice in them. (Sec. 54)...As I behold [Christ, in this colloquy]...I shall ponder upon what presents itself to my mind. (Sec. 53)

Readers familiar with Jung will note the close similarity to the technique of *active imagination*. They will also note the difference from Freud's technique of *free association* which involves following a thought or feeling wherever it may lead, making no attempt to return to the original image. In *active imagination*, however, as in the Ignatian method, one does follow the original *matter* wherever it may lead, but then returns each time to the subject, continuing in this way until no new material is forthcoming (or until one is tired or prohibitively uncomfortable). At this point one has a wide circle of associations around the central image, thoughts and reflections which amplify it, and give a deeper, richer sense of its meaning in one's own life. It will be apparent that although Ignatius himself did not conceptualize it in such terms, the results of his techniques would include what any depth psychology would term the emergence of unconscious contents.

Indifference is another frequent Ignatian term. It is similar to, but not identical with, the Buddhist concept of detachment. The difference between the terms is probably mainly at the theoretical level and therefore may, as East and West make progress in discussion, disappear. Although I have not had the opportunity to investigate this in detail, I suspect from preliminary inquiry that *as experienced by the contemplator* the two are the same. Ignatian *indifference* does not mean that the thing or idea in question is not cared about. The meaning is much more like the correct use of the word *disinterested*. That is the attitude a judge should have—intense interest, but with no axe to grind in terms of which side wins. *Indifference* may include acute interest and care, but private personal bias, conscious or otherwise, about possible outcomes is entirely absent. One aim of the Exercises is to secure this attitude about all possible persons, situations and material objects. Practice in acquiring detachment will facilitate true love of God, which in turn will make detachment easier.

For a long time, the Jesuits interpreted the idea of detachment in such a way as to exclude "particular friendships" for themselves, though not for lay exercitants. If one were too close to another person, this might become a "disordered attachment" preventing one's primary allegiance to God. In the last twenty years or so they have come to understand that this was a mistake. Without friendship emotions dry up or become twisted, and so are unavailable for the Great Work. Revision of the former attitude was facilitated by reconsideration of the actual relationships obtaining among the original band. It was quickly perceived that these were close and sustaining. The idea of "disordered attachment" between persons is now understood to mean possessiveness, and other attitudes constricting one's own or the other's freedom, thus inhibiting maturational possibilities—in short, the very interpersonal attitudes which a modern psychotherapist would call "unhealthy."

Ignatius uses the term *fruit* to refer to the result of each prayer period and of the Exercises as a whole. There is a time following each prayer period when one applies one's intellect to the experience. Did it bring something helpful? What were the high points? What were the low points? What was boring? What was difficult? Were there strong desires or other feelings associated with it? We will examine later how the answers to such questions are evaluated in determining the *fruit* of the work.

The Rules for Discernment of Spirits (Secs. 313-36)

Jesuits frequently speak of the necessity for *discernment*, particularly when complex decisions need to be made. This term is derived from Ignatius' *Rules for the Discernment of Spirits* at the end of the Exercises. The spiritual director (to whom the book is addressed) must be both subtle and expert in this process. After making the Exercises, the exercitants will have acquired this skill as well, and be able to apply it themselves. From time to time thereafter they may, in times of difficulty, wish to consult another who is similarly skilled.

Although Ignatius' vocabulary is antique, at least one underlying meaning of the process he describes is surprisingly modern:

St. Ignatius distinguished three kinds of thoughts: first, those which were strictly his own, which he felt arose from his own free will and from logical process. The other two kinds of thoughts he said did not come from within, but from without, from beyond his control, and he referred to them as the "good spirit" and the "evil spirit." Even though he assigned to these spirits an origin utterly external to the mind, he recognized that they must appear through the psyche. He emphasized the importance of becoming aware of these spirits and thought they would appear most clearly during periods of silence and prayer. Psychotherapists of any school would refer to the first category of Ignatian thoughts as the contents of the conscious mind. Those of the Freudian school would not agree to the external origin of the spirits, but would speak of material coming up spontaneously from the unconscious. They would emphasize the importance of making this material conscious, and would agree that a definite period of time set aside, preferably daily, and free from other distractions, is necessary to encourage the appearance of such material. Psychotherapists of the Jungian school might be more willing to assign at least in some instances, an external origin to unconscious contents, and would surely be more willing to assume that the unconscious contains health-promoting and growth-producing elements (the "good spirit"), as well as neurotic and destructive ones (the "evil spirit").[3]

This psychological interpretation illustrates, but by no means exhausts, the modern application of this apparently outmoded language.

Ignatius varies the rules during each Week of the Exercises. The director is most active in the early phases, leaving more to the interaction between the exercitant and God as the work progresses. The terms *consolation* and *desolation* are used throughout to describe the subjective responses of the exercitant. But each of the "spirits" can give either *consolation* or *desolation* depending on the state of the work. This approach presupposes that the person has learned affective prayer—the kind of total involvement described above. Unless prayer is affective, there will be no inner *movements* whose significance needs interpretation. Not everyone is capable of this, and the decision about the prospective exercitant's ability is made by the director during the Principle and Foundation. Modern directors frequently (but not always) find that persons unable to enter affectively into prayer can benefit from some professional psychological help.[4]

The "good spirit" gives consolation when exercitants are on the right track, and desolation when they are not. The "bad spirit" does the opposite. How to tell the difference? Through discernment, the prayerful process of sifting through felt needs and desires, spontaneous impulses and inclinations, and the conflicting interior reactions that one experiences when one confronts deeply the situations and events of one's life. One learns to distinguish those that move one to choose loving actions from those that move one to choose selfish actions. That is the all-important criterion. One thus finds God in this integrating process *within* the self. That is what leads one to God's will.

In what follows, it will become apparent how important it is to cultivate the kind of *detachment* or *indifference* upon which Ignatius lays so much stress. The less one's emotions are bound up in defending mundane attachments, be these to things or to ideas, the more they are able to be attuned to the infinite, the divine. The techniques of discernment, taken together with their application to the various parts of the Exercises, form the exercitant in accordance with this desirable end.

The First Week (Secs. 24-90)

In the original, general confession and Holy Communion precede the making of the Exercises. In addition, there is a preparatory prayer and a closing prayer for each exercise. The function of these is not just the practice of piety. As will be appreciated from the description of the techniques, those making the Exercises are embarking on an exploration which is not without risk. Much of it is interior, but it also opens up the possibility of making connections with aspects of the Unseen which many conceptualize as being exterior to the human psyche. This formal point cannot be discussed in this essay, as responsible theologians and philosophers differ widely in their interpretation of the phenomena which are involved. Those accepting Jung's concept of the *collective unconscious* find it a useful bridge between the various positions. But whether the Unseen is postulated as interior or exterior to the human psyche, experience has shown that care in making the contacts is wise.

Beginning with a prayer or other form of conscious intentionality about the desired goal provides protection against dangerous or chaotic contacts being made when the psychic centers are opened, something the Ignatian techniques are well capable of doing. Letting go with fantasy, abandoning ordinary reality is safe provided one has proper guidance. One has chosen the channel, and has not simply made a random venture into the unknown. Concluding with a prayer assists exercitants in returning to the ordinary reality and in reestablishing the usual ego boundaries. That process is further facilitated by the immediate application of the intellect to the experiences undergone. This is perhaps a good place to point out that one of the important functions of fasting is that it opens up the psychic centers—it is not just a masochistic form of self-denial. Eating something is helpful in closing those centers and resuming ordinary contact with the manifest world.

These considerations apply, of course, to the entire Exercises, but because of the peculiar dangers and difficulties of the First Week are especially important there. This is why:

> One may say that the *overall* rubric under which the Exercises function is "You shall know the truth, and the truth shall make you free." But some kinds of truth are very hard to take, and cannot be unflinchingly regarded unless there is a safe place on which to stand while one is examining them. In these terms, the function of the Principle and Foundation is to ensure that the exercitant has a secure sense that freedom is really possible. Without this sense, it is too difficult or even impossible really to contemplate the subject matter of the First Week, one's own sin and that of the fallen world. It is also during this preparatory phase that the teleological character of the entire work is established. The goal is in the future, outside of oneself, in God. And this future goal shapes and qualifies the entire work. Furthermore, it establishes the paradox that to be truly free, one must be willing to give up control, which is ultimately in the hands of God.
>
> From this vantage point, it is possible to proceed to the work of the First Week...the contemplation of one's existential tendency to sin, as well as of one's particular sins, all in continuous interaction with the sin and sins of the world... Without the security of the Principle and Foundation this would either be impossible...or else it would lead to a catastrophic state of despair.[5]

Ignatius begins this process with an *examination of conscience*.

The function of this is to make one's actual attitudes and behavior conscious. Only that which is conscious is subject to scrutiny and possible change. No modern director would take an exercitant through the *examination of conscience* in the rigid, not to say compulsive, routine described in the Exercises. But the goal is no different than when the Exercises were first written and practiced.

The first *matter* is world sin. Ignatius begins by considering first the sin of the angels, then of Adam and Eve, then of humanity in general. About this Stanley says:

> Whether or not one presents this meditation as formulated by Ignatius, it is paramount to note that he seeks here to induct the exercitant into a true, personal experience of salvation-history. He wishes to give him an existential appreciation of what existence outside the gospel actually means.[6]

This modern Christian interpretation can be extended: What is life like without an organizing principle which transcends the ebb and flow of short-term human affairs? Different religions consider this issue in different ways, both propositionally and metaphorically or mythologically, but they all consider it.

There are numerous obstacles to this kind of opening meditation in modern consciousness. The very idea of sin has been badly contaminated by concepts of action morality, scruples, and by numerous persons with poorly formed consciences (or super-egos, if you prefer). Another obstacle is what Doherty calls "the four great un-freedoms: fear, anger, guilt and prejudice." All sin is derived from one or more of these "unfreedoms." If the attitudes and disposition of particular exercitants require such modification, it is entirely possible to go through the whole First Week effectively without mentioning the word *sin*.

Many alternatives can be found. For example, to get people to contemplate the sin of the world, one can have them spend some time in the emergency room of a big city hospital; or have them go through the slums of their community; time can be spent in court or in jail. Of course this will not work for everyone. Some may think—perhaps even say—"Only low class people get into that kind of trouble, and of course I don't!" For others, seeing films of the Holocaust or of Hiroshima may be a better way. But the imaginative director who is responsive to the particular exercitant can always find some way to induce a real *experience* of—not just thoughts about—the sin of the world. In directing Christians such experience is always combined with meditation on appropriate scripture passages. Of course the holy writings of other religions have passages which lend themselves to similar use. In evaluating Ignatius' original formulation it is helpful to remind oneself that in the sixteenth century persons asked to contemplate the sin of Lucifer or of Adam and Eve were not immediately assaulted by the inner question: "Is this story really true, or is it *only* metaphorical?"

The next task in the First Week is to get the exercitants involved in the examination of their own sins. About this Stanley says:

> Here the aim is to bring home to one a realistic picture of himself as a personality deformed by his past. At best he has an almost overwhelming inclination to ratify, by actual sin, the original sin of Adam and Eve.[7]

Any psychiatrist could pronounce the first sentence of that statement with conviction. Modifying the language only slightly, in the second sentence what Freudians call the repetition compulsion can be recognized. That is a Western, subjective description of what Easterners refer to more objectively as *karma*. But even persons whose past wrong choices have not been of such degree, or constellated in such a way as to produce symptoms requiring psychiatric intervention, are governed by the same principles. Everybody's life compass is a little off, and one must make the effort to discover the magnet full of "sin" which is deflecting the compass from its true course.

The Ignatian meditation on hell is problematic for moderns. Many directors just omit it. Others do not agree. The point is to visualize what life without God would be like. The ancient symbol of the lake of fire is not the only way. Each exercitant can be asked to develop a personal image of Godless life (or death) which is experientially meaningful, and for some the feared modern lake of fire, nuclear holocaust, may be the effective image.

Ignatius suggests various forms of penance, including deprivation of food, discomfort in sleeping, and actual self-flagellation. Unlike many of his contemporaries he is careful to insist that none of these should be carried to the point of causing serious harm or illness. Modern directors ignore these particulars. But for many people some outward act signifying their recognition of their misdeeds is extremely helpful. The sympathetic imagination of the director responsive to the condition of the particular exercitant can find something suitable.

The First Week is purgative. It can be very painful. But the worthwhile fruit is a real increment of freedom, a true sense of freedom from sin—a release from sin in the past and a better sense of how to cope with sin in the future. A related fruit is an increment of closeness to God, before whom one has acknowledged the worst and has found that one is nevertheless deeply and personally loved.

The Parable of the Kingdom (Secs. 91-100)

A day of repose comes after the rigors of the First Week. Influenced by Ignatius' early experience as a soldier, this is described in highly militaristic terms, comparing the call of God to the call of an earthly king asking his subjects to fight for him. But Ignatius also gives us the underlying principle which makes it possible to translate the exercise into modern terms:

> I will ask for the grace I desire. Here it will be to ask of our Lord the grace not to be deaf to His call, but prompt and diligent to accomplish His most holy will. (Sec. 91)

Exercitants are invited to look forward, to dream the impossible dream, to look beyond themselves in order to imagine larger possibilities for their own lives than have hitherto seemed possible. The rest of the Exercises are to be focused on the life of Jesus, and this day of cheerful repose is calculated to give an overview of that life. Jesus went through trials, temptations, danger, even death, and yet overcame all. Exercitants are urged to see this triumphant life as a model of possibility for themselves. For some, consideration of the life of Jesus in this specific way will not be a good model, if only because of all the terrible sermons they have endured on the subject!

But the "call of the King" can be seen in other terms. "Come and work with me, be my companion in spreading the kingdom's good news." Exercitants are now ready to learn that they can be a vital part of the human family in and through whom God can work. If this is to be effective, it is essential for there to have been a *thorough* First Week experience. If not, some hidden sins (or unfreedoms, if that term is preferred) will still be pulling one off course. This may happen in various ways, including the distraction of the thought that "God couldn't really use *me*, I'm not sufficiently worthy"; or the obverse of that which is to be so arrogant as to have a Messiah complex.

One director I know uses the "fiction" of J. R. R. Tolkien as an entree to this meditation, on the theory that Tolkien did not so much invent the hobbits as "stare them into visibility." Another uses the image of the clown, or the recent drama "Godspell." The central question is this: what could my life be like if I were truly free of all the impediments now preventing me from participating fully in God's marvelous plan? One is not at this time making a final choice of life pattern, but one *is* considering possibilities which have seemed out of the question until now. The underlying assumption is that God's plans for one's life will be far better than one's own. Put more colloquially, God has a much better imagination than we do!

The Second Week (Secs. 101-189)

In the Second Week one learns to give up one's own will and to let God take charge. To the secular mind this may sound as though passivity, if not actual masochism, is sought. But that reflects the narrow view that conscious choice is exclusively bound to personal wishes. The religious outlook, however, whether ecclesiastically grounded or not, is that one's necessary orientation is not merely to the human plane but also to that which is eternal and divine. In that case, when faced with decision, it is only common sense to secure as much input as possible from the larger dimension since to do so expands one's options. This is the liberating insight so well expressed in the Collect from the Book of Common Prayer: "Almighty God...in whose service is perfect freedom."

The meditations of this week are designed to bring directly into the exercitant's experience the vision of the Parable of the Kingdom. The *matter* is the life of Christ from the Incarnation to Palm Sunday. The Week begins by considering the Incarnation as the paradigm of divine initiative in reaching out to suffering humanity. Excerpts from the Preludes to the meditation follow:

> ...how the Three Divine Persons look down upon the whole expanse or circuit of all the earth, filled with human beings... They decree in Their eternity that the Second Person should become man to save the human race...This is a mental representation of the place. It will be here to see the great extent of the surface of the earth, inhabited by so many different peoples, and especially to see the house and room of our Lady...This is to ask for what I desire. Here it will be to ask for an intimate knowledge of our Lord, who has become man for me, that I may love Him more and follow Him more closely. (Secs. 102-4)

The last sentence is taken from a prayer first written by Dennis, Bishop of Chichester two centuries before Ignatius. The most recent version was in "Godspell": "Day by day, three things I pray, to see thee more clearly, love thee more dearly, follow thee more nearly day by day."

Following this first meditation, the rest of the Week is illuminative, helping exercitants to know what they are *free to* do with their lives now that they are *free from* the burdens dealt with earlier. It is in this part of the Exercises that life choices are made. For Jesuits, the first making of the Exercises includes the final decision, after several years of preparatory training, about joining the Order.

With the Parable of the Two Standards, Ignatius illustrates the need to come to grips with our conflictual history as we face real decision making in our lives (Secs. 136-48). He imagines two armies, one under the banner of Satan, the other under the banner of Christ. Exercitants must choose which army to join. Obviously one can consider the governing principles of right and wrong under other images.

Once again the importance of a deep First Week experience becomes clear. Without that one would still be in the grip of various disordered attachments, things or ideas which one was pursuing for their own sake rather than in the service of God. An illustration may clarify the point. I have heard many clergy say such things as "I know I ought to speak out for such-and-so, but my congregation wouldn't like it. I don't dare offend them, or take them faster than they are ready to go." Such a statement may be literally true. But even if true it may conceal attitudes which should not influence the final course of action, such as a wish not to rock the boat, not to be out of favor, not to spoil chances for political advancement in the church, not to risk losing a big pledge—the list is endless. Yet the decision not to do the right thing could easily be rationalized in terms of the congregation's defects to avoid the necessity of considering one's own. The Ignatian process of discernment helps identify and clarify those hidden attitudes which could lead to dishonesty about one's true motives. The exercitant who has gotten this far in the work will not be afraid to consider all of those self-centered motivations. There will be no unreasonable fear of punishment, and there will be confidence that God has a way to implement the right course of action. One will not have to go through difficult circumstances alone.

Ignatius expresses the grace sought in this meditation in terms of gaining insight into the workings of the evil one. This works, no matter how one conceptualizes the reality which he symbolizes by the term "evil one." What these workings of the evil one have in common is that they interfere with the exercitants' ability to allow full scope to God's initiative in their lives. Understanding and learning to respond to God's initiative is the hallmark of the Second Week experience. Ignatius illustrates this with a description of "Three Classes of Men," excerpts from which follow:

> This is the history of the Three Classes of Men. Each of them has acquired ten thousand ducats, but not entirely as they should have, for the love of God. They all wish to save their souls and find peace in God our Lord by ridding themselves of the burden arising from the attachment to the sum acquired, which impedes the attainment of this end. (Sec. 150)

Note carefully that it is the *attachment,* not the money itself, which produces the burden. He goes on:

> The First Class. They would like to rid themselves of the attachment they have...but the hour of death comes, and they have not made use of any means. (Sec. 153)

> The Second Class. They want to rid themselves of the attachment,

but they wish to do so in such a way that they retain what they have acquired... (Sec. 154)

Here the hidden attitude is that God must adapt to their wishes rather than the reverse. But the Third Class is different:

These want to rid themselves of the attachment, but they wish to do so in such a way that they desire neither to retain nor to relinquish the sum acquired. They seek only to will and not will as God our Lord inspires them... As a result, the desire to be better able to serve God our Lord will be the cause of their accepting anything or relinquishing it. (Sec. 155)

This is characteristic, and extremely important. It illustrates Ignatius' recognition that God does not say the same thing to everybody; that conduct, whether virtuous or otherwise, cannot be exclusively judged by its external appearance. This highly personal emphasis is one of the main reasons why the Ignatian method is so peculiarly well suited to modern application. The central insights have an adaptability which the author could not have imagined, and that is the hallmark of all great thinkers.

In summary, the *movement* of the Second Week is to understand that divine initiative must always precede human response if choices truly suited to the individual are to be made. The Incarnation, which is the original Ignatian *matter* to convey this lesson, is seen as the primary as well as the most accessible manifestation of divine initiative. That is not, however, the only image capable of carrying this crucial lesson.

The Third Week (Secs. 190-217)

Fortified by the fruits of the previous work, the exercitant is now ready to learn true compassion. Doherty describes the *movement* of the Third Week as follows:

Compassion, the grace asked for here, is the highest form of love for neighbor. The one who experiences compassion for another not only looks on the loved sufferer's ills as his own, but he also looks at his own goods as something at the sufferer's disposal for dispelling the ills.[8]

The *matter* Ignatius suggests for attaining this grace is the Last Supper, Passion, and Burial of Christ. During this time exercitants are particularly urged not to console themselves with anticipatory thoughts of the Resurrection, but to stay with the sorrowful material, identifying as fully as possible with our Lord's sufferings.

True compassion is extremely difficult to attain, and few do. The reason it is so hard is that it means being able to enter fully into another's experience without giving up the sense of one's own identity and personal responsibility. A glance at our state hospitals for the mentally ill or at our jails makes the point. Those entrusted with the care of the unfortunate inmates tend to make two mistakes. They may withdraw emotionally and take refuge in feeling superior, either morally, emotionally, or both. The other common error is to lose track of their own standards and stability in the effort to empathize fully. In neither case is it possible to be of real help. Many of the problems which so frequently attend reform movements can be traced to the absence of true compassion. The problems of many Northern white liberals who came South to help during the civil rights movement are a good illustration. Their efforts were frequently contaminated by more or less conscious feelings of superiority and condescension, and eventually such attitudes led to charges that they, too, were racist.

Although the cultural context was so different as to make specific comparison with the present impossible, Ignatius was well aware that one could not carry out the commandment "love thy neighbor as thyself" without true compassion. The Third Week is a unitive way, a full identification with God's own suffering, recognizing that in the last analysis, love of God and love of neighbor are inseparable.

You will have noticed that there are only twenty-seven sections in the Third Week, as compared with sixty-six in the First Week. Of those twenty-seven, only nineteen are devoted to the actual meditations for the week. The directions are extremely meager in comparison to the rich detail of the earlier parts.

> Why is so much left up to the combined imaginations of the exercitant, God and the director? It is because it is not easy to be specific about how to do good. Sin, on the other hand, is basically simple, and so it is not hard to give First Week directions.

The reason there are only ten commandments is because there are only ten sins. But, just precisely because each of us is unique, there is an infinite variety of ways to do good. Each person going through the Exercises is going to get a different assignment from God on how best to fulfill their own potential, and how best to contribute to the life of the company of all faithful people, and how best to do the work of "bringing in the Kingdom."[9]

It is impossible to know in advance where the Spirit is going to lead exercitants once they have acquired the ability to hear that Voice. This is why the directions get increasingly vague, and more and more adaptation to the needs of individual exercitants is suggested.

Three times during the Exercises, exercitants consider their disordered affections and inordinate attachments, root tendencies which block the effectiveness of grace and prayer in the process of discernment. In the First Week sin was considered. In the Second Week money was the principal Ignatian example, as a metaphor for any object or attitude which hinders a full response to God's initiative. By the Third Week, exercitants have made a deeper commitment to serve God through a life choice informed by prayer. The consideration of inordinate attachment here is correspondingly more subtle. Exercitants are asked to consider their attitude to something in life which one is not free to dispense with; something which is not intrinsically a block to growth, but the proper use of which requires discernment.

The example Ignatius uses is food, in the "Rules for Eating." His terms are almost unusably old-fashioned were we to try to take them only literally. Somewhat paraphrased, he suggests that food should be taken in the presence of the Lord and according to His example; some spiritual activity should be joined to the refreshment of the body; self-control should be maintained both regarding the quantity and manner of eating.

One modern interpreter sees these rules as principles for the consumer, and it would be difficult to imagine anything more needed in contemporary America.[10] Using Ignatius' guidelines, one is brought to consider not only one's standard of living, but the higher set of values against which that standard is measured. It was during the 1950s that we were told that in order to support the consumer society, alleged to be necessary to prevent another depression, we must have planned obsolescence. In short, we were told "waste is good for you." Unfortunately, religious leaders did not immediately reply, as they should have, that "waste is wicked"! And yet, much has been written about the theology of the Eucharist, suggesting that this is one of its meanings.

Nor is the connection with compassion, with true love of neighbor, difficult to discern. Ultimately, everything wasted is stolen from someone in need, somewhere in the world, but that is an insight to which most Americans have been systematically blinded. I speak here of real *waste,* not of appropriate *use.* To grasp the Ignatian viewpoint, one must remember his basic principle of detachment as exemplified in his discussion of money. None can know, except through a process of prayerful discernment, exactly what disposition should be made of anything, whether in the service of self or others. But a society which says, for instance, that to run a successful restaurant one must serve people three times as much as anybody needs, and far more than most can manage to eat, is hardly in a position to find Ignatius' instructions outmoded— even were they to be taken literally!

This wonderful fruit of the Third Week, true compassion, is achieved by classical exercitants through the unitive way of incorporating more and more into themselves the virtue and love of the Christ. Ignatius also suggests at this stage that there can be profit in reading the lives of the saints. This provides a possible modernizing paradigm for those wishing to use the basic structure of the Exercises outside classical Christianity. Every tradition has its saints.

The Fourth Week (Secs. 218-37)

The directions here are even sparser than for the Third Week. The *matter* suggested is the life of Christ from the Resurrection to the Ascension. The various post-resurrection appearances and their effect on the persons so visited form part of the meditations. As throughout the Exercises, each meditation must incorporate its subject matter into the exercitant's own experience.

Although it is part of the Fourth Week from the temporal point of view, the mysterious "Contemplation to Attain the Love of God" is set apart, taking up the last seven sections. One is at last free to love God, not just to receive God's love. The fruit of this heightened capacity for love manifests as loving and redeeming action in the world. Ignatius says, in the introduction to the Contemplation, that "love ought to manifest itself in deeds rather than words" (Sec. 230). Without this return to full, conscious participation in the wider community, Ignatius felt that the work of the Exercises was not complete. The director who notes that an exercitant is trapped in ecstatic experience, not impelled to come back to earth and pick up the course of life in a new and productive way, knows that something has been missed somewhere along the line.

This is not a system whose desired endpoint is merely a personal feeling of bliss or joy. Such feelings occur, but constitute a by-product of grace, not a goal in themselves. Ignatius was a firm believer in balance between contemplation and action. I believe that all genuinely religious systems of development embody this balance, though all do not conduce to the same level of action, as most moderns understand that term. But our cultural definition of action suffers from extraverted distortion, and most of us no longer understand what is meant by the saying, "they also serve who only stand and wait." The hermit who considers only his or her own development is not a true hermit.

In summary the Principle and Foundation and the First Week develop a new vision, and much of the effect is to change the way one uses one's cognitive faculties. The Second Week develops a new heart, and growth in affective life. The Third Week brings head and heart together, while the Fourth Week enables the integration of one's new being into the task of ongoing life. The subtle and individualized application of the Rules For Discernment throughout makes such development possible.

Discussion and Conclusion

Comparison of the Exercises with contemporary depth psychology is perhaps inevitable. To some extent the fact that such comparison is at least implicit throughout this paper reflects my professional training. But there is also another reason. American culture is unusually conscious of mental and emotional pathology, as the most superficial comparison of our outlook with that even of other Western nations (not to speak of Eastern and Third World countries) is sufficient to show. More than any other culture on earth we have substituted the concept of sickness for those of evil and sin. Any system of personal amelioration and development is therefore bound to be examined, at least in part, through psychological filters.

Psychiatrists make much of the infant's primary narcissism, which must be supplanted by other, more socially based attitudes if successful maturation is to occur. But have we really gained anything by substituting a concept of "original pathology" for that of "original sin"? I do not think so. And the social affiliations which are urged on us for the sake of mental health are surely only a limited and secularized version of the great commandment: "Love the Lord thy God with all thy heart, soul, mind and strength, and thy neighbor as thyself." True religion knows that love of neighbor apart from love of God is not fully possible, particularly when "neighbor" is correctly defined as every single member of the entire human family. Psychiatric theories are inadequate to the task of teaching us to love people we do not like, or people we do not know. And yet, if we are to survive as a species, the need to do just that is urgent.

What the psychoanalytic theories have done is to expose the anatomy and physiology, so to speak, of original sin. Some misperceive that doctrine as embodying God's sadistic curse on his children. I take it to be a succinct way of referring to the obvious fact that no human being is able to avoid making wrong choices—probably many times a day. In the Christian tradition, at least, sin has usually been dealt with inefficiently, and often counterproductively. Psychiatry, when not going beyond its sphere of expertise, can be very useful in correcting such mistakes.

The Ignatian system is especially interesting because it offers one of the best ways of dealing with sin to be found anywhere in the Christian tradition. And the modern concept of sin as an impediment to freedom, directly derived from Ignatius' own insights in the matter, is particularly liberating. The focus, then, is not on sin for its own sake, but merely as an obstacle in the true path of joy and fulfillment.

C. G. Jung has explained simply and convincingly why a reference point for one's value system beyond the human plane is, in the long run, the only effective protection against mass-mindedness which always means diminution of individual consciousness

212

and conscience.[11] Becoming freer through some substantial increment of control over one's sinful tendencies is only the beginning. It is a beginning which leaves one with nowhere to go if there is no definite idea of what one is *free for,* not just what one is *free from.* Without some anchor in the divine, the tendency to lapse into some degree of selfishness is irresistible. A value system needs a firmer base than one's unexamined natural inclinations. Jung also believed that every neurosis is at bottom a moral problem, and that the neurosis is always a substitute for legitimate suffering— the true cause being too painful or difficult to face.[12]

Most spiritual masters can be convincing about where they are, but usually leave one in confusion about how they got there. This is not true of Ignatius. His system is unusually lucid. His structure is developmental in a way which coheres well with what contemporary students of human growth have discovered through research. More remarkably still, it can be adapted effectively for use by persons from religious traditions other than his own without doing violence to his goal—a mature individual with a heightened capacity and desire to engage in loving and redeeming action in the world.

It is one of the marks of genius that its work is not bound to its own perforce limited cultural outlook, but is accessible to others, generation after generation. The Spiritual Exercises of St. Ignatius of Loyola meet this test: they constitute a workable model for today.

NOTES

1 Louis J. Puhl, S.J., *The Spiritual Exercises of St. Ignatius* (Chicago: Loyola University Press, 1951). All references to the Exercises are from this translation.

2 Robert Doherty, S.J. (unpublished seminar notes).

3 Ruth Tiffany Barnhouse, "The Spiritual Exercises and Psychoanalytic Therapy," *The Way*, Supplement 24 (Spring 1975).

4 Ibid.

5 Ruth Tiffany Barnhouse, "Spiritual Direction and Psychotherapy," in *The Journal of Pastoral Care* 33, no. 3 (Sept. 1979).

6 D. Stanley, S.J., *A Modern Scriptural Approach to the Spiritual Exercises* (Chicago: Loyola University Press, 1967).

7 Ibid.

8 Doherty.

9 Barnhouse, "Spiritual Direction and Psychotherapy."

10 John Futrell, S.J., "Communal Discernment," in *Studies in the Spirituality of Jesuits* 4 (Nov. 1972).

11 C. G. Jung, *The Undiscovered Self* (Boston: Little Brown, 1958).

12 C. G. Jung, in Erich Neumann, *Depth Psychology and a New Ethic* (New York: Harper & Row, 1973), Foreword.

A SCHEMATIC COMPARISON OF THE SPIRITUAL EXERCISES OF ST. IGNATIUS WITH THE SYSTEMS OF FREUD AND JUNG

	SUBJECT MATTER	FRUIT	FREUD	JUNG
PRINCIPLE & FOUNDATION	Creaturehood / identity as child of God	Establish teleology / "Freedom seen as possible" / Preparatory	Establishment of Basic Trust / Possibility seen of Cure/Relief / No teleology	Establishment of Basic Trust / Possibility seen of Cure/Relief / Teleology
FIRST WEEK	Sin / self and world	"God loves Me" / "Free from" / Purgative	Neurotic Guilt / Primacy of Instinct / Consciousness: individual only (Reductionistic)	Shadow Archetype / Search for Wholeness / Consciousness: Personal and collective (Not Reductionistic)
SECOND WEEK	Life of Jesus / Birth—Palm Sunday	"God's Initiative" (2 Standards) / "Free to" / Illuminative		
THIRD WEEK	Life of Jesus / The Passion	"Compassion" / "Free because" / Unitive		
FOURTH WEEK	Life of Jesus / Resurrection and Ascension	"To Attain the Love of God" / "Free for" / Redeeming & Loving Action in the World		

conscious choice

Individuation Process

conventional religion

215

The Balance of Transcendence and Immanence in Tsong Khapa's Presentation of Buddhist Spiritual Discipline

Robert Thurman

*A*ll founders of religions have based their determinations of ultimate reality on their own experiences as mediated by their own reasoned interpretations. They exemplify for us the human possibility and even necessity of experiencing the Ultimate in some way. Because their lives and teachings subsequently never depart from their awareness of that Ultimate, their lives become ideal models for the members of their traditions and their teachings become enduring precepts of perfection, liberation, or salvation. Reminding ourselves of these simple points helps us to focus our attention on the crucial importance of the metaphysical quest of ultimate reality as the principle and foundation of all spiritual disciplines.

Religious traditions have basically two ways of referring to the Ultimate, the negational or apophatic which calls attention to its transcendence, and the affirmational or kataphatic, which bears on its immanent dimension. We can distinguish religious doctrinal systems on the basis of their apophatic and kataphatic character, the infini-theistic systems being apophatic and the theistic systems kataphatic. Among the religions that stress the apophatic are various forms of Buddhism, Taoism, and Jainism, perhaps Confucianism, and some forms of Hinduism, while among those that stress the kataphatic are the "Abrahamic" traditions, Judaism, Christianity,

Islam, the theistic forms of Hinduism, Shintoism, Bon, Yoruba, and innumerable tribal religions. There is in fact a mutual indispensability of affirmational and negational languages concerning the Ultimate in all these religions. This needs emphasis because the theistic systems tend very much to avoid their own negational underpinnings, while the infini-theistic systems tend to ignore their own affirmational implications. Thus in the present climate of encounter and mutual enrichment of the world religions, each can be a mirror for the other in those elements less noticed in each itself. As the theist may love to thunder away about how "God" is this and that, said this and that, revealed this or that scripture, he or she may need reminding that the center of the temple has no idol, the crucifix is a symbol of redemption and not itself an idol, and the mosque allows no anthropomorphic or deo-morphic representation of any kind. The great monotheisms of India always retain central awareness of the unqualified Absolute underlying all incarnations, the *nirguṇa* beyond all *saguṇa* embodiments. Monotheism itself has invariably been a powerful apophatic negation of the claims of ultimacy invested in the idols of polytheistic pre-existing religions. The doctrine of the transcendentality of "G-d" (his un-nameability, inconceivability) is completely apophatic in thrust, and the commandment against idolatry is a clear safeguard against forgetting that, as communities tend to do. On the other hand, as the infini-theist may love to immerse himself in emptiness, in the infinity and transcendentality of the Ultimate, may wish to excuse himself from decision and difficult action in times of crisis, wishing to wait to first attain enlightenment, the powerful images of immanence of the tradition should be brought to mind: the dynamic compassion of Amitabha, Boundless Light Buddha, the tireless and omnipresent activity of Avalokiteshvara, the Bodhisattva of effective love and total self-sacrifice, the play of Krishna, or the selfless activity of the just ruler animated by the inexhaustible Tao. These are ultimate models of ethical and spiritual involvement in the relative and immediate world, and they call the infini-theist out of his tendency to lounge in exquisite samadhis into a more active engagement in compassionate activity.

In this essay I shall speak as infini-theist to theist, calling forth some of the resources of the Buddhist tradition to the task of making more effective paths of spiritual discipline concerned with the confrontation with the ultimate reality. To this end, I will sketch, with the help of the great Tibetan Lama Tsong Khapa (1357-1419), the *Lam Rim,* or "Stages of the Path of Enlightenment," teachings. These teachings organize the major doctrines of the Individual Vehicle (Theravada, etc.) and Universal Vehicle (Mahayana) forms of Buddhism into a graduated path for any individual to proceed from his or her own starting point to the highest goal of unexcelled, perfect enlightenment, or Buddhahood. The earliest versions of *Lam Rim* spiritual exercises date from the days of Nagarjuna and Aryadeva (ca. 1st-4th centuries CE), and every generation of Buddhist Masters developed them more and more. Saint Asanga (ca. 4th-5th centuries CE), and the brilliant Shantideva (ca. century 8th CE) were two of the foremost Masters in this line. The last great Indian Master was Atisha Dipamkara Shrijnana (ca. 982-1054 CE), who brought the teachings to Tibet, during the period of the destruction of the Buddhist monastic universities in India. They descended eventually to Tsong Khapa, and his masterwork, the *Lam Rim Chen-mo* is universally acknowledged as the fullest synthesis of these teachings.

Tsong Khapa also wrote a very concise set of verses, given to him in a mystic revelation from the Khidr of Buddhism, the Bodhisattva Manjushri, known as the *Three Principles of the Path.* I will follow his exposition therein, covering the first two sections only briefly, and concentrating on the third, that concerned with the contemplation and realization of the ultimate reality—that is, the attainment of the transcendent wisdom of subjective and objective selflessness.

The three principles of the path are known as transcendent renunciation, the spirit of enlightenment of love and compassion, and the wisdom of selflessness. It is logical that they be central principles, since the central human addictions that prevent liberation and enlightenment and cause all suffering are the three poisons—lust, hate, and delusion. Transcendent renunciation is essential to conquer lust, love is essential to conquer hate, and wisdom is essential to conquer delusion, the core delusion being the misknowledge about and misperception of a real, fixed, self-sufficient self at the base of egocentric habits. The three principles also correspond to three stages of development, sometimes called the three personalities—the inferior, mediocre, and superior. The

inferior personality is the worldly person, attached to the enjoy-
ments of egocentric living, at the lowest level in the present life,
and even in the future lives if they are somewhat religious. The
mediocre personality has realized the inherent misery of egocentric
or cyclic existence, and seeks liberation in Nirvana, but only for
himself alone. The superior personality is vividly aware of the
horror of egocentric living and totally concentrated on liberation,
but he also is simultaneously aware of the predicament of all
other sentient beings trapped in the prison of delusive self-concern,
and so he aspires for the simultaneous liberation of both himself
and others. The inferior person, who is dominated by lust for life,
needs to practice renunciation; the mediocre person, dominated by
hate for life, needs to practice love; while the superior person,
detached yet empathetic, needs to practice wisdom.

The opening verses of Tsong Khapa's work are addressed primarily to the inferior person:

Reverence to the Holy Gurus!

I will explain as best I can
The essential import of all the Victor's Teachings,
The path praised by all the holy Bodhisattvas,
Best entrance for those fortunates who seek freedom.

Listen with clear minds, you lucky people,
Who aspire to the path that pleases Buddhas,
Who work to make meaningful your leisure and opportunity,
Who are not addicted to pleasures of cyclic life.

Lust for existence chains all corporeal beings,
And such addiction to egocentric pleasures
Is only cured by transcendent renunciation.
So first of all, you must seek transcendence.

Leisure and opportunity are hard to find,
And there is not time in life—keep thinking on this,
And you will reverse your concern for this life.
Contemplate the inexorability of evolutionary effects
And the sufferings of egocentric life—again and again—
And you will reverse your concern for future lives.[1]

In the most abbreviated way, Tsong Khapa refers to a number of major themes of meditation, which usually occupy the first few weeks of a typical *Lam Rim* meditation instruction course. Before beginning the reversal of preoccupation with worldly goals, a context is established in the opening verses, a context of taking refuge in the Three Jewels of Buddha, Dharma, and Sangha (the Teacher, his Teaching, and the Community of its practitioners). In the Tibetan system, these Three are made immanent, personal to the practitioner in the Guru, or Lama, who represents the Lineage of Teachers which brings the Teaching across the centuries to the moment of practice. There are elaborate visualizations and prayers, of course, to invoke these liberated and compassionate presences to bless the struggling practitioner.

Under the theme of leisure and opportunity, one contemplates the extreme preciousness of one's present embodiment as a human being, endowed with intellect, free will, and the access to liberative teachings. A clear vision of the factuality of the multi-life, or spiritual, perspective is deemed essential here. Thus, it is impossible, or very difficult, to practice this path under an ideology of materialism, wherein there is no form of personal spiritual continuation from one life to the next. This is not because nothingness is frightening; on the contrary, it is too easy to expect a mere anesthesia of oblivion to arise automatically at death. A healthy terror of an unpleasant future life, a life deprived of the leisure and opportunity one now has, a life of hellish misery, is considered essential to develop the intensity of will to achieve transcendence. This terror is heightened by the next series of meditations, those on the immediacy of death, coming to the realization that "there is no time in life." Thus, one comes to a vision of one's present, living, conscious self, perched on a shaky evolutionary limb of life, over an abyss of an infinite past evolutionary struggle up from inconceivably difficult lives in the hells, limbo-realms, and animal kingdoms, as well as more difficult human embodiments and a possibly infinite future series of more such lives. Such a vision causes the reversal of concern for fame, wealth, strength, power, etc.—worldly goods which cannot help one beyond death—and one's total commitment is toward those spiritual goods that may help one's spiritual continuation, i.e., self-control, love, wisdom.

Still, one may yet preserve a hankering for future lives, thinking that through merit and wisdom one may be assured of a new life in one of the many heavens, or in an even better human rebirth, at which point one will be in a better position to attain enlightenment, practice the difficult self-transcending practices. So, the next themes are introduced to reverse such concern for future worldly goals. The "inexorability of evolutionary effects" brings up a still more detailed and vivid contemplation of the workings of evolutionary (*karmic*) causality, until it becomes apparent that the network of causes is so vast, subtle, and all-encompassing, one cannot be assured by any mere works of really improving one's situation. One might have done so much evil in so many lifetimes its effects might ripen horribly at this death, no matter how much virtue one was to enact in this lifetime. This is combined with a meditative travelling of all the six realms of living beings. For these meditations, the original context (mentioned above) of refuge in the Three Jewels, etc., is essential, since the evolutionary reasoning and cosmological descriptions are so compelling and vivid that the sensitive person is guided delicately into a state of cosmic horror, until, as it is said, one perceives all of egocentric life as if it was on fire, as if one's own hair, clothes, and body were on fire and the only water was the ocean of liberation and enlightenment. Tsong Khapa concludes:

> By constant meditation, your mind will not entertain
> A moment's wish even for the successes of life,
> And you will aim for freedom all day and night—
> Then you have experienced transcendent renunciation.

At this point if one has successfully meditated, he has developed the "mediocre personality" that earnestly wishes only for liberation from the egocentric life cycle, and the contemplations that generate the superior personality need to be introduced:

> Transcendence without the spirit of enlightenment
> Cannot generate the supreme bliss
> Of unexcelled enlightenment—therefore,
> Bodhisattvas conceive the supreme spirit of love.

> Swept away in the currents of four mighty streams,
> Bound tightly by chains of evolution, hard to break,
> Locked in the prison of the iron cage of self-concern,

222

Totally enveloped in the darkness of misknowledge,
Born and born again in endless egocentric lives,
Uninterruptedly tormented by the three miseries—
Such is the state of all beings, all just your mothers—
From your natural feelings, conceive the supreme spirit.

While the practitioner still reels from the cosmic horror of the vision of unliberated life, wishing for nothing but personal release, he is guided to regard all other beings as being in the very same situation. A contemplation of the beginninglessness of the evolutionary cycles of all beings is brought into psychological alignment with one's deepest feelings about one's mother or father of the present life, at the stage of the earliest infancy, and all one's primal love for that object is brought forth and then diffused over all beings, gradually widening the circle of identification until one can see all beings as having been one's mother in one life or another. Then, one's primal gratitude for their loving-kindness is generated, and one's powerful drive to repay that kindness and save them from their dreadful plight. The details of these contemplations, conducted over the next few weeks of a typical *Lam Rim* course, are too numerous to describe fully. In sum, though, with the sixth stage, known as "excessive resolve," literally, an intense messiah-complex should be generated, wherein the individual practitioner feels bound to take upon his or her shoulders the full responsibility of saving all living beings, out of the very sense of gratitude and debt the most filial child should feel in saving his or her own parents from disaster.

The emergence from this stage is calmed, and a premature self-martyrdom is forestalled by a seventh stage called "spirit of enlightenment of love and compassion," wherein the practitioner contemplates the fact that infinite hosts of Bodhisattvas have trodden this path, have come through this resolve and realization, and hence there are infinite forces for salvation as well as infinite beings to be saved. One is brought to reflect upon the fact that one must develop the ability to makes one's new drive effectual, that only a Buddha has such ability, that one must therefore become a Buddha, and this can only be accomplished through wisdom of ultimate reality. Additionally, at this stage many practical methods of the Bodhisattva ethics are taught, giving guidance in more ordinary ways of helping others in smaller ways, on the stages before Buddhahood, in "ordinary" life.

Returning to the path, however, one then enters the path of the wisdom of selflessness, emerging from the double intensity of an excess of cosmic horror pushing one toward transcendence combined with an excess of cosmic compassion pushing one toward fulfilling one's love for all beings:

> Though you experience renunciation
> And cultivate the spirit of enlightenment,
> Without the wisdom of realization of emptiness,
> You cannot cut out the root of egocentric life—
> So, you should strive to understand relativity.

Of the three poisons—lust, hate, and delusion—delusion is the root. Once delusion causes one to misperceive subjects and objects, lust or hate will arise for them inevitably. Detachment and love can moderate or temporarily suppress lust and hate, respectively, but they will lie there in latency and will emerge again eventually so long as their objects remain, and so long as a deluded subjectivity misperceives their true nature. Therefore only the wisdom of selflessness, the ultimate reality, can eradicate the egocentric samsaric life cycle. "Relativity" (*pratītyasmutpāda*) is a kataphatic way of referring to Emptiness (*śūnyatā*), as I will explain below.

Tsong Khapa continues:

> Who sees the inexorable causality of all things
> Both of cyclic life and liberation,
> And gets rid of any convictions of objectivity—
> Thereby enters the path pleasing to the Victors.

Misknowledge (*avidyā*) is defined as a wrong knowing, a misknowing of actual reality. Thus the deluded person sees the wall before him, and knows that it is "really" there, perceives it to be "ultimately" there. He can have all sorts of theories (e.g., that only God is Ultimate, that only Emptiness is, that matter is actually a buzzing, blooming confusion of electrons and quarks zipping around a mostly empty space), but he still misperceives the wall as if it had intrinsic reality, intrinsic objectivity, intrinsic identity, at the subtlest level. Therefore he lives by the wall, for the wall, against the wall, and not by God, by Emptiness, or by physics. In Buddhist language, he considers the wall to have a real, fixed, self-sufficient, objective self. More important than the wall are the phenomena constituting our own bodies. And perhaps most important of all, or ultimately equally important, is the self.

We feel our "selves" as real, self-sufficient, undeniably really there. My "self" is my "first fact," self-evident to me. Descartes stopped with his thinking doubter, his *cogito*. Most of us never get so far as to thinking through to our thinking, finding the bedrock of our existence there, even though we feel it to be there, habitually live by it, through it, and for it. And this is indeed the first step, called the "first essential." It is to observe the "self" that is imagined in the daily habit of self-preoccupation. It is said that it is best observed in the heat of being falsely accused of something. "You did that awful thing," thunders our accuser, when we know we are innocent. Then arises the naked force of egotism, "*I* did not!" we stammer. A tightness of throat and chest, a heat from the solar plexus, a tension in the face, the whole complex overwhelms us. The normal incessant murmur of "I" "I," "me" "me," "mine" "mine," becomes a roar, riding the energy of righteous indignation. It is not a question of the mere capability of using the pronoun "I," of responding to "you." This is merely the learned ability to organize the conventional self (*vyāvahārika-ātma*) to interact intelligently with others. It is the excessive emotion called forth, the special intensity, anxiety, outrage that emerges with the "I." It is a complex knot of concepts, percepts, emotions, perhaps even neural patterns, that is built around an assumed real, independent, fixed object that is us, that is our identity. So the first essential is to observe the impact of this assumed real presence.

The next essentials have to do with trying to discover if the "I" does indeed truly exist as it seems to exist. In this sense, the quest of ultimate reality is not just a self-conditioning to bring oneself to an experience of another assumed reality one may have a theory about. It is rather a rigorous critical inquiry into those assumed ultimate realities one already mis-knows to be the case. And one cannot even take for granted they are mis-known, just because some supposedly enlightened persons said they are. The fact to be faced is that I know this wall has objective existence. I know this wall of self has objective existence. Now, if I wish to really know myself, I must examine this sense of knowing, to discover if it is indeed knowledge, or if it is misknowledge.

The second essential, which is called the "ascertainment of logical pervasion," is a commitment to respect the outcome of the inquiry. For instance, if I examine a gem to see whether it is diamond or glass, then if it tests out as a diamond, I accept it, but if it tests out to be glass, I do not. If it does not appear to be a diamond, I do not buy it anyway at a diamond's price, on some vague idea that it must be something even more rare which I do not yet have the skill to test. So also in the quest of the real "self," I commit myself to the fact that I live as if it were really there in the way it habitually feels as if it were. If I examine more deeply introspectively and find it solidly there, I will accept it as real. If I do not find it to be there, I will accept the fact that it is not there, that my assumption of its presence is false. I will not allow myself some vague third option, some ineffable presence that I shall just continue to assume, even though I have found nothing to correspond to my habitual feeling. This essential is important to forestall the inevitable trickery of our egocentric habit.

Beyond this essential, there are numerous techniques of inquiry in the Buddhist tradition; sometimes there are two more essentials, sometimes five, sometimes one. All of them involve introspective contemplation of the constituents of our being, usually inventoried for convenience into "five heaps" (*skandha*)—the heaps of forms, sensations, concepts, volitions, and consciousnesses. These are elaborately detailed in the 2500-year-long Buddhist tradition of introspective psychology. When four essentials are elaborated, in the third, one introspectively superimposes this model of five heaps on one's own inner sense of being through patient inner observation. One becomes familiar with his body, its skin, hairs, flesh, blood, bones, inner organs, circulations of energies, breathing, etc.—all the forms that one identifies as one's self. Are they, or any one of the them, that fixed, real self I assume as a core? No one has yet found anything thus resistant to the dissecting scalpel of introspective analysis. Well, then, the heap of sensations, the pains in my legs, the tinglings in my chest, the pleasure of the cool wind on my face, the sense of heaviness in the stomach from my good breakfast, the warmth of my lungs, the pulse of my heart—is anything fixed, solid there? Hardly. Then my idea-heap, the flow of concepts, images that pop in and out of my inner monologue, are any of them fixed? Well, do certain words remain the same? But everyone else knows them too, they are part of the language, can they be my *self*? Perhaps not satisfyingly so. Well, then my wills, my emotions, but they fluctuate—now I am mad, now sad, now glad, now calm, now restless. Are any of them constant, suitable as a fixed, real self-identity? Well, then, at last we come to consciousness. There seems to be a constant awareness underlying all this, for who is watching all these other heaps? But is there anything contentless there? Are not all moments of consciousness responding to different physical or mental objects? Do I not get lost in looking at myself looking? Who is looking at whom? It is said that when we pursue this analysis intently without becoming distracted (which one can eventually learn to do), we experience a sense of pure, clear emptiness finally; we seem to sink away from any clear sense of definiteness, even losing self-awareness for a moment or even for a longer while. This fading of consciousness can be blissful or neutral. But is it suitable as the self? Can we claim consciousness as the self only when it is unconscious? This kind of self would certainly not satisfy our original assumption of a hard core of identity which we habitually feel ourselves lugging around and living and dying for. We may then come to the conclusion of the third essential, that there is no fixed, etc., self that is the same as the heaps, either any one of them or all of them in combination.[2]

We then begin the fourth essential, which is more subtle and indeed intellectual in tenor. We now begin to inquire into whether our putative self can exist meaningfully as something different from the heaps. Here we may quote Tsong Khapa from another work:

> If the self were objectively different from the heaps, it would become devoid of the created nature of the heaps, and would have no production, duration, and destruction, just as a horse does not have the nature of an ox, established as a different thing. But one here objects, "Well, isn't that how it is, after all?" But then it is not logical for the innate mental habit to perceive such (an

absolutely different permanent, aloof self) as the object that is the basis of the conventional designation of "self;" because it is not a conditional thing (i.e., not subject to ordinary relations) just like a sky-flower or like Nirvana. Furthermore, if it were really different from the nature of heaps, etc., which is formful, etc., it would have to be perceived as such, just as matter and mind are perceived as different. But since it is not perceived in any such manner, the self is not a thing different from the heaps.[3]

In another approach, the third and fourth essentials mentioned above are combined into one. This one is called the "royal reason of relativity," and is considered the most direct method, though difficult for beginners in practice. It is simply the contemplation of the syllogism: "all subjective and objective things are empty of any intrinsically established self-reality, because they are relatively occurrent." This brings powerfully before the intellect the simple though far-reaching fact that it is simply a misconception to think of a *non-relative*, i.e., absolute, independent, self-sufficient, permanent, changeless, etc., thing as *relating* to things that are obviously relative, dependent, and fluctuating. It is a misuse of language, a self-contradictory assumption. Using this reason as the third and last essential, one contemplates the heaps exhaustively and observes their complete flux and relativity, thereby realizing the total lack of anything substantial, nonrelated, which yet serves as core of those things.

Whichever of these approaches one employs, eventually there ensues a contemplative state known as the "space-like equipoised samadhi," in which subject and object merge like water poured in water, and one has an experiential, nonconceptual taste of emptiness of intrinsic identity. Of course, as this experience dawns in one's consciousness, one's intensity of analytic inquiry focuses on it, too, as well as on the subject that is experiencing it, since after all, this emptiness might itself be the permanent self one has been seeking. A very subtle portion of consciousness is thus mindful that, whatever appears to be taking place, since one is crossing a threshhold of a mental state, "the state" itself can have no *absolute objectivity* (i.e., it is itself empty of any putative intrinsic reality of its own; it, too, is subtly relative insofar as one is relating to it by entering it). Therefore, one is aware that this is a last illusion of

substantiality among others, that it is no more emptiness of intrinsic reality than the previous experienced subject-object realm is
emptiness of intrinsic reality.

This insight is essential to avoid a fear of the illusion of
dissolution, and is important to guard against indulging in various
marvelous, formless trances. Though sometimes practitioners may
stay for some time in the space-like equipoised samadhi, almost
immediately in subjective time sense they emerge into what is
called the "dream-like aftermath samadhi," wherein subjects and
objects appear as before, but now everything seems like a dream,
like an illusion. Tsong Khapa is very clear on the point that the
dream-likeness is not because everything seems fuzzy or foggy or
ghost-like; things are even more crystal sharp than they ever were.
But now one's habitual misperception is accompanied by an intellectual intuition that they are not objectively real as they appear
to be, the latter now operating with equal intuitive force. One's
sense of "real self" returns, as before, but the intuition that there is
no substantial self, that the "I" is merely a conventional designation, habit balances the sense of self, tempers therefore the
intensity of self-preoccupation.

Although this experience might be thought of as a kind of
enlightenment, *satori,* or peak experience, it is by no means necessarily very profound at first, Usually the practitioner is guided to
return to the state through an analysis of phenomenal objects,
physical, mental, and uncreated, or intellectual, such as space
or even emptiness, and to reenter the space-like samadhi through
focusing on objective selflessness (i.e., by sustaining the non-finding
of phenomenal or noumenal objects through and beyond the
dissolution experience). There is a long training in the oscillation
between the space-like and the aftermath dream-like samadhis,
gradually trying to even out the sense of imbalance on both sides.
In this sense, Buddhahood is defined as the point wherein dissolution and resolution are experienced simultaneously as two aspects
of the one inconceivable non-dual reality, and where, therefore,
wisdom and compassion are in perfect integration. This can be a
long, slow process, and there are many phenomenologies of these
higher reaches of the path. It is an enormous literature which we
require perhaps another half a century to master and bring into

our culture, even with our modern universities and computers, although there are already a number of worthwhile studies available in English.

To return here to Tsong Khapa's *Lam Rim* exercise, we must remember that this third principle of the path, while it gets to the root of the egocentric life cycle and brings the practitioner face to face with ultimate reality, in no way obviates the continuing need for the other two principles, renunciation and love. Indeed, the development of the wisdom of selflessness, even in the early stages, lends yet more power to the other contemplations. Let us recall that the practitioner entered the quest of wisdom from an uncomfortable state of being pressured by two intensities, that for transcendence and that for immanence of loving expansion to free all beings from suffering simultaneously. Now, with wisdom initially acquired, this double intensity is offset by another creative tension, that of the double exposure of a continuing dream-like misperception of self and others, subjects and objects, combined with an intellectual intuition of the emptiness or selflessness of everything. The former, gradually-lessening misperception aides the practitioner to remain in contact with his overflowing resolve of love and compassion in that he can widen his scope of embrace of his mothers, other living beings. And the latter, gradually-deepening intuition of universal emptiness begins to satisfy his drive for transcendence in that he has developed a core intuition of the liberatedness of all things, himself included. The personal relief he feels at this immediately flows out as joy, in that he begins to discern the solution of the problems of other living beings. And the grief he empathetically feels ever more widely at the fact that these beings themselves still do not feel the freedom they themselves have in their own very marrow, serves to intensify his drive to deepen his own wisdom, the wellspring of his joy with which to shower them.

Tsong Khapa beautifully describes the non-dual perseverance in wisdom from this stage:

Appearance as inevitably relative,
And emptiness free of all assertions—
As long as these are understood apart,
The Victor's intent is not yet known.

He refers to the initial stage of oscillation, or rather an initial misunderstanding of the oscillation, as if there were two separate realities and one was moving back and forth from absolute to relative. But such an ultimate duality, he asserts, is not the intent of the Victor, the Buddha.

> But when they are simultaneous without alternation,
> The mere sight of inevitable relativity
> Becomes sure knowledge rid of objectivity-habits,
> And the investigation of authentic view is complete.

Without explicitly mentioning it, Tsong Khapa is actually teaching here the Tantric understanding of emptiness and non-duality, the Tantric view being defined as a procedure that "intimates" the Buddha-stage via an act of the imagination by cultivating the "double-exposure" approach of perceiving objects and their emptiness simultaneously, rather than focusing on one or the other in alternation, as in the exoteric approach. And this is indeed the fullest use of the royal reason of relativity, wherein the perception of the precision of the logical sign, relativity, immediately reinforces the understanding of the thesis, emptiness of intrinsic objectivity. And of course, *vice versa*, the intuition of emptiness immediately, without a second thought, reinforces the perception of relativity. As the Eleventh Dalai Lama remarked, "It is like a man whose senses are addled by liquor; he looks up and sees two moons in the sky in a drunken blur, and he says to his friend without need of reflection, 'Ah, there's the moon!' "

Tsong Khapa continues:

> Further, while appearance eliminates absolutism,
> Emptiness eliminates nihilism,
> And you know emptiness manifest as cause and effect—
> Then you will not be deprived by extremist views.

We may note here how the non-duality of Ultimate and relative has been sealed by yet another reversal. Originally, the contemplation of the royal reason of relativity focused on the thesis, emptiness, to counteract the habit of absolutism, the reification or objectification of relative things as absolutes which obscures Suchness, the transcendentality of the Real. And it focused on the reason, relativity, to counteract the tendency to nihilism, the repudiation of things or the objectification of their transcendentality as nothingness, which obscures Thatness, the immanence of the Real. Contemplation of this royal reason, thus, takes us beyond the grosser habits of dualism. But now, as we continue along the path, now mobilizing wisdom as a powerful noumenal intuition gradually deepening to replace the intuitiveness of our misperception, our central way is braced against extremisms from the opposite sides as well. Thus the mere appearance of things, the fact that they do relate to us by arising even in our habitual misperceptions as if they still had intrinsic reality, itself counters our tendency to absolutism; they relate to us by appearing, confirming our intuition of their non-ultimacy without a second thought. And the intuited emptiness of things, our constantly confirmed sense of their relative non-ultimacy, itself counters our tendency to nihilism; there is no independent thing, not even an intrinsically real emptiness, which confirms our commitment to relativity without a second thought.

We have here in outline form a path of spiritual discipline. Ideology or doctrine is important in providing the context of the path, and the doctrine here is that of Buddhism of the Universal Vehicle, which honors as basic within itself the Individual Vehicle of renunciative self-liberation. But there are certain purely disciplinary elements here that are useful to anyone, irrespective of religious tradition. I am particularly struck by parallels to the Ignatian Exercises, as limned by Professor Barnhouse so eloquently. Thus, the context of an initial place of 'refuge' seems essential to each path, as well as the sense of guidance and protection of a Lama or spiritual perceptor. And so does the first principle of transcendent renunciation, generated by contemplation of evanescence and death, to detach one from mundane preoccupations. Further, a cosmic terror occasioned by a vista of personal responsibility for some sort of future existence seems likewise essential for generating the necessary spiritual intensity. Here the atheistic traditions have their major problem, from the Buddhist perspective, for by denying the spiritual essence of living beings, they provide an ideological guarantee of immunity from future terrors for the practitioner, promising automatic anesthesia at death. All they think they can lose is this immediate life, and, while that might seem terrible if they are relatively happy, it is not at all so terrible to those undergoing any sort of serious suffering. There would be some Lamas who would say that under these ideological convictions it is impossible to develop the transcendental attitude essential for spiritual transformation. And that may be so. Or it may be that some parallel ideas of responsibility to the future can be cultivated to work around this ideological block, since every being at least subconsciously still fears that "undiscovered country from whose bourne no traveller returns," no matter who tells them or how much they assert there is no such place. Beyond this, the contemplations of the sufferings of egocentric life cycles and the inexorability of evolution can be extremely inspiring under other ideologies, since the vivid depictions of extreme forms of biological distress at least serve to get us to count our blessings energetically, while also developing a wider empathy with the true condition of other forms of life.

The second principle, the meditation of love and compassion, is essentially valuable to any spiritual tradition, or even to any secular social system. No system of law or mechanism of control can ever replace people's inner loving motivation not to injure one another and to strive to bring each other benefit. And it is useless to resort to cynicism ("people are just plain mean, out for number one!," as they say), as if love and compassion were quanta distributed insufficiently to each person by some inept cosmic planner. The fact is that love is a positive emotion and creative activity every human being has had to develop in great degree, just to have evolved into humanity from lower, more aggressive forms of life, and these emotions and activities can be developed, increased, or allowed to atrophy and decrease. Thus all methods of cultivating love and compassion through spiritual discipline should be carefully studied, refined, developed, and applied to current people in all situations.

Members of other religious traditions have usually shied from gaining benefits of the contemplations of selflessness, the systematic, critical, yet yogic and experiential confrontation with the question of ultimate reality, because of the forbidding labels attached to these disciplines, such as "selflessness" and "emptiness." "Who wants that awful problem? We should steer clear of that sort of nihilistic idea." But now we should be in a position to get beyond such superficial reactions. Certainly, most other traditions posit the existence of a "soul," an immortal spiritual essence in each person. So it seems it is simply an ideological opposition, "soulfulness" *versus* "soul-lessness." But before we settle on this, we must examine what sorts of souls are involved.

Is there some negational aspect in the spiritual soul concept, and is there some affirmational aspect in the soul-lessness concept? Right away we can see that the spiritual soul is not the mundane ego, its immortality not the immortality of the egocentric personality. Indeed, the teachings direct the disciple to see the sinful, despicable nature of the egocentric, petty personality, the egotistical will, and turn within to find the real, pure, redeemed spiritual essence of the immortal soul. Those not embarked on spiritual paths are nevertheless directed ritually in this direction, through baptism, communion, prostrations, prayers, initiations, etc., in the various traditions. Therefore, the soul traditions all strongly negate the egocentric delusion, and seek a second birth in a higher self, a pure and selfless self that is pure love, one with the Ultimate, God or Brahman. The calling of this higher self ("Self") is comforting to those engaged in the struggle, reassuring them at the outside that their loss of ego-defenses is more than compensated by a far greater spiritual gain: "who shall lose his life for my sake, shall find life everlasting!"; "through *Islam,* surrender of the egotistical self, one enters the Garden of the community of believers." The drawback in this form of terminology is that those not engaged in a path of spiritual discipline, the mouth-believers, can too easily use the language of self to rationalize their assertions of their petty egotistical self, let the rituals take care of the higher soul and live through the petty ego.

On the other hand, where is the affirmational part of the "selflessness" approach? To the fore, of course, is the work of negation of the egocentric self, the cruciality of transcendence of the delusion of egocentrism. We have had a glimpse of the vast array of techniques available in this endeavor. And precisely to forestall the casual practitioner's appropriation of any "soul" or "self" language to rationalize petty egocentrism, the "selflessness" doctrine is everywhere present. But there is another self also everywhere present. This is the self that must restrain the selfish appetites and aversions. It is the self that must act generously, ethically, tolerantly, must do good to others out of love and compassion, must devote itself to the cultivation of great compassion, must attain wisdom and even Buddhahood. This is the relative, or conventional self, the changing, alive, suffering, and transcending self. It is the self that can become perfectly fulfilled in Buddhahood, once liberated from the egocentric self-habit, from the delusion of identifying with the egocentric, fixated, petty personality as if it were the true self. It is even called, by Maitreyanatha, the "supreme self of selflessness," not a simpleminded paradox, but precisely meaning the free spiritual self that is rid of the petty egocentric self. Of course, there is a drawback in this form of doctrinal emphasis, just as the opposite form has the drawback that it can be too easily misunderstood as meaning that there is no self at all, which misunderstanding can reinforce the rationalizing of any sort of selfish, irresponsible behavior as allowed, since there is no self to experience the consequences, either in oneself or in others. In short, the doctrine of selflessness can be misunderstood as nihilism, as well by its proponents as it has been so frequently by its opponents.

The usual Buddhist decision in this weighing of drawbacks has been to consider this disadvantage less costly than the other, since a thoroughgoing nihilism has been rarer, harder to rationalize than thoroughgoing absolutisms. This is true historically, in most cultures, but it is not necessarily the case in modern societies. Buddhist Masters are rethinking this exclusive emphasis in the modern situation, wherein nihilism is a much more serious ideological problem. Luckily, there is room to maneuver pedagogically, since the great Pioneers of the Central Way, Nagarjuna and Aryadeva had said: "The Buddhas mention 'self,' and also teach 'selflessness,' as well as teaching that there are no such things as 'self' and 'selflessness,' " and "The Buddhas teach 'self,' 'selflessness,' 'both self and selflessness,' and 'neither'; these are conventional expressions used in accordance with the needs of the disciples." A good example of the modern adaptation to a different ideological climate is that of the Kyoto School of modern Buddhist thought, wherein Nishitani and others have beautifully elaborated a language of the "Great Self" primarily out of the Zen tradition, to lead the modern mind out of the seduction of continental nihilistic existentialism.[4] Nishitani develops this language in the course of probing into the question of self, in the context of the "I"-"Thou" encounter, beginning from a famous Zen *koan* wherein two Masters manifest their encounter as great selves unafraid of small selves, delighting in liberation, yet sensitive to its lack in others. We might also witness this encounter by hearing Kyozan's roar of liberative laughter!

> Kyozan Ejaku asked Sansho Enen, "What is your name?"
> Sansho said, "Ejaku!"
> "Ejaku!" replied Kyozan, "That's *my* name."
> "Well then, "said Sansho, "my name is Enen."
> Kyozan roared with laughter.

NOTES

1 Cf. *Life and Teachings of Tsong Khapa,* ed. R. Thurman (Dharmsala: Library of Tibetan Works and Archives, 1982).

2 William James narrowed down his quest for the self to a "warm feeling" in the area of the throat, which much impressed Wittgenstein. And David Hume reports: "For my part, when I enter most intimately into what I call 'myself,' I always stumble on some particular perception or other...I never can catch 'myself' at any time without a perception, and never can observe anything but a perception. When my perceptions are removed for any time, as by sound sleep; so long am I insensible of 'myself,' and may be truly said not to exist." *Treatise of Human Nature* (Oxford: Clarendon, 1980), 251-52.

3 Thurman, 134.

4 Cf. *The Buddha Eye,* ed. F. Franck (New York: Crossroad, 1982).

CONTRIBUTORS

Dagfinn Aslid Ph.D. Candidate, Claremont Graduate School, Claremont, California

Ruth Tiffany Barnhouse Professor of Psychiatry and Pastoral Care, Perkins School of Theology, Southern Methodist University, Dallas, Texas

Arabinda Basu Professor of Philosophy, Sri Aurobindo International Centre of Education, Sri Aurobindo Research Academy, Pondicherry, India

William Cenkner Professor of History of Religion, Catholic University of America, Washington, D.C.

James Duerlinger Associate Professor of Philosophy, University of Iowa, Iowa City, Iowa

James Gaffney Professor of Ethics, Religious Studies Department, Loyola University, New Orleans, Louisiana

Ursula King Senior Lecturer in Theology and Religious Studies, The University of Leeds, Leeds, United Kingdom

Robert Kress Associate Professor, Department of Systematic Theology, Catholic University of America, Washington, D.C.

Seyyed Hossein Nasr Professor of Religion, Temple University, Philadelphia, Pennsylvania

Philip Novak Assistant Professor of Philosophy/Religious Studies, Dominican College, San Rafael, California

Huston Smith Professor of Religion, Emeritus, Syracuse University, Syracuse, New York

Robert Thurman Associate Professor of Religion, Amherst College, Amherst, Massachusetts